P9-BZV-828

GUARD US,
GUIDE US

GUARD US, GUIDE US

DIVINE LEADING *in*
LIFE'S DECISIONS

J. I. PACKER AND
CAROLYN NYSTROM

BakerBooks
Grand Rapids, Michigan

Published by Baker Books
a division of Baker Publishing Group
P.O. Box 6287, Grand Rapids, MI 49516-6287
www.bakerbooks.com

Printed in the United States of America

Library of Congress Cataloging-in-Publication Data
Packer, J. I. (James Innell).
    Guard us, guide us : divine leading in life's decisions / J. I. Packer and Carolyn Nystrom.
      p. cm.
   ISBN 978-0-8010-1303-4
    1. Decision making—Religious aspects—Christianity. 2. Providence and government of God—Christianity. I. Nystrom, Carolyn. II. Title.
   BV4509.5.P325 2008
   248.4—dc22
                                                 2007039885

To some friends
at
All Souls
and at
Immanuel Presbyterian
where God's guidance has been
sought and found:

Martin and Carolyn
Dan and Sharon

Mark and Maggie
Mateen and Cindy

Contents

Lead us, heavenly Father, lead us
  O'er the world's tempestuous sea;
Guard us, guide us, keep us, feed us,
  For we have no help but thee;
Yet possessing every blessing
  If our God our Father be.
Savior, breathe forgiveness o'er us;
  All our weakness thou doest know;
Thou didst tread this earth before us,
  Thou didst feel its keenest woe;
Lone and dreary, faint and weary,
  Through the desert thou didst go.
Spirit of our God, descending,
  Fill our hearts with heavenly joy;
Love with every passion blending,
  Pleasure that can never cloy;
Thus provided, pardoned, guided,
  Nothing can our peace destroy.

James Edmeston (1791–1867)

Prologue

The Taste of Fear

Fear of imminent bodily harm has an unpleasant flavor in the most literal sense. Bile rises from the stomach and plants in one's throat a sharp, bitter, metallic taste. So it was with J. I.'s American friend as he and the birthday girl drifted out to sea off the coast of Maui on a capsized catamaran with a large shark swimming quietly round and round them. So it was with his Canadian friend as she trod water in the chilly Pacific after the boat had sunk. J. I. has known the taste himself, and probably you have too; you would be a remarkable person if you have not.

Other forms of fear may not leave the same bad taste in the mouth, but metaphorically they can spoil the taste of your life. They cloud your spirit by day, they keep you awake at night, they undermine your concentration at all hours, and they make you run scared on a regular basis. Of all the modes of drivenness that human life embraces, being driven by fear is perhaps in the long run the most uncomfortable and the most damaging; it spoils your relationships by draining your capacity to live, it robs you of wisdom by keeping you looking sideways rather than straight ahead, and it is a very hard disability to overcome.

During the past century and a half, the topic of guidance from God has become a focus of just such fear in many Christian hearts. Christian people have always rejoiced in the certainty that God in his omniscient wisdom and grace is working out his plan for our lives, and that he helps us in our decision making and strengthens us to do what obedience to his revealed will requires of us. But in some quarters the exuberant, outward-looking holiness modeled by such men as John Wesley and William Wilberforce shrank into a legalistic pietism. Pietism, which means living by the belief that nothing in life matters so much as my personal relationship with God, is right and good, but legalism, which means living by the belief that the quality of my relationship with God depends on my turning in some form of correct performance, is neither. In this case, two specific things went wrong. First, the notion spread that getting and following direct guidance from God, as something above and beyond making commonsense decisions in Christian terms, was a matter of great importance in the Christian life. Second, God's plan for the Christian individual's life came to be thought of like a travel itinerary in which making planned connections is crucial and missing a connection wrecks the plan and spoils the rest of the journey. For now a second-rate plan B must be formed to replace the original ideal, but now impracticable, plan A, and this will certainly involve some measure of loss.

In consequence, fearful (fear-full) and perplexed anxiety with regard to decision making became widespread among evangelical people. Believers felt unable to make far-reaching decisions until they had received some special personal indication from God as to what they should do. Fear of making what from God's standpoint would be wrong commitments vocationally, professionally, socially, relationally, and matrimonially induced a kind of inner paralysis that resulted in good and desirable commitments not being made, because people could not bring themselves to make any commitment at all (which was, of course, an instance of decision making in itself, though it was not usually seen that way). This has not been a happy state of affairs.

The irony of the situation was that teachers (there once were many of them) who warned against sentencing oneself to the second-rateness of a plan B through not asking God's guidance diligently enough and so failing to make the right decision, were trying to ensure that Christians would face up to Christ's call to embrace costly, self-denying service of others for his sake. At one time it was almost axiomatic among evangelicals that all who aimed to be first-class Christians should become either missionaries overseas or ministers/ministers' wives or medical personnel (doctors or nurses) or masters/mistresses in schools. All other walks of life, however legitimate, were viewed as second-class by comparison with these. So young Christians were urged to seek personal guidance into one or other of the favored four, rather than into any more lucrative line of work.

None of this, to be sure, was wholly wrong. These four forms of service do in fact ordinarily offer more opportunities for doing good and bringing immediate benefit to people than do many other trades and professions; so they should be seen as privileged, and young people should be encouraged to aspire to one of them on this account. But the idea that they set you in a higher plane spiritually is a new form of the medieval superstition that God sees the professionally religious as a cut above everyone else. And the idea that you would need a special sign from God, over and above interest, aptitude, and the estimate of your fitness by others, to warrant your committing yourself to serve in one of these fields, or in any other employment for that matter, is superstition too.

But believers still feel anxious about guidance and find decision making spiritually uneasy and problematical. Fear, it seems, is still here. It is to try to help in this area of tense sensitivity that the present book has been written.

Fear-full Saints

One last preliminary point. Ministering over the years has shown us that the redeemed community includes two sorts of people, as does also the wider world: those who run silly and those who run scared. In terms of the ancient doctrine of the four temperaments, those who run silly tend to be the sanguine and the choleric, while those who run scared tend to be the phlegmatic and the melancholy. In modern language, we would label the two types the impulsives and the depressives. The impulsives are not thoughtful enough in the service of God, being too hasty and superficial and happy-go-lucky to reach wisdom's full seriousness, while the depressives, feeling that things are against them, are not sufficiently trustful of God to enjoy wisdom's full stability. The pervasive fear of being somehow wrong-footed and let down is always with them, and weakens their spiritual life more than they are aware. In terms of the classic cardinal virtues, the first type lacks prudence, the second type lacks courage, and both make mistakes about God's guidance to them by reason of their own particular weakness. We have written this book in hope of helping both sorts of believers. The reason why our expositions swing as widely as they do is our desire for maximum usefulness. It is our prayer that everyone who reads this book will gain from it. God grant it! Amen.

J. I. Packer
Carolyn Nystrom

1

The Shepherd and His Sheep

Be thou our guardian and our guide,
   and hear us when we call;
Let not our slippery footsteps slide,
   and hold us lest we fall.

Isaac Williams (1802–65)

We begin by pursuing the point that our prologue has just made.

Guidance is a word, as we saw, that for many Christian people evokes both fascination and fear. The fascination is felt because Christians do in fact want to be divinely guided and know that there are many places in the Bible where guidance is promised to faithful believers. The fear arises because they suspect that it is hard to get guidance right, and they anticipate disaster should they get it wrong. They know of cases where guidance has been claimed for crazy and ruinous conduct, and this knowledge keeps fear very much alive. The fascination and the fear are fed by a nagging sense of uncertainty regarding God's ways in guidance and of his elusiveness in fulfilling the promises he has made about it. As it is said of some people that you never know where you are with them, so some believers come to feel about God because of what they or their friends experienced when they sought God's guidance at a difficult time in their lives. When they thought they were following clear guidance or when they felt requested guidance had not been given, trouble came, things went wrong, hopes were dashed, and their sincerity in seeking to be guided seemed to go for nothing. This has left them bewildered and sore, as if they had been let down. It is bad for believers to live with such feelings, and it dishonors God when they do. Part of the purpose of the present book is to give help at this point.

Guidance through History

The first thing to say is that this syndrome of troubled and hurting perplexity about guidance is a relatively recent arrival among evangelical Christian people. It is the fruit of a particular belief about God that blossomed in the world of pietistic experientialism in mid-nineteenth-century America that followed two generations of Wesleyan mission work and the Second Great Awakening. The belief was that immediate guidance from God in the form of voicelike thoughts and strongly inclined imaginings and inner urges was regularly given to Bible-believers who really needed it and humbly sought it. To be sure, voices and visions of this kind had been claimed as guidance by some on the margins of seventeenth-century Puritanism, but mainline Puritans had dismissed them as "enthusiasm" in the bad sense—that is, fanaticism. Now, however, against the background of sustained emphasis on the ministry of the Holy Spirit to the individual, this conception of God supernaturally telling people what to do came to be thought of as guidance at its clearest and best and as an experience that all zealous believers might hope to know sooner or later.

Two twentieth-century developments reinforced this notion. The first was the teaching of Frank Buchman and his colleagues in the personal spiritual renewal movement between the two world wars that was called the Oxford Group. Buchman taught that one should set aside time daily (ideally, half an hour or more) to listen to what God had to say to one's conscience about living out Christ's four absolutes: honesty, purity, unselfishness, and love. The phrase "quiet time" came to birth as Buchman's label for this exercise. The practice of a daily quiet time with God for prayer, meditation, reading Scripture, and self-examination that leads to confession and renewed commitment to holy living, though not directly mandated in Scripture, has become a vital spiritual discipline for Christians generally. Its lifelong practice has led them to become spiritually mature men and women, able servants in God's kingdom. By contrast, neglect of these quiet time exercises of heart makes for flat, dry, stunted, barren Christian living. But a regular "quiet time" should not be seen as a magic formula for receiving personal guidance from God.

The second development was the spread of Pentecostalism with its claim that all the giftings and dimensions of New Testament Christian experience were now being restored to the church, words of direct guidance among them. The worldwide charismatic movement of the last third of the twentieth century embraced much of this, including expectation that words of guidance for particular persons would from time to time be given to other Christians as messages for them to deliver, often publicly, as when Agabus told Paul publicly what the Holy Spirit was saying about how his trek to Jerusalem would end (Acts 21:10–14). Note that Paul did not treat Agabus's message as guidance not to go to Jerusalem, but instead said a firm no to his friends when they urged him to change his plans. When Luke tells us that his friends finally gave up trying to persuade him, saying, "Let the will of the Lord be done," he means us to understand that they had come to see Paul's resolve to go ahead and suffer as God's authentic guidance to him (compare Acts 20:22–23). God-given warnings of trouble to come are not necessarily admonitions to take avoiding action; they may rather be tests of our sincerity, requiring of us continued obedience with eyes wide open to the consequences. In John 21:18–19, we watch Christ test Peter in this way. More later on that subject.

Now we see how it has come about that many in our Western Christian world take the true essence and definition of guidance to be God somehow telling us, in words or as if in words internally in the mind, or else by prophetic messages duly delivered, what we should do: we can embrace ends to which we must now seek means (example: Paul's company taking ship for Greece, Acts 16:9–12); or make specific moves in a situation where God's end is not yet clear (examples: Paul's company stopped from evangelizing as planned in the provinces of Asia, Mysia, and Bithynia, Acts 16:6–8; Philip led into the desert to meet the Ethiopian, 8:26–29); or take specific steps as means to a specific foretold result (examples: directions for safety given to and through Paul in the storm, Acts 27:22–26, 31, 34; Jesus instructing Peter about the fish and the coin, Matt. 17:27). We see too how guidance comes to be thought of as a potential disaster area, where a mistake or a misstep can deprive us forever of God's best. We can see how anxious uncertainty about guidance becomes a sore spot, often made sorer by dramatic tales from pulpits, platforms, and printed sources, telling how guidance was given and followed in particular cases with marvelous results. It is into this world of wonderment and worry that we now speak.

And what have we to say? Negatively, that a good deal of what we have sketched out is badly wrong. Positively, that God's guidance is one aspect of his covenant care. Let us explain.

To clear the ground, we would begin by stating our recognition that God on occasion in Bible times communicated with some people in the manner described above, and that he has not said he will never do so again, and that some at least of the glowing stories about guidance of this kind that are told can hardly be doubted. Some see reason to deny that God ever did, or will, communicate this way now that the canon of Scripture is complete, but that view seems to us to go beyond what is written and to fly in the face of credible testimony. It is not for us to place restrictions on God that he has not placed on himself! Certainly, no messages from God of the kind we are discussing could be regarded as canonical in the sense of carrying authority for universal faith and life in the way that Scripture does, and as we noted above, Scripture shows us, from the case of Paul and Agabus, that fresh information from God about the future is not always meant to change our convictions about what we should be doing in the present. This, however, is not to deny that "private revelations," as the Puritans used to call them, ever take place nowadays. On that question we keep an open mind. Though we know that self-deception here is very easy, we would not short-circuit claims to have received words from God; we would instead test them, as objectively and open mindedly as we can, in light of the teaching of Scripture itself. Scripture teaches that principle of testing in such passages as Deuteronomy 18:21–22 where God's people are told to listen to supposed prophets with discernment: "When a prophet speaks in the name of the LORD, if the word does not come to pass or come true, that is a word that the LORD has not spoken; the prophet has spoken it presumptuously. You need not be afraid of him." Similarly Paul instructs the church at Thessalonica in 1 Thessalonians 5:20–21, "Do not despise prophecies, but test everything; hold fast to what is good."

Covenant Context

But now, the things we want to say against this background are, first, that personal messages from heaven are not and never were God's usual way of leading and guiding, and, second, that even should such words appear as part of the story, God's work and ministry as our guide always involves far more. On the first point, we contend that God's regular way of showing us what he calls us to is by appropriate application of the once-for-all revealed truths of the Bible. On the second point, we hold that God's guiding of us is, as we said above, one aspect of his active covenant care of us, and as such has much more to it than simply telling us what to do and then, so to speak, standing back to see what we make of his instructions.

Let us be clear about God's covenant with believers, the covenant of grace as theologians call it, which is the context and frame of all God's guiding action. *Covenant* is the biblical word for the all-inclusive mutual commitment of God to us and us to him. It is not a negotiated partnership between equals but a relationship imposed through God's initiative. It is rightly termed a covenant of grace because God's undeserved kindness is at the heart of it. The change of arrangements for maintaining covenant fellowship when Christ's mediation as priest and sacrifice superseded the typical setup that was previously in place did not change the nature of the relationship itself. That is portrayed in Scripture as a *royal* covenant, comparable to the ruler-subject bond created in the ancient world by suzerainty treaties; also as a *marriage* covenant, a husband-and-wife commitment, in which each party pledges all that they are and have to the other and promises to serve the other in love; also as a *family* covenant, a parent-and-child relationship, an unchangeable bond of parental care binding the parents and their children together; and also, in an image that illustrates all three of these analogies, as a *shepherd-and-sheep* reality, involving affection, protection, leadership, and provision—in short, everything the shepherd can devise that makes for the welfare of his flock. The often-repeated biblical formula, "I will be your God, and you shall be my people," sometimes called the slogan of the covenant, is to be expounded in terms of all these relationships side by side, just as light is to be explained in terms of all the colors of the spectrum together. Our knowledge and experience of the reality of God's grace, including his guidance, is in truth covenantal throughout.

Look, now, in more detail at the picture of God as shepherd and believers as the Lord's sheep—including Christ's depiction of himself in John 10 as the Good Shepherd. The image here is of the owner of the flock shepherding his sheep himself, looking after them and caring for them in every way not only because they are his livelihood and so need to be kept safe, well fed, and healthy, but also because their very silliness and helpless dependence on him generate a strong sense of affectionate responsibility toward them. I (J. I.) know this firsthand, having watched it over many years in my friend John, a sheep farmer in Wales, and the same patient commitment to each sheep's well-being shines through the sweet and simple book by Phillip Keller, *A Shepherd Looks at Psalm 23.*[1] Keller ran sheep ranches in British Columbia for eight years, and wrote his book directly out of that experience. There is no reason to think that the empathetic bond that develops between owner-shepherds and their sheep was any different in the biblical world from what we see it to be today, nor is there any reason to think that the basic techniques of shepherding are different now from what they once were. All the evidence, in fact, points the other way.

Right Paths

The task of this initial chapter is to establish a perspective and lay a foundation for all that is to come, and Keller's title takes us straight to our chosen way of doing this. We propose now to expound Psalm 23 in a way that will show it to be a biblical classic on guidance, countering all the anxiety we may feel on the subject with all the assurance and reassurance which in that case we need. "He leads me in paths of righteousness for his name's sake" (v. 3). We shall try to bring out the full force of this statement. But to do that we must see it in its place in the psalm as a whole; and that means remembering that the Psalter is a God-given songbook, the lyrics of which are poetry written in the Hebrew manner; and that means we must be ready both for sudden switches from one thought and image to another and for what we may call secondary imagery, the use of a new image to illustrate and develop the further meaning of an image already present in the text. This very Eastern procedure may at first stumble our prosaic Western minds; we have to learn that good biblical interpretation involves discerning and luxuriating in the imagery as well as distilling the logic of each passage. Biblical communication regularly engages both our logic and our imagination. We shall try to bear this in mind as we dig into the psalm.

The first four verses sustain the picture of the psalmist (David) as the sheep and the Lord as the shepherd, walking ahead to guard and guide, as ancient shepherds did.

> The LORD is my shepherd; I shall not want.
>> He makes me lie down in green pastures.
> He leads me beside still waters.
>> He restores my soul.
> He leads me in paths of righteousness
>> for his name's sake.
> Even though I walk through the valley of the shadow of
>> death,
>> I will fear no evil,
> for you are with me;
>> your rod and your staff,
>> they comfort me.

The shepherd provides a quiet and safe place to eat, drink, and rest, and to find inward refreshment and renewing of contentment. Also, he protects his sheep from real harm and danger, however threatening the terrain through which they have to pass. And now, following this, the quite different image of VIP treatment at a banquet is superimposed, to amplify the picture already given of the sheep having all the food, drink, and sense of security that their well-being requires.

> You prepare a table before me
>> in the presence of my enemies;
> You anoint my head with oil;
>> my cup overflows.

Banquets in Bible times were occasions for friendly fellowship and relaxed enjoyment. Here David speaks of God the faithful shepherd doubling as God the generous host, bestowing these blessings on one whom he treats as an honored guest. The oil on the head no doubt refers to the blob of a sweet-smelling olive oil compound that a good host would dab on all his guests' foreheads as they arrived, so as to mask body odors (this was before the days of showers) and to make their faces shine while producing what we may call the cologne effect ("fragrance for men"). In light of what Keller tells us, however,[2] it is natural to guess that what suggested this detail to David's mind was the recurring need throughout each summer for the shepherd to apply to the sheep's heads the traditional Palestinian mixture of olive oil, sulfur, and spices that was designed to relieve the itching caused by nose flies and other such pests, and to stop the spread of scab when the sheep rubbed heads, as it is the way of sheep to do. The detail of enemies' presence was likely suggested by David's memories of predators (lions, bears, and wolves) spying on and stalking him and the sheep as they moved around in the wild. In any case, the picture of David happily banqueting with his enemies close and watching, but unable to interfere, carries the thought of perfect protection bringing perfect peace, which is the thought David means to express.

"It takes one to know one," we say. Sheepfarmer Keller discerns that David, who began as a professional shepherd in his father Jesse's service, builds up his account of God the shepherd out of his own experience of a full season's work on the job—from the time he led the sheep out of the fold to the Judean hills in the spring to the time he brought them back in the fall. Our appreciation of God's pastoral care is enlarged and deepened by what he tells us, nonshepherds that we are. For instance, we learn that sheep simply refuse to lie down (v. 2) until they are quite free from fear, from disturbance by troublemakers in the flock, from active harassment by flies and parasites, and from hunger and thirst; so the shepherd must be willing to work in order to shield them from these things when resting-time comes.[3] We learn of the planning and preparing that must be done so the shepherd can always lead his sheep along paths that bring them to good grazing in green pastures and to places where still waters provide good drinking.[4] Knowing something of Palestine's climate, geography, and sheep-farming heritage, Keller is able to help us imagine how David would lead the family flock uphill in the spring to high meadows and then, as winter approached, take them downhill through dark ravines where predators prowled, back to the family fold (v. 4).[5] He explains to us also about the shepherd's rod (club) and staff (stick with a hook-shaped crook at one end), and how they would be used to service and protect the flock.[6] Readers end Keller's book wiser both about shepherding and about the patient, painstaking quality of God's love.

"My cup overflows," says David (v. 5). This is a picture of abundance. So much wine is provided that those who fill the guests' cups can afford to be prodigal, pouring it out up to the brim and then adding a little more. God's goodness (generosity, that is, according to the constant Old Testament nuance that the word carries) is such that the streams of his gracious giving never cease to flow to the guests at his banquet, who are both his family and his flock—his children, who are also his sheep. Verse 6 reads:

> Surely goodness and mercy shall follow me
>   all the days of my life,
> And I shall dwell in the house of the LORD
>   forever.

So now the guest at the banquet, silly sheep that he or she is, is to be a permanent resident in the home where the banquet took place, where the host-owner-shepherd himself lives. God's hospitality to his servant in the place of his own presence is unending.

It would be hard to imagine a more reassuring, heartwarming sequence of images than this. Small wonder that Psalm 23 has always been a favorite of Christian people, that it is constantly used at Christian sickbeds, deathbeds, and funerals, and that it exists in several versions in a whole series of Christian hymn books. Perhaps the finest of all the versions (and the least well known) is this, by Isaac Watts:

> My Shepherd will supply my need,
>   Jehovah is his name;
> In pastures green he makes me feed,
>   Beside the living stream.

He brings my wand'ring spirit back
    When I forsake his ways;
And leads me for his mercy's sake
    in paths of truth and grace.

When I walk through the shades of death,
    Thy presence is my stay;
A word of thy supporting breath
    Drives all my fears away.
Thy hand in sight of all my foes
    Doth still my table spread;
My cup with blessings overflows,
    Thine oil anoints my head.

The sure provisions of my God
    attend me all my days.
O may thy house be mine abode,
    and all my work be praise!
There would I find a settled rest,
    While others go and come,
No more a stranger or a guest
    But like a child at home.

Substantively and canonically, the Bible is a unity, and the Old Testament, which lays conceptual foundations for all that is to come, should be interpreted by the light of its New Testament fulfillment. How then do we achieve a fully Christian understanding of Psalm 23, as we, with Phillip Keller, Isaac Watts, and countless others have already begun to attempt? What are the rules for doing this?

Theological Framework

First, the psalm must be set in an explicitly Trinitarian frame, and the work of God being celebrated must be seen as the joint operation of the Father who cares supremely for his family, the Son who identifies himself as the Good (*kalos*) Shepherd of his sheep (*kalos* meaning gloriously beautiful as well as functionally excellent), and the Holy Spirit who directly generates faith, peace, joy, and praise in believing hearts.

Second, the psalm must be set in an explicitly covenantal context, so as to be seen as a realizing of the truth that the one-and-only three-in-one is now and forever *our* and therefore *my* God, and that I among the rest am *his* through all eternity.

Third, the psalm must be set in an explicitly soteriological, that is, salvation-centered frame, so as to be read as witness to aspects of what God does to rescue us who believe from the guilt and enslaving downdrag of sin, and to prepare us for heaven, where we shall be at home with the Lord in joy unbroken by unfulfilled desires or unhallowed dreams or lapses into unlove.

Fourth, the psalm must be viewed, as we have already started to view it, in terms of the human realities of shepherding. As we noted, godly young David became a professional shepherd, an expert in sheepkeeping strategy, before he became anything else, and the interpreter therefore must catch up cognitively with David's expertise in this in order to grasp the full implications of the imagery he develops in his poem.

With these rules in our mind, let us look through the psalm again. Look first at the *relationship* within which God guides. In verse 1 the psalmist, picturing himself as a sheep, a silly, stubborn, needy, dependent, vulnerable creature, unable to look after himself properly, makes two statements. The first declares, in a tone of evident gladness, that he is in fact under the personal care of the divine shepherd, Yahweh (Jehovah, as our forebears used to render the name), the sovereign God of creation, providence, and grace. A shepherd is essentially a caregiver as we have seen, and because sheep get into all sorts of scrapes, pick up all sorts of infections, and are unable to defend themselves against attack, being shepherd to a flock of sheep in ancient unfenced Palestine was no light work. The shepherd needed to be with the sheep all day, every day. He had to inspect them regularly to make sure they remained in good condition. He had to be ready to defend them against predators from the wild. He had to inspect the terrain where they were to graze, to make sure no poisonous greenery grew there. He had to be equipped to relieve itching and pain caused by insects and parasites, and to supply remedies for body sores and internal discomforts. And every day he must ensure that each sheep had all the pasture and watering that she needed; which meant that he had to keep moving the flock on, lest they ruin pastureland by overgrazing it. The spiritual counterpart of all of this comes to me from God, says David—for "The Lord is my shepherd." So forgiveness, protection, freedom from fear, inner health and strength, enjoyment of life, and much more are ours today as children of the Father, beneficiaries of Christ the Son, and sharers in a new, God-centered life imparted and sustained by the indwelling Holy Spirit.

The second statement spells out the happy fact that this will go on endlessly. "I shall not want": not now, not ever. The shepherd's comprehensive care for me will never cease, says David. Every Christian's hope is based on the certainty that nothing that makes for real, long-term well-being will ever be lacking in our lives. Such is the grace of our God.

In verses 2 through 4, the picture of God's constant covenant care is filled in. Green pastures (places of sufficient and satisfying provision) are guaranteed, and security while there is guaranteed too. "He makes me lie down." Keller has already told us that sheep will not lie down to sleep until peace and quiet reign and there is no disturbance. Failing this, Keller adds, sheep keep moving restlessly from one spot to another; they lose sleep, become irritable, lose weight, and end up comprehensively substandard. His own presence among them, engaging their attention in order to soothe down the tensions they were feeling, was, he notes, regularly the decisive factor in getting them to lie down and go to sleep.[7] There is evidently a maternal quality in the care good shepherds give, and our minds go straight to Psalm 4:8: "In peace I will both lie down and sleep; for you alone, O Lord, make me dwell in safety."

In verse 3, David speaks directly of his own person to bring out the force of these images. "He restores my soul." While the verb may have been suggested by the shepherd's recurring task of setting right way up sheep that have rolled involuntarily on to their backs and now cannot move and are suffering as a result (it happens today and must have happened in David's day too), the thought is evidently of hope renewed in place of despair, of confidence in God's goodness and promises renewed in face of the stunned apathy brought on by bad experiences, of love to God and man restored in times of bitter resentment, of self-control regained after surrender to an urge that craves to become a regular bad habit, and so on. And leading beside still waters, where drinking brings pleasure in the quenching of thirst and health through inner lubrication and flushing of the system, clearly signifies God leading the believer along paths of righteousness—justice and fairness, honesty and honor, integrity and fidelity—"for his name's sake"—that is, to bring to himself honor and praise that are both God's desire and his due.

In verse 4, we find David developing further the image of the shepherd and his sheep. Following the shepherd as he leads her back to the fold, each sheep sometimes walks through the dark valleys where death stalks. David makes two points relevant to us. First, *danger of loss* faces Christ's followers—loss of quiet untroubled life, loss of stable circumstances, perhaps economic loss, perhaps even loss of life itself. To follow Christ faithfully Christians must swim against the cultural stream in all sorts of ways. As we do this we find ourselves facing threats to our well-being that, if we were not Christ's servants, we would have avoided. For example, we read that the panic-struck disciples awoke Jesus, screaming as they watched the boat fill with water, "Teacher, do you not care that we are perishing?" and we remember that they were only out on the lake in the storm because Jesus had said, "Let us go over to the other side" (Mark 4:38, 35). Had they not been his followers, this moment of facing death would not have come their way. Discipleship often works like that.

Second, *deliverance from evil* is promised to Christ's followers. The sheep draws comfort (reassurance, calm, and sustaining strength) from the shepherd's use of rod and staff. David no doubt wielded his club to deal with the lions and the bears (1 Sam.

17:34–37), and smaller predators too, and Keller describes how shepherds use their crook to lift newborn lambs and return them to their mother without putting human scent on them, to help sheep out of tangles with thorn bushes, to guide them along difficult and dangerous tracks, to draw them close to himself when he needs to look them over, or simply to give them a sense of their closeness to him.[8] David would have used his crook in similar beneficent ways, evoking in his sheep a sense of safety, certainty, and enjoyment. The knowledge of being protected by Jesus, our Good Shepherd, along with his Father and his Holy Spirit, does the same in us (John 10:14–15).

Verse 5 now celebrates the joy that all believers are meant to know as we receive into our hearts, thoughts, and mentalities the full abundance of what the apostle Paul calls "the unsearchable riches of Christ" (Eph. 3:8). Pictured here as sumptuous food, drink, and hospitality banquet-style, these riches include: the knowledge of one's forgiveness, acceptance, new birth, adoption, and abiding fellowship with God; the knowledge of being loved, rescued, renewed, and claimed by a sovereign Savior; the knowledge of a sure hope of happiness with God beyond our power at present to imagine; a glowing contentment as one basks in the reality of God's favor; a sense of triumph and empowerment through Christ and the Spirit as one faces up to life's problems and pressures; and, as advertisements so often say, much, much more. The reference to enemies watching as one feasts is a reminder of spiritual battles against the world, the flesh, and the devil still to come, but the knowledge that one is on the victory side as one moves forward with Jesus Christ sustains the spirit and keeps one in peace as the conflicts approach. Finding oneself to be one of a fellowship—a flock—of individuals whom the Good Shepherd is leading in the same direction is also one of the enrichments that are ours in Christ; the experience confirms over and over that in the flock of God, as indeed in all of human life, a joy shared is a joy doubled.

Verse 6 now rounds off the psalm by reminding us that divine goodness and mercy—kindness, generosity, care for us, patience with us, and helpfulness toward us—will be our portion throughout life, and enjoyment of what we may dare to call home life with the Father, the Son, and the Spirit will be ours literally forever. The privileges, pleasures, and prospects of those who have the Lord as their shepherd are in truth more than words can tell.

Shepherd-Guided

How does all this bear on guidance? The three points that follow show us the answer. The *doctrine* of guidance appears as one of the *principles* of what Isaac Watts termed God's guardian grace, and what we have referred to as God's covenant care. "He leads me." *Lead* is the verb that here carries the promise that our God will bestow the discernment of decision and direction that we need in order to keep moving with him along the path of life. Our certainty, as believers, of God's guardian grace and covenant care should always undergird our quest for guidance.

The *ethic* of guidance appears in the *parameters* that qualify the promise. God leads "in paths of righteousness," nowhere else. God's guidance never violates the principles of uprightness and integrity, nor will he ever prompt us to irresponsible decisions and actions. He guides us, rather, to obey his Word and to choose between options by the exercise of the Christlike, God-honoring, farseeing wisdom that is modeled for us in the Bible, the wisdom that always aims at what will please God best.

The *spirituality* of guidance appears as a purpose and policy, not simply of keeping in touch with our Shepherd incidentally as we review the range of possible decisions, but of pursuing our *personal relationship* with him just as closely as we can when we have decisions to make. The Shepherd "leads me in paths of righteousness for his name's sake"—that is, to show his faithfulness and to be honored for it by our thanks and praise. Praising and thanking God in advance because he has promised so to lead us is often a means of coming to a clear discernment of what is the scope of his leading into present decision and action.

These are the three basic concerns that we shall explore in the following pages. Our aim, as we have said, is to put the topic of guidance back where it belongs, namely in the guardian-grace, covenant-care context in which Psalm 23 sets it. This means that we shall have no time for any version of *fortune-telling* (the appeal to arbitrary signs and humanly designed "fleeces" to tell us what to do); nor for primary reliance on something best termed *"feeling-itis"* (the appeal to strong feelings and hunches, however sudden and sustained, to tell us what to do); nor for any form of *fear* lest a guidance mistake irrevocably ruin God's plan for our life. If the sheep strays off the path, the shepherd brings her back again. That is how guidance under God's guardianship plays out. Like all the rest of Psalm 23, this is wonderfully good news. Let us rejoice in it as we move forward.

2

Some Tangled Tales

Lead, kindly Light, amid the encircling gloom,
    Lead thou me on!
The night is dark, and I am far from home;
    Lead thou me on!
Guide thou my feet; I do not ask to see
The distant scene; one step enough for me.

John Henry Newman (1801–1890)

He leads me in paths of righteousness for his name's sake.

Psalm 23:3

The two song writers quoted above, though in eras nearly three thousand years apart, each gives us wonderful insight into God's guidance. Newman shows the troubled circumstances, dark and gloom, when we most long for the "kindly light" that only God can provide. And poet-shepherd-king David reveals something of the purposes of God as he extends to us the kindly light of his guidance into right paths. It is "for his name's sake." The people of God, as his sheep, wear his name as part of their identity (Rev. 7:3; 14:1; 22:4). So God wants us to wear his name well and take it along routes where his name will receive honor because of the kind of people he is growing us to become through the work of Jesus Christ. The purpose of his guidance at all times is to enable us to do that.

Personal guidance, then, is an aspect of God's covenant care, now exercised through the faithful shepherding ministry of the covenant mediator, our Lord and Savior Jesus Christ. He, the self-identified Good Shepherd, leads each believer in paths of righteousness, and if we stray off track, he rescues and restores us. Though the restoring process may be traumatic and tearful, depending on how much thoughtlessness, willfulness, presumption, and rebellion went into the folly that now makes correction necessary, the restoration is always complete; though we may now have to live long-term with the sad consequences of our mistakes, we shall be back on the path, chastened but forgiven through our shepherd's atoning death, and facing forward once more. Our Shepherd will continue to ensure that our souls are fed and that when spiritual predators surround us we are protected, and no one will be able to wrench us out of the firm grip of his hand (John 10:27–30). So we shall be led safely home into a state of unimaginable bliss in which we shall be unimaginably close to the Lord Jesus and to the Father and to the Holy Spirit forever. A grasp of these bedrock certainties about God's gracious guardianship is the point of departure for exploring the further things about divine guidance that we have to say in this present chapter.

The Nature of Righteousness

Our first task now is to understand the nature of the righteousness into which the Good Shepherd leads us. In the Bible, righteousness in its primary meaning signifies personal behavior that is truly admirable and morally purposeful. Righteousness in both God and humans means doing what is right, in the sense of meeting all obligations and displaying all relevant forms of virtue, goodwill, and enterprise. Righteousness thus shows up the good person's goodness and calls forth praise from discerning observers, both angelic and human. We may receive this praise into ourselves and thus be encouraged along this right path, but the praise will more rightly be redirected to Christ, whose name we wear whenever we term ourselves *Christian*.

Righteousness in God centers upon his faithfulness in keeping his Word, both his promises to give good things to those who trust and obey him and his warnings that he will deal with those who ignore or defy him as they deserve. (Thus it is that salvation and judgment are set forth in Scripture as equal expressions of God's righteousness.) God's holiness is his righteousness in intention, and his righteousness is his holiness in action.

Human righteousness, under God, which is our present concern, is essentially a matter of honoring, obeying, and pleasing God—in other words, living the life we were all made to live—and of dealing with people (relatives, partners, friends, colleagues, fellow believers, and fellow human beings as such) in an honest, respectful, well-wishing, Christlike way, serving them, helping them, treating them the way one would wish to be treated by them, and putting ourselves out to meet all the genuine claims they have upon us and to supply their genuine needs every way we can, never settling for the fairly good, or the "not bad," in place of the best that the situation permits. This is neighbor-love as Christ taught it, and as all Scripture presents it. A Christian traveling in Buddhist Thailand saw an accident occur right in front of the tour bus and asked why they did not stop to help. He was taken aback (so he told J. I.) when the driver explained to him that Buddhists recognize no obligation to involve themselves in other people's troubles. Christian righteousness, however, according to the New Testament sets love of God and neighbor at center stage, and so requires precisely this involvement, just as it requires us to know that God regularly shapes our circumstances so as to draw us out in showing neighbor-love at its fullest. Here our models are the Samaritan in Jesus's story, as well as Jesus himself, both in his service of the needy during his public ministry and then supremely in his dying at the Father's direction to save us all. Righteousness is love with wisdom; love is righteousness with goodwill.

Guidance, as we have seen, is often discussed as if discerning the specifics of God's plan for one's own life and making positive decisions within the frame of that plan is the whole of what guidance is about. For an adequate notion of guidance, however, we must add to this that God's plan for us is to lead us in paths of righteousness, which means that the decisions we make should always have in view the twin goals of maximum service to others and maximum pleasing of God. All real human righteousness, so far from being self-centered as stereotypical Pharisees thought and taught, is both God-centered and others-centered, and it is into righteousness of this kind that our Good Shepherd leads us. Our purpose is to show as clearly as we can how he does it.

"He leads me" along paths of righteousness, says David. *Lead* in itself is an umbrella-word covering many modes of direction: thus, the dictionary suggests that *lead* means to guide by the hand or by showing the way; to have preeminence and control, as in an orchestra, an army, a team, or a project; to draw, entice, allure, influence, and prevail on other persons to act in a certain way; and more. So we have to ask, "What sort of leading is in view here?"

In the picture that the psalm draws, the shepherd's leading includes all the procedures whereby he induces the sheep to go where he wants them to. Walking ahead of them, he sets them an example and stirs them to follow it—that is, to follow him. Walking behind them as a modern shepherd would do, with trained dogs padding alongside to head off any sheep that start to stray, would be our picture of the same process; but trained dogs were not, it would seem, any part of the ancient shepherd's equipment. What corresponds to this in the life of Christian discipleship? The answer is, God's own instruction from and through his written Word. Direct guidance as to things we should and should not do is found in the Ten Commandments and the case-law based on them, in the oracle-sermons of the prophets recalling Israel to God's standards, in the wisdom books of Proverbs and Ecclesiastes, in the teaching of Jesus, and in the many treatments of Christian behavior in the Epistles. And through the Word, via honest commitment to live by the Word and humble experience of the Word's transforming power, God gives wisdom to discern his will in all situations that call for reflective thought.

Elisabeth Elliot has such situations in mind as she describes her own prayers for guidance. Having quoted "Tell God every detail of your needs" from the J. B. Phillips rendering of Philippians 4:6, she continues: "Sometimes to make sure I don't forget the details, I make a list. The necessity of recalling all the things that have any bearing on my need for guidance—the pros and cons of all the possible courses which seem open, the circumstances which look to me significant, the reasons I have for wanting one thing above another—help me to sort out exactly what it is I am asking."[1] Paul too, points us along this path when he writes in Romans 12:1–2: "I appeal to you therefore, brothers, by the mercies of God [as expounded and thought through in his letter thus far], to present your bodies [your entire selves] as a living sacrifice. . . . Do not be conformed to this world, but be transformed by the renewal of your mind, that by testing [options] you may discern what is the will of God, what is good and acceptable and perfect [on each occasion]." This will be the fulfillment of God's promise to the godly in Psalm 32:8–9: "I will instruct you and teach you in the way you should go; I will counsel you with my eye upon you. Be not like a horse or a mule, without understanding. . . ." God's promise to guide us is first and foremost a promise to give discernment.

Sometimes God leads and guides his people by his providential provision of leaders. Writes the psalmist: "You led your people like a flock by the hand of Moses and Aaron." "[God] chose David his servant and took him from sheepfolds; . . . to shepherd Jacob his people, Israel his inheritance. With upright heart he shepherded them and guided them with his skillful hand" (Ps. 77:20; 78:70–72). God sent Nehemiah to lead the people in rebuilding Jerusalem's wall (Neh. 2:17–20), and he looked to them to follow his lead, which they did. The writer to the Hebrews admonishes: "Obey your leaders and submit to them, for they are keeping watch over your souls, as those who will have to give an account" (Heb. 13:17). Paul expects to be obeyed as a pastoral leader and a role-model: "Be imitators of me, as I am of Christ" (1 Cor. 11:1;

cf. 4:16); "You became imitators of us and of the Lord" (1 Thess. 1:6); "As you have always obeyed, so now, not only as in my presence but much more in by absence, work out your own salvation with fear and trembling" (Phil. 2:12). What is discerned in cases of this kind is a leader guided by the authority of God. Where there is no living leader to indicate the will of God, God regularly uses circumstances to nudge us in the right direction and make the proper path obvious to us. Out of the circumstances, seen in biblical light, the discernment comes.

Prayer to be led by God, as sheep are led by their shepherd, is a recurring feature of the psalms. "Lead me, O LORD, in your righteousness" (5:8). "Lead me in your truth and teach me" (25:5). "Lead me on a level path" (27:11). "Send out your light and your truth; let them lead me" (43:3). "Lead me to the rock that is higher than I" (61:2). "Lead me in the path of your commandments, for I delight in it" (119:35). "Lead me in the way everlasting!" (139:24) "Let your good Spirit lead me on level ground!" (143:10). The same petition, expressed in the same image by the same word, appears in the Lord's Prayer: "Lead us not into temptation" (Matt. 6:13; Luke 11:4). Here our Father is for the moment viewed as our shepherd, and we, his children, as his sheep. Finally, when (twice) Paul speaks of being "led" by the Holy Spirit (Rom. 8:14; Gal. 5:18), what he is celebrating is not recurring exotic experiences, but the reality of lives in which these prayers in the Psalms are fulfilled, ordinarily through our taking note of what the Bible teaches, accepting advice, and exercising sanctified common sense. In so doing, we prove for ourselves the truth of the vision in Isaiah 40:11: "He will tend his flock like a shepherd; he will gather the lambs in his arms; he will carry them in his bosom, and gently lead those that are with young." We learn in experience the meaning of Isaiah 42:16: "I will lead the blind in a way that they do not know, in paths that they have not known I will guide them. I will turn the darkness before them into light, the rough places into level ground. . . . I do not forsake them." And repeatedly we realize that Isaiah 57:18 has yet again been actualized in our lives: "I have seen his ways, but I will heal him; I will lead him and restore comfort to him. . . ." How unimaginably good to us our Lord is!

Guidance: Scope, Shape, Specifics

We are now in a position to explore some affirmations about the scope, shape, and specifics of God's guidance.

The scope of guidance. The guidance of God—his leading of us, that is—extends to the whole of our lives. Personal life is a unity, embracing character, skills, relationships, initiatives, goals, plans, and problems; use of time, money, and opportunities; choices of home location and wage-earning profession; long-term, life-strategy decisions (like the decision of J. I.'s friend who decided to spend his twenties learning, his thirties and forties practicing what he had learned, and his fifties and sixties writing out of his knowledge and experiences, or the decision of anyone who buys a house on a twenty-five-year mortgage); investment of energy in sports, hobbies, and general interests; and coping with various kinds of disability in oneself and one's dependents. Scripture tells us that God guards believers within this larger context of complexity and assures us that God is under promise to be our guide in all of it too.

The shape of guidance. God's guidance has various modes and comes to us in more than one form, but the bottom line in the guided life is always discernment and acceptance of the will of God so that our attitudes and reactions express joyful submission and faithful obedience to his leading. As the shepherd allures and reassures the sheep whom he is bringing into line, so does our fatherly God as he draws us to himself and moves us on with himself. Discernment comes through listening to Scripture and to those means of grace that relay biblical teaching to us in digestible form—sermons, instruction talks, hymns, books, Christian conversations, and so forth. Discernment comes as we judge alternatives, calculating the probable consequences of each, and testing each to find the best option (which, in cases where no happy options exist, will be the least evil, the course that makes the best of a bad job). Discernment comes as we wait on God, laying before him all the aspects of, and angles on, perplexing situations as we see them and asking for help to discern the proper path. Discernment comes too as God alerts us to the pitfalls of prejudice and impressions—pressures, that is, from untested, sacred-cow assumptions and insistent irrational desires, both of which belong to the confusion of mind about spiritual things that is inseparable from our fallen existence and that is guaranteed to induce temptations along these lines for every single one of us sooner or later.

A simple example of this sort of derailment is the following experience recorded by Elisabeth Elliot: "I knew a girl in college who looked on circumstances as nothing more than the devil's pitfalls. She felt she had to inquire of God before making her bed or helping her roommate with the cleaning. Once she had to borrow shampoo because, halfway to town to buy some, she received a divine direction to go back. This kind of piety is hard to live with, to say the least."[2] Theological prejudice and error, and irrational, obsessive inner urges can of course produce, and have in fact produced, much more serious aberrations in practice than the oddities here described with such charitable restraint. But we leave out the horror stories; this is not the place for them.

It is true that God sometimes told his prophets to do crazy-looking things in order thereby to bring his people a message (see for example Isa. 20:1–3; Jer. 13:1–7; Ezek. 4:1–5:4), and it would be going beyond Scripture to speak as if we knew that God will never do anything of this kind again. But it is entirely biblical to distinguish rules from exceptions, and to say that for New Testament Christians, biblical warrant rooted in apostolic teaching should accompany all claims that particular courses of action are being taken in accordance with the will of God. The regular shape of guidance is that God teaches us to apply revealed principles of action, both positive and negative; to observe parameters and limits of behavior that the Bible lays down; and thus to follow the path of faithful obedience and true wisdom, in fellowship with the Lord our shepherd who by his Spirit leads us so to do.

The specifics of guidance. The decisive moments in human lives are the moments of decision and commitment whereby we embrace a course of action that excludes alternative possibilities. We call such moments of commitment "making up our mind." In human lives that are guided by God, the same applies—ideally in the following way. As we collect and survey all the available facts that are relevant for making a decision; as we search the Scriptures for the relevant principles and parameters of decision and action; as we ask fellow Christians for words of wisdom and advice on the matter in hand; as we come to terms with the limitations and non-negotiable alternatives, working out the likely consequences of each possibility open to us so as to make sure we will not unwittingly choose the merely good in place of the best, we should constantly ask God to judge, correct, and direct our thinking—heading us off from deciding badly and granting us the Spirit-wrought reality of his peace in our hearts as we move into what we see to be the wise way into which he is leading us. We should be willing, and (like the psalmists) tell God we are willing, to wait on him patiently till the desired discernment comes.

Paul, writing as he always did by the light of revelation as a spokesman for the Father and the Son and as enabled by the Holy Spirit, gave the Philippians the following promise, which is there for us all: "In everything by prayer and supplication with thanksgiving let your requests be made known to God. And the peace of God, which surpasses all understanding, will guard your hearts and your minds in Christ Jesus" (Phil. 4:6–7). The ineffable, and to outsiders incomprehensible, *peace* of God of which Paul speaks, using a Greek word freighted with all the overtones of well-being that belong to the Hebrew word for peace, namely *shalom*, is the Holy Spirit's gift of awareness that one is the lamb that the divine shepherd is carrying in his arms, beloved, protected, and kept safe from spiritual danger—whatever physical hazards one may have to face. The word Paul uses for *guard* carries the picture of "a besieged citadel . . . the castle of the mind of the Christian . . . garrisoned strongly. Its walls are constantly patrolled. Its sentries never sleep at their posts. The troops are the Household Guards of the King of kings and they march behind the standard of the peace of God."[3] If the specifics of guidance, listed above, are followed out in sustained prayerful dependence on God, looking to him throughout for certainty on what to do, the fulfillment of this promise of *peace* is guaranteed both as one waits and also when God reveals the path ahead.

Signs and Certainty

"But what about signs?" asks someone. "Should they not have a place in a list of the specifics of guidance? Does not Scripture show us God giving guidance by means of signs?" Yes, it does, just as it tells us of God giving guidance by means of the Urim and Thummim, whatever they were (scholars can only make guesses), and also by means of dreams and visions as well as the casting of lots. A prime example of a guiding sign was the pillar of cloud by day and fire by night that led Israel out of Egypt through the wilderness to the promised land (see Exod. 13:17–18, 21–22; 40:36–38; Num. 14:14; Deut. 1:33). But does Scripture encourage individual Christians to ask for and expect guiding signs in their personal decision making? That God may on occasion prompt us to perceive particular events or circumstances as guiding signs is granted without dispute; what God had done before he can do again, and many can testify to the reality of such signs as among God's happy surprises for them at certain points in their pilgrimage. Whether we *should* as a matter of policy look out for signs to show us the will of God is, however, a different question.

"But what about Gideon?" it is asked. "In the roll call of Hebrews 11:32–34, he heads a list of heroes who 'through faith conquered kingdoms, enforced justice, obtained promises . . . were made strong out of weakness, became mighty in war, put foreign armies to flight'—so evidently Gideon is a man for us to admire and treat as a model. Gideon asked to be shown God's will by a sign, and God gave him one. The fleece he put out was wet after a dry night, and dry after a dewy one. God answered his request, twice over, just as he made it, and thereby brought him the certainty he needed. Isn't there an example here for us to follow? Isn't it to give us that example that the story is recorded?"

Well, is it? Consider the following. First, in Gideon's day most of the Bible had not yet been composed, and there is no reason to think that what there was (the books of Moses and maybe Joshua) adorned the home of country farmer Joash and had been the regular study of his youngest son Gideon, a laborer on the family farm. In modern tribal situations, where converts are new and do not yet have the Bible and sometimes in the lives of new converts in other situations too, God is found showing himself to people and dealing with them in ways outside the parameters of the rules he has given for ordinary adult Christian living. Something similarly special appears in God's dealings with young Gideon.

Against this background we should feel the force of what Phillip Jensen and Tony Payne describe as "a crucial distinction . . . to set out how God *can* guide us (or how he has guided people in the past) does not tell us how God *does* guide literate people of today or how he *will* guide them in the future. This is worth repeating: to set out how God *can* guide does not tell us how God *will* guide in our daily lives."[4]

Second, God had already spoken to Gideon in a theophany (the angel of the Lord in the Old Testament is God acting as his own messenger). God had told the young Gideon to overthrow the local Baal-worship, centered on the farm, and restore Yahweh-worship, which Gideon with his heart in his mouth had done, and now God had told him to raise an army to overthrow Israel's Midianite overlords—which also he had done. The destiny of the nation was thus the agenda item, not some private personal decision. A battle for the deliverance of subjugated Israel was now pending. Novice commander-in-chief Gideon still has his heart in his mouth, however, and that is why he asks for the sign of the fleece to confirm that God will truly "save Israel by my hand, as you have said." That sign will give him the confidence for battle that he and probably his troops with him had not so far managed to sustain. (See Judges 6:36–40 in context.) Bruce Waltke observes: "Many have taken the concept of a supernatural sign, a 'fleece,' and made it normative for all their decisions. I have heard Christians speak of 'putting out a fleece' on whether to purchase a car, invest in a new product, and select a school. Those kinds of decisions, while certainly important to the individual believer, are not on the same scale with determining the course of a nation whom God has selected for blessing."[5] Gideon's situation and ours hardly match.

Third, the essence of "putting out a fleece" for guidance about a private and personal decision, such as those Dr. Waltke refers to, is to devise a test to which God is asked to submit in a specified way, so that he dances to a tune that this or that believer composed for him. This comes close to the devil's second temptation in the desert, which Jesus dismissed by saying: "It is written, 'You shall not put the Lord your God to the test'" (Matt. 4:7 citing Deut. 6:16). Gideon's words introducing his second request, "Let not your anger burn against me," sound as if Gideon knew there was something presumptuous about what he was doing. Young and untried as he was, however, he desperately needed personal encouragement and something encouraging to tell his troops, and it would be a frigid and feeble comment if we were simply to say that God's promise to him (Judg. 6:16), coupled with the early sign (fire from the rock, v. 21), should have been enough. "Lord, I believe; help my unbelief" was what Gideon was expressing, and the searcher of hearts knew that. God met Gideon where he was, in what we would call a blue funk, and by answering his request kept him going as Israel's generalissimo. What we see here is God's gracious, shepherdlike compassion for the self-confessed weakling, making him strong for the huge-looking task ahead. It would be wrong to see in Gideon's plea for reassurance evidence of an irreverent and presumptuous heart, but it would be a different story if you or we "put out a fleece" for guidance in buying a car or choosing a school. Gideon's was clearly a special case.

Fourth, to treat the Old Testament account of someone's action or experience as a model for ourselves without taking account of the difference made by the coming of Jesus, and the completing of revelation, and the writing of canonical Scripture, plus the present reality of the full post-Pentecost ministry of the Holy Spirit, is always a mistake. It was natural that spectacular signs of God's presence, purpose, and promises should abound in days when resources for inward knowledge of God and discernment of his will were less than they are for us, and it is equally natural that in view of the richer resources that we Christians have for this knowledge and discernment, outward signs should be fewer, as no longer needed in the same way. The apostles never tell Christians to seek signs of God's will for their decisions, as though the gospel and its ethical corollaries are not in themselves sufficient to guide our steps, and Jesus warned the Pharisees explicitly against the irresponsibility of seeking signs when they should be facing up to his words. After Jesus had fed some four thousand people with seven loaves and a few fish we read, "The Pharisees came and began to argue with him, seeking from him a sign from heaven to test him. And he sighed deeply in his spirit and said, 'Why does this generation seek a sign? Truly, I say to you, no sign will be given to this generation.' And he left them, got into the boat again, and went to the other side" (Mark 8:11–13). We might need a similar warning. And if our hearts still hanker for the kind of spectacular signs we read of in the Old Testament, we may need also to open our ears to Dallas Willard's point that longing and indeed lusting after the spectacular in any form at all

> generally goes along with the *less mature* levels of the spiritual life—though the mere absence of such spectacular events must not be taken as indicating great spiritual development. After all, such an absence is consistent with utter deadness. . . .
>
> When the spectacular is *sought*, it is because of childishness in the personality. Children love the spectacular and show themselves children by actively seeking it out, running heedlessly after it. It may sometimes be given by God—it may be necessary—because of our denseness or our hardheartedness. However, it is never to be taken as a mark of spiritual adulthood or superiority. If spectacular things do come to them, those who are more advanced in the Way of Christ never lightly discuss them or invoke them to prove that they are right or "with it" in some special way.[6]

Was Gideon spiritually immature? Undoubtedly. Did his immaturity restrict God's blessing of him in his God-appointed leadership role? Not in the least. But is his immaturity something for Christians to cultivate and imitate? Surely not.

Fifth, pastorally, over and above concerns about inward maturity, there is a further angle to be noted on the quest for fleeces. Bruce Waltke expresses it like this: "I think 'laying out a fleece' is generally the lazy man's way to discern the will of God. It requires no work, little discipline, and almost no character development. God has a different program of guidance."[7] God has blessed Christians in this quadrant of the earth with ample opportunity to know God's character, his priorities, and the principles recorded in Scripture by which he expects us to make our decisions. God has also given us vast opportunity for knowledge of how Scripture has been interpreted by devoted scholars over two thousand years—and further how Christians throughout that time have lived God-guided lives. It is possible that God provides simplified means of guidance for his children who lack such wealth of knowledge. But we who are privileged by these opportunities must seem lazy indeed if we short-circuit them in search for a sign.

Sixth, the future coming of Antichrist, wrote Paul to the Thessalonians, will be accompanied "by the activity of Satan with all power and false signs and wonders, and with all wicked deception" (2 Thess. 2:9–10). This reference to Satanic deception makes explicit what Jesus himself had in view when he said: "False christs and false prophets will arise and perform signs and wonders, to lead astray, if possible, the elect" (Mark 13:22). It thus appears that the quest for guiding signs, which is at best a blind alley and an obstacle to spiritual maturity, can be at worst setting oneself up to be deceived by Satan, the archetypical specialist in lying and deception, who is only too ready to foul up our decisions and commitments by setting false signs before us and leading us to misinterpret our circumstances and make ruinous decisions. And if bad does not in this way come to worst, the mindset that seeks signs and hesitates to act without them is bound to paralyze us morally and keep us from making commitments that we ought to make, and that in all conscience is something that truly limits what God will do in and through us.

From no standpoint whatever, then, are we to expect signs to litter a properly God-guided path. If God gives signs, as he sometimes does, they are to be received as a bonus and an encouragement, but we should be seeking guidance via the specifics noted earlier and not by any form of a quest for signs.

Guided Endurance

A myth, that is, a nonfactual fancy, which for some surrounds the subject of guidance, is the idea that as one follows God's guidance everything falls neatly and pleasantly into place, so that the headaches and heartaches that unbelievers have to cope with do not arise. Thus the guided ones lead a charmed life. The wide currency of this notion is, we think, further evidence of our immaturity, the naïve magic-carpet view of living that Dallas Willard illustrated for us a few lines back, when he spoke of being addicted to the spectacular. We round off this chapter therefore, by categorically denying that either in the Bible or in life, today or any day, are those whom God guides shielded from hardships and bewilderments.

This denial should not be problematical to any believers; for surely we all know, first, that it did not work out this way for Jesus, the Lord whom we follow, and, second, that God uses stretching and sandpapering experiences both to teach us truths and to shape and, if we may so speak, polish our souls. Says the psalmist; "You have dealt well with your servant, O LORD, according to your word. . . . Before I was afflicted I went astray, but now I keep your word. . . . It is good for me that I was afflicted, that I might learn your statutes" (Ps. 119:65, 67, 71). These are words that every believer will have reason to echo sooner or later. To Christians being hammered for their faith the writer to the Hebrews says: "It is for discipline that you have to endure. God is treating you as sons. For what son is there whom his father does not discipline?

. . . He disciplines us for our good, that we may share his holiness" (Heb. 12:7, 10). This regimen of character training is appointed for all who follow Christ. The Pentateuch shows Israel experiencing hardships (lack of food and water along with periodic conflicts) as they trekked where the pillar of cloud and fire led; and the story of Jesus walking on water starts with the disciples caught in a wind storm because they were obeying Jesus's instructions to cross the lake to Bethsaida (Matt. 14:22; Mark 6:45; compare Mark 4:35–41 for a similar situation).

Micaiah and Jeremiah also brought trouble on themselves by obeying God, in their case by saying what he gave them to say, and infuriating their hearers by so doing. Wicked King Ahab summoned the Lord's prophet Micaiah to his presence and asked if he should lead his people into battle against Syria. In the background, four hundred prophets were already telling Ahab to go for it. Prophet Zedekiah was dancing around with iron horns on his head saying, "Thus says the LORD, '. . . you shall push the Syrians until they are destroyed.'" But Micaiah spoke a true, though unwelcome message: "I saw all Israel scattered on the mountains, as sheep that have no shepherd" (v. 17). Zedekiah gave Micaiah a resounding slap on the face for his trouble, and Ahab clapped him into prison to exist on a diet of bread and water "until I come in peace" (v. 27). In fact, Ahab did not return at all; he died in battle, as Micaiah had foretold. (See 1 Kings 22.)

The prophet Jeremiah fared no better. Instructed by God, Jeremiah warned Jerusalem, "Thus says the LORD of hosts, . . . I am bringing upon this city and upon all its towns all the disaster I have pronounced against it" (Jer. 19:15). Pashhur the priest did not find these words particularly inspiring; so he beat Jeremiah and put him in the stocks for a day. Upon release, Jeremiah spoke again—this time against Pashhur himself. "Thus says the LORD: Behold, I will make you a terror to yourself and to all your friends. . . . I will give all Judah into the hand of the king of Babylon. He shall carry them captive to Babylon. . . . Moreover, I will give all the wealth of the city . . . and all the treasures of the kings of Judah into the hand of their enemies. . . . And you, Pashhur, and all who

45

dwell in your house, shall go into captivity. To Babylon you shall go, and there you shall die, and there you shall be buried, you and all your friends" (Jer. 20:4–6).

Oddly, by human standards at least, Jeremiah does not then go off to gloat about God's curse on his evil rival. Instead he grieves the fate of his city and prays a haunting prayer of lament: "O LORD, you have deceived me, and I was deceived; you are stronger than I, and you have prevailed. . . . For the word of the LORD has become for me a reproach and derision all day long. . . . Cursed be the man who brought the news to my father, 'A son is born to you.' . . . Why did I come out from the womb to see toil and sorrow, and spend my days in shame?" (Jer. 20:7–8, 15, 18). At each turn, Jeremiah was faithfully following God's guidance, but each guided turn took him deeper into despair. And his troubles continued. By chapter 38, we find Jeremiah and Pashhur still in conflict, with Jeremiah now under threat of death. Even King Zedekiah turns Jeremiah over to his rival prophets, and they dump him into a cistern so full of mud that Jeremiah sinks down to his armpits where he is left to die of thirst and starvation. Jeremiah is rescued—again. But he rises out of the cistern to face a ruined city. All who receive God's guidance and seek to live by it must expect experiences of this kind, to instruct, test, correct, purge, deepen, and strengthen them. For it is by these means that God trains, matures, and toughens his children, increases their faith, and makes them grow in Christ.

To illustrate this further, we now offer excerpts from the tangled life-stories of three contemporaries, all born within the same two-year period: J. I.'s friends Denys and Elisabeth, and J. I. himself. We do this with some hesitation, not presenting these persons as role models or as anyone special, only as individuals whose experience helps to show how living under God's guidance may work out, and we ask our readers to confine their interest in the narratives to precisely that question; for we offer them not as human interest stories, but simply as testimonies to God in action in three people's lives. No intrusions into privacy are involved, for Denys is now in glory, Elisabeth has put her own story into print,[8] and J. I., who is drafting these paragraphs, has already had the external facts of his life up to 1996 made public.[9]

Denys's story illustrates how harrowing the business of making decisions may become as one seeks to live a guided life. The last time I (J. I.) saw Denys we had been friends in Christ for a quarter of a century and were both in our midforties. He came to our home, where I was bed-bound with an ulcer on my leg, and we talked in the bedroom. Denys had come to Christ in Oxford, a year after my own conversion, and we had walked together through the first months of his new life. Called by God, he was sure, to be a medical missionary, he switched from chemistry to medicine as his academic study, and started making plans. A Brethren missionary in Ecuador named Wilfred Tidmarsh, recruiting replacements for a mission station he had had to abandon, sparked in Denys's mind a vision of pioneer solo service in South America,[10] but, guided by his own constant need of medical attention, he finally became an anesthetist in a hospital in Africa. His disability was iritis, a chronic inflammation of the eye, which he had picked up when, as head boy of his school and also a strong swimmer, he had dived into a tank of dirty water to retrieve a younger boy's spectacles. Regular medication and dark glasses thus became necessary for him, and, to enable him to keep functioning professionally, the dosage had to be steadily increased. Now, back in England, so he told me expressionlessly from behind his dark glasses, he was suffering from a long-term depressive condition that made him zombielike both at home and in all his nonprofessional relationships. He knew it, but could do nothing about it. He had come to talk over with me the medical choice that had been set before him: whether to accept an increased drug dosage that would counter the depression and keep his eyes going for work at the hospital, but would also strain his heart and almost certainly shorten his life, or to settle for the status quo, a steady though slow reduction of his emotional and visual capacity. We explored the pros and cons, and he went away to make his decision. I do not know who else he consulted or what if anything he said to his family or how finally he made up his mind; I only know that in a few months he was dead. "But for those months," his widow said to me, years later, "I had my husband back." I cannot doubt that he made the better decision.

We think it widely assumed that when God guides us we shall be shielded from ever having to make agonizing decisions of this kind. Not so, however. Dallas Willard speaks trenchantly to the point.

> In recent years innumerable spokespeople for God have offered ways we can use God and his Bible as guarantees of health, success and wealth. The Bible is treated as a how-to book, a manual for the successful life in the way of the Western world, which if followed will ensure that you will prosper financially, that you will not get cancer or even a cold and that your church will never split or lack a successful minister and program. . . . The word of God does not come just to lead us out of trouble—though it sometimes does this—or to make sure that we have it easy and everything goes our way. . . . We must not be misled by wishful thinking. We are going to go through the mill of life like everyone else. We who are disciples are different because we *also* have a higher or additional life—a different quality of life, a spiritual life, an eternal life—*not* because we are spared the ordinary troubles that befall ordinary human beings.[11]

Exactly so.

Elisabeth's story illustrates the way in which the God of mercy will mercilessly pulverize—the word is not too strong—our imperfect, naïve, and prejudiced humanity so as to work in us, whom he guides, meek and self-negating submission before his greatness (that is, humility of heart); contented ignorance of his strategies in face of his wisdom (that is, humility of mind); unfailing love for others in light of Jesus's self-giving love for us on the cross (that is, humility of soul); and unflinching obedience to God's Word and leading at whatever cost (that is, the humility of true strength). Elisabeth is a brilliant and magnetic writer, with the gift that Bunyan and C. S. Lewis also had of objectifying her thoughts and experiences so as to write about them as if they were somebody else's, and I guess I (J. I.) am one of her most appreciative readers. Years of friendship have not augmented for me what she has already said in print but have simply enabled me to understand it better and value it more. Because her own books lay everything out so clearly and fully, my survey of her story will be brief.

Nurtured in pietistic circles where missionaries were idealized, Elisabeth was sure from early on that mission work was God's way for her. Being linguistically gifted, she qualified at Wycliffe's Summer Institute of Linguistics on reducing languages to writing for Bible translation and went to the Colorado tribe in Ecuador for that purpose. But her informant, the only person fluent in both Spanish and Colorado, was killed in a brawl, and the suitcases containing the entire fruit of nine months' unremitting linguistic labor were stolen.

This was not to be her only loss. In due course she married fellow missionary Jim Elliot, who with four colleagues was killed in 1956 by the Waorani[12] tribal people whom they had gone to evangelize. Elisabeth stayed in the area working now on the language of the Quichua tribe. A couple of years later Elisabeth Elliot and Rachel Saint (sister of Nate Saint, who also died in the massacre) were invited to live among the Waorani. Taking this as an answer to prayer, Elisabeth and her small daughter lived among her husband's killers for two years, after which circumstances dictated a return to America. There she found she no longer fitted into the evangelical subculture from which she had come; she was cold-shouldered and sometimes treated badly. Elisabeth remarried, but her new husband soon died of cancer, and that led to a third marriage some years later.

Out of all of this has come a significant ministry about being real with the real God in various departments of life. The road has been rough for her all along. From first to last, Elisabeth has sought to find and follow God's guidance. On the pressures and perplexities that arise for all who follow that goal, she has this to say:

> When I lived in the forest of Ecuador . . . I always had with me a guide who knew the way. . . . Trails led often through streams and rivers which we had to wade, but sometimes there was a log laid high above the water which we had to cross.

I dreaded those logs. . . . But the Indians would say, "Just walk across, senorita," and over they would go. . . . I was barefoot as they were, but it was not enough. On the log, I couldn't keep from looking down at the river below. I knew I would slip. I had never been any good at balancing myself on the tops of walls and things, and the log looked impossible. So my guide would stretch out a hand, and the touch of it was all I needed. I stopped worrying about slipping. I stopped looking down at the river or even at the log and looked at the guide, who held my hand with only the lightest touch. . . . But his being there and his touch were all I needed.

. . . The lesson the Indians taught me was that of trust.[13]

G. K. Chesterton declares with blithe abandon that Christians when they cannot see where God is taking them, which is quite often, "go gaily in the dark." How can anyone do that? Because we can trust the God who leads us as Elisabeth learned to trust the Indians who led her across the logs. The deepest question with which Elisabeth's story, and, we hope, this whole book confronts us is: do we really *trust* the Father, the Son, and the Spirit, the Triune God who guards and guides?

J. I.: What, now, of my own story? I do not think there is anything out of the ordinary about it, but I sketch it out here because I think it illustrates something of real importance, namely the responsibilities that divine guidance imposes and the sense of partial failure that it generates.

As I review God's steering of my life, one thing that stands out is the element of surprise at all the crucial points. I was never expecting what came; I was always projecting something else. This was true of my conversion to Christ in 1944, at a time when I thought I knew what a Christian was and had been one for years. It was true of the certainty that God wanted me in pastoral ministry, an awareness that broke in when I was expecting to end up as a schoolmaster. It was true of my discovery that educating adult Christians for ministry was an activity after my own heart, for which I had some instincts and natural skills; this realization came through being providentially pitchforked into seminary teaching for a year, at a time when my sights were set on local church ministry and my own theological studies had not begun. It was true of my further discovery that I could write books, a discovery made through trying to fulfill a request to write a pamphlet. It was true of the time that Kit and I first met, at a retreat where neither of us had expected to be. (It took me all of forty-eight hours plus an entire sleepless night to discern that under God she was the one for me. She was not in the least like the wife I had imagined myself finding some day.) And it was supremely true of the conviction, forced on me in my fifties by a complex of circumstances when I was expecting to serve out my time in England, that we were to become Canadians and that I should take in hand the work that has occupied me since 1979 at Regent College, Vancouver. In all of this my heavenly Father has proved himself a God of happy surprises and has engineered for me a personal fulfillment beyond my dreams.

All of that no doubt sounds wonderful; but it has its flip side. Gifts and opportunities are given to be used, and the more one is given the more will be required of one, in both quantity and quality terms. The underside of the guided life as I have experienced it for almost two generations is failure to do all that I could and should have done, whether as a grateful child laying himself out to please his Father and serve his siblings or as a public performer actualizing his full potential for honoring God and helping other people. Like all my fellow believers, I have fallen and do fall short of what with more alertness, concentration, and self-discipline I might have done for Christ and his kingdom, and I can only live by being forgiven on a daily basis.

That is surely enough about Denys, Elisabeth, and me.

What is the point, now, that we are laboring to make in all this? Simply that, though the principles of God's guidance, and his guardianship are universal, the guided lives of believers are as different from one another as are the believers themselves, and the reality of God's guardianship and guidance, while glorious in itself, brings no immunity from any of the pains and problems of everyday human life in a fallen world.

The closing comment shall come from Cornell Capa, the hard-headed photographer who covered the Waorani massacre for *Life* magazine. Almost half a century ago he wrote:

> I wondered how Betty [Elisabeth] could reconcile Jim's death at the hands of the Aucas and the Lord's apparent failure to protect him from them. Her answer came back without hesitation: "I prayed for the protection of Jim, that is, physical protection. The answer the Lord gave transcended what I had in mind. He gave protection from disobedience and through Jim's death accomplished results the magnitude of which only Eternity can show.[14]

There are many Christians among the Waorani today, and the Elliot story has had the enormously wide impact of inspiring young adults to pioneer mission work. Truly we can set no limits to the potential significance of lives in which God guides and guards the heart.

3

Your Good Health

I appeal to you therefore, brothers, by the mercies of God, to present
your bodies as a living sacrifice, holy and acceptable to God, which
is your spiritual worship. Do not be conformed to this world, but
be transformed by the renewal of your mind, that by testing you
may discern what is the will of God.

Romans 12:1–2

The title of this chapter is a form of words that you might expect
to hear at a party as people around the table drink toasts to each
other. We borrow the phrase because it pinpoints what this chapter
deals with. In the first place, you who read these words are people
whose overall spiritual health we hope and pray God will use our
book to promote. And secondly, what we must now explore is the
certain truth that our power to discern and follow God's guidance
in our making of both short-term and long-term decisions will be
reduced if spiritually we are out of sorts. Ordinarily, as we know
from experience, our best brainwork is done when our bodies are
fit and we feel good, but bodily disorders diminish the balance
and power of our minds—and there is a spiritual counterpart to
that. As business people who want always to be at their best make

a point of taking regular exercise to keep their bodies healthy, so Christians who desire always to be sensitive to nudges from God, in whatever form they are going to come, need to take appropriate action for keeping in good spiritual shape. To show how this may be done, and to point out as we move along some of the pitfalls that threaten if this is not done, is thus our next task.

Facing the realities of our present condition is the first step for all of us. All athletes must endure a regular "sports physical." This is a checkup designed to show if the athlete's body is set for the rigors ahead and to spot any potential weaknesses that might jeopardize his or her well-being or (perhaps more importantly) the well-being of the team. The sports physical is intended to uncover these weaknesses and lead to treatment for strengthening what is not up to the mark *before* major damage is done. So it is with spiritual checkups. They are a part of our training for "wellness" in our life with God. The New Testament pictures the Christian life as running a race (see 1 Cor. 9:24, Gal. 5:7; Phil. 3:13–14; and Heb. 12:1) and makes clear that checkups are part of the discipline required. "Examine yourselves. . . . Test yourselves," writes Paul (2 Cor. 13:5).

Why Checkups?

Why do we need regular checkups of our spiritual health? During off-season, an athlete doesn't always notice when he or she has drifted into a state of being below par—a little weight gain, a little flab on the haunch, a little more windedness at a dead run—it all goes unnoticed. Everything still feels right—and that is precisely the problem. Similarly, perfectly ordinary people, when weakened by flu or some other scourge, begin to forget what it felt like to be really well. "Didn't I always have to lean on the chair on my way to the couch? Wasn't I always out of breath walking to the kitchen? Yes, I guess so. Was that really I who ran laughing down the hallway just last week, then rolled around on the floor with the children? Surely not!" Being sick, or less than well, begins to feel "normal." The same thing happens with regard to spiritual health. Just as we can begin to lose our athletic conditioning (if we ever had it), so we can begin to lose our spiritual edge, the edge that brings joy and confidence, peace, love, and productivity, and we hardly realize what has happened. Our spiritual languor begins to feel normal. What we need is the jolt of a checkup.

There are all sorts of reasons for a below par spiritual state in which energy for God and for God's glory is simply lacking, but its outcome is always the same. The peace, the active goodwill, and the joy that we once knew are no longer a part of our regular condition of life. William Cowper, who lived much of his life in acute depression, wrote "Where is the blessedness I knew when first I saw the Lord?" This question is often echoed by people who drift into a spiritual lassitude. Such folk may feel physically and mentally exhausted. Sometimes they lapse into an ongoing attitude of irritation at other people, irritation at the church, irritation at husband or wife or children or employer. Of course these symptoms may represent some medical condition or chronic exhaustion due to overwork. But whatever else is happening, these folk have come to be *spiritually* out of sorts, and they now need spiritual guidance for their recovery, over and above the other forms of help that they may also need.

It is our strong conviction that the guidance of God will only be reliably received by those whose hearts are right with God, and whose motivation is the glory of God—which are both signs of good spiritual health. If people who are not in good spiritual health seek the guidance of God, as many do, they are going to find frustration, disappointment, delusion perhaps, and certainly distress; for things simply won't come right. Many books take up the subject of God's guidance, some of them offering a wide range of excellent insights, but few speak to the prerequisite of spiritual health: that guidance from God is only to be expected when spiritually you are in good shape. This however seems to us a matter of crucial importance, and so we stress it here.

One of the first things that happens during a spiritual drift is that we slip under the power of pride, which is the basic expression of original sin that regularly takes over in such cases. Pride says in some form, "Me first, I want my choices, just as I want everything else, to put me on top." Then our pride expresses itself in all sorts of attitudes and maneuvers contrived to put other people down so that we will indeed be on top. To trace all the ins and outs of the attitudes people adopt in the service of pride is like mapping the Mississippi Delta—the complex of bayous and backwaters, and the quantity of mud one meets, are both very great. Meanwhile the delinquent Christian hardly knows that he or she is spiritually substandard. This absence of spiritual awareness is the beginning of the problem, one that cannot be solved until people frankly face the fact that pride has got hold of them and that pride is now what is making the mess, which they feel in some broad unfocused way, that their life has become.

Bible biography provides many object lessons about this, and two of the fullest and clearest are in the life of the man who wrote Psalm 23, David himself. Look at David for a moment. He was a godly shepherd boy who became a godly king. The prophet Samuel celebrated him at the outset as a man after God's own heart, and the apostle Paul confirms that this was God's final estimate of him. (See 1 Sam. 13:14 and Acts 13:22.) Magnetic leader and man of action, gifted musician, and deeply devotional poet, tenderhearted friend and generous foe, ardent, adoring, single-minded servant of God, constantly concerned to honor God and bring benefit to God's people, David deserves his place in the heroes' gallery of Hebrews 11 among those who "through faith conquered kingdoms, enforced justice, obtained promises . . . became mighty in war, put foreign armies to flight" (Heb. 11:32–34). And Psalm 23 shows that through all his days he saw himself as a sheep whom God was leading "in paths of righteousness"—ways, that is, as we have seen, of holiness, integrity, wisdom, and virtue (v. 3). Yet David's life of service to God was marred by two great lapses, like near-fatal illnesses punctuating a life of normally robust health. In both of these episodes, as it seems, pride egged David on into really ruinous folly. The first concerned Bathsheba and Uriah; the second was the national census-taking.

To understand the wretched story of David and Bathsheba, we must realize that royal polygamy was at that time a status symbol. It was taken for granted that kings would have a plurality of wives and concubines, and God did not make an issue of this with either David or Solomon. What was so bad here, however, over and above David's indulgence of lust, which in itself was bad enough, was that he impregnated a woman whom he knew to be another man's wife, thus breaking the seventh and tenth commandments. Having failed to fool the husband into thinking the coming baby was his, David sent the man off to certain death so that he might marry the lady himself, thus in effect breaking the sixth, eighth, and ninth commandments as well. We might well ask, "What was happening inside David?" The evident answer is that his bodily laziness (he had not led his men out to the war, but was taking it easy at home) had induced spiritual unconcern and vacancy; he was thinking, not about what he could and should do for God, but like any other king at that time what he might do to please himself. Proud egoism had taken over and put his conscience to sleep. As we know, God judged David for this: Bathsheba's child died, and David's home life as well as his public life was ravaged by Absalom's rebellion. (See 2 Sam. 11–12, and with 12:11 compare 16:20–22. For David's eventual repentance, see Psalm 51.)

The taking of the census, from which Joab tried unsuccessfully to dissuade David, also expressed a lapse into pride while conscience slept. There was no reason to do this other than the arrogance of a monarch who wanted to be able to tell the world how many people he governed and how large an army he could raise when he had to. In the temptation to act thus, which Satan administered (1 Chron. 21:1–8), God's displeasure with Israel for unspecified sins was being expressed (2 Sam. 24:1), and God's judgment on David for his own sin in taking the census was to make him choose which of three forms of public diminution his people, along with their king, should now suffer. (See 2 Samuel 24 and 1 Chronicles 21 for the whole sad story.)

In both these instances the saving grace for David was that when alerted to his sin and rebuked for it, he acknowledged his wrong, humbled himself, made no secret of his guilt, repented, threw himself on God's mercy, sought forgiveness, and thus came back to spiritual sanity. When servants of God fall into sin, either with eyes wide open to the wrongness of what they are doing or, seemingly like David, not letting themselves realize that it is sin until after it is done, this is the only way they can be restored. All of us believers need to learn this lesson, for we shall all of us make mistakes and slip into sins of one kind or another, and we shall all from time to time need to tread the pathway back that David trod before us, where the rule is that the greater the folly the more radical the repentance needs to be. Wisdom, however, tells us to try to avoid such lapses by knowing and not losing sight of our own vulnerabilities. But for that we need both faithful friends and periodic health checks, which bring us back to the topic now before us.

Looking Backward

Before we go any further into our explorations, we need a further glance at the places where we have walked in the first two chapters. We started by looking at Psalm 23 and identifying ourselves as sheep under the guardianship and guidance of our divine Shepherd. We saw that God's guardianship and guidance covers the whole of our life. From one standpoint his guiding guardianship is his work of leading us "in paths of righteousness for his name's sake." From another standpoint it is guardianship and guidance in the path of spiritual wellness. God's sheep are wonderfully blessed! The psalmist changed the imagery in order to make that point. "You prepare a table before me in the presence of my enemies; you anoint my head with oil; my cup overflows." Here is abundance, an overflow of good things, all gifts from the Shepherd. "Goodness and mercy shall follow me all the days of my life, and I shall dwell in the house of the LORD forever." All this is a picture of spiritual wellness, the ideal. That is what may be ours if we humbly hold our position as the Lord's sheep.

At the heart of living, as we also saw, is decision making. We are to make our decisions in our character as the sheep of the Lord Jesus Christ, moving through life under the guidance of our Good Shepherd. First a warning: bad decision making can take the form of following impressions—hunches masquerading as messages from God. "I feel" is a red-flag phrase in this matter of guidance; self-proclaimed holy hunches can be a source of real danger. True, our Lord does indeed *sometimes* gently nudge his sheep in one direction or the other—particularly those who know him well and are used to recognizing his voice within. But this is less the norm than many people assume, and it is not the place to start when seeking guidance from God.

Healthy decision making isn't a matter of thinking what we want to think, and then acting as if it were true. It isn't a matter of following our feelings, although if, by the grace of God, we make wise decisions for the living of our life, good feelings and even joy regularly follow. But the wise Christian seeking God's guidance doesn't start with impressions and subjective fantasies. Wise Christians start with the written Word of God, which they receive as their guidebook, as from the hand of Jesus Christ himself. We make our decisions in the light of what Scripture actually says and then, following on from that, in the light of wisdom that comes to us as we soak ourselves in God's Word. The Word and the wisdom: these are the first two basic resources for good decision making, the activity that promotes and sustains true spiritual health.

From the Scriptures we learn parameters. We learn where it is wrong to go; we see the outline of the path that we must stay on. Following the principles taught in the Word, we seek to obey the revealed directions of God for living our lives to his praise. This is not always as straightforward as it sounds. There is quite an art involved in unshelling biblical principles from their context in Scripture and applying them (reapplying them) to the specifics of our lives. The classic Christian name for this art is *casuistry*, the resolving of cases of moral decision by the Word of God. Christians need basic skills in casuistry, and that will be treated later in this book.

Healthy Wisdom

We have also looked briefly at the kind of wisdom that comes from soaking yourself in Scripture. Wisdom produces the good life, the life of responsible relationships, the life which is lived in the joy and peace that come from God. Joy and peace will mark our life, flowing to us in the first instance from our reconciled relationship to God and remaining ours as long as at the heart of our living is the sense that, "Yes, God has prompted me to follow this path. I am judging, I am deciding, I am moving, I am acting according to his wisdom. God is with me, then, in what I am doing." This is healthy Christian experience. But in order to live in wisdom, we have to learn from God to understand people and situations, and to work out the consequences of different courses of action, and to see the creative possibilities that are there for us as well as for those who depend on us—the people we live with and are nurturing and advising. Wisdom discerns what constitutes faithfulness to God, respect for others, and prudent behavior in difficult situations. Wisdom covers all of that—and much, much more.

The way of spiritual health, then, is to learn to live and make decisions under the Word, in the light of God's wisdom as the Bible itself presents it. Certain books of Scripture are classified as wisdom writings, and these are not always as well appreciated as they should be; so we pause for a moment to say something about what they give us. Wisdom literature in the Old Testament includes the Proverbs collected or composed by Solomon and others (a compendium of shrewd sayings about life, perhaps echoing the words of Jewish grandmothers to their grandchildren for generations, but presented as from father to son); the book of Job (which shows us how to suffer); the book of Ecclesiastes (which, in the person of Solomon, teaches the way to enjoy life in this fallen world); the Psalms (modeling praise and prayer); and the Song of Solomon (which sings the exuberance of love). With these belongs the New Testament letter of James, as we shall see.

Some people may be startled to find Song of Solomon listed as "wisdom literature," but the Bible is quite robust about the fact that love between a him and a her is of enormous importance in human existence. It is meant to be, and of course it still is; and a great deal of wisdom is needed to know how best to express it. Furthermore, this uninhibited love song images the love between the Lord and his people: the love that he shows to them and the love that they must show to him. True, the book is essentially a torrid love song, but so it had to be in order to become the vivid parable of self-giving, two-way love between the Lord and his own that it most certainly is.

Christians often neglect the wisdom literature of Scripture, but it is an important part of God's guidance to us. According to these books, we must learn, at all costs, to avoid folly, which the book of Proverbs in particular pictures over and over as the opposite of wisdom and which is the chronic condition of so many benighted members of the human race. The preamble sermon which fills the first nine chapters of Proverbs guides us away from folly and toward wisdom. Throughout Proverbs the "wise man" (Solomon) admonishes his "son." In the first chapter he warns his son against ever lapsing into violence for fun:

> My son, if sinners entice you,
>   do not consent.
> If they say, "Come with us, let us lie in wait for blood;
>   let us ambush the innocent without reason. . . ."
> My son, do not walk in the way with them.
>
> Proverbs 1:10–11, 15

Then in chapter 5 he admonishes his son against lapsing into unmarried sex merely for short-term entertainment while he praises sensuous joy in married love:

> My son, be attentive to my wisdom; . . .
> For the lips of a forbidden woman drip honey,
>   and her speech is smoother than oil,
> but in the end she is bitter as wormwood, . . .
> Let your fountain be blessed,
>   and rejoice in the wife of your youth,
>   a lovely deer, a graceful doe.

> Let her breasts fill you at all times with delight;
>> be intoxicated always in her love. . . .
> For a man's ways are before the eyes of the LORD,
>> and he ponders all his paths.
>
> Proverbs 5:1, 3–4, 18–19, 21

In Proverbs 7, the wise man continues his warnings about appropriate and inappropriate sex, this time warning his son against succumbing to the temptation of prostitutes and thus becoming so much the prisoner of his own passions as to follow her "as an ox goes to the slaughter" (7:22). Why all of this restraint? Why not enjoy the thrill of violence against a weaker person, or of sex with any willing partner? It is not that God is a dour killjoy willing misery and deprivation for us; it is rather that the results of these forbidden actions are harmful to those who perform them. At the same time, the writer affirms the goodness and joy of sexuality within marriage, under the benevolent oversight of God the Creator who is not whimsical or random in judgment but who "ponders all [each person's] paths" and matches outcomes to choices (Prov. 5:21).

Violence and promiscuous sexuality are extraordinarily prevalent in today's world, but God says that they are ruinous folly. This is a kind of folly which, whatever it does for other people, brings personal and spiritual decline to anyone who falls into it. It is the way of spiritual bad health leading to death. The personified Wisdom of Proverbs says, "Don't follow it." Alas, people did pursue folly, and people do still. The opening chapters of the book of Proverbs are thus very much words for our time: they remain guidance (to us) from God.

These are just a few examples of how the wisdom writings give guidance to us who believe. We will return to them throughout this book. For the moment, our point is simply that lapsing from God's revealed ideal is like contracting a degenerative disease, with disfigurement and dysfunction soon appearing, and that to maintain spiritual health and fortify us against such infection we need regular checkups.

The checkup process for spiritual health is something we can usually manage with God's help on a do-it-yourself basis. Some Christians, however, look for human help through a process called spiritual direction. As Catholics have always known, and evangelicals are beginning to learn, the task of a spiritual director is to enable a person to discern what the Holy Spirit is doing in his or her life and then to cooperate with that; their task is also to observe anything that is deficient or going wrong in a person's spiritual life and to put their finger on it with the purpose, by God's grace, of bringing correction. In a way the spiritual director's job is like the midwife's: presiding over the birth, checking that the process is going along as it should, and blowing whistles straightaway if something begins to go wrong in the delivery process. The question "Should I seek out a spiritual director?" is like the question "Should I tell my sins to another person?" In both cases the answer is "All may, none must, some should."

The rest of this chapter is devoted to setting out four key principles that belong together as a kind of chain. To help the memory, we state the four principles using four words that begin with the letter *H*: Health, Habit, Heart, and Holiness.

Health

Principle One: Health for the soul is the fruit of holiness in the heart. Psalm 86:11 shows us the meaning of this principle. "Teach me your way, O LORD," says the psalmist "that I may walk in your truth." Here is the basic purpose of seeking God's instruction. We labor to learn his way *so that* we may walk in his truth. Motive, as always, ranks high in God's value system. Seeking God's guidance in order to decide later whether or not we will follow what he reveals is out of the question. We must ask that God teach us his way in order that we may walk in it, even if his way is not the route we had first intended.

And now verse 11 goes on to say, "Unite my heart to fear your name." That is a breathtaking, revelatory prayer. The heart is the very center, the energy center, of the person. Our desires, purposes, plans, attitudes, according to Scripture, all come out of the heart. Jesus set the Pharisees straight on that one. They said, "Well, holiness is a matter of (for instance) washing your hands before meals." Jesus said, no. The disciples asked him what he meant, and he said that the bodily functions have nothing to do with real purity or impurity; what comes out of the heart is what defiles a person. (See Mark 7:1–13.) On another occasion he berated the Pharisees for the hidden greed, self-indulgence, hypocrisy, lawlessness, and injustice that was the inside story of their lives (Matt 23:23–28). All that constitutes a person (life, energy, attitudes), all of this and more come out of the heart, as if the heart is a factory in which all personal qualities are constructed. What then does it mean for God to *unite* my heart? The psalmist shows an awareness that the fallen human heart needs integration, a kind of uniting which naturally it has not got, and which, even in the person like himself who is born again and has a new heart, still does not fully appear. How are we to understand this?

When a person becomes a Christian by putting faith in the Lord Jesus through the work of the Holy Spirit within, a new creation takes place. We have a new heart. The very core of our person, the basic inner self, the factory production line as we might say, is changed. The Holy Spirit has renovated us and now indwells us to sustain our new life at all points. And all the attitudes and desires and purposes and expressions of energy that are part of our new personal life, what the new heart pumps out when we are born again, center first and foremost upon the desire to be Jesus-like, the desire to love and honor and obey and please and exalt our heavenly Father, and most of all to glorify our Savior by sharing our knowledge of him. This desire, or group of desires, is what we mean by holiness in the heart. But the difficulty is that those good desires are opposed by the old egocentric, self-seeking, self-serving desires that controlled us before we became Christians. They are still there in our system, even though they are no longer controlling our life. "Dethroned but not destroyed" is the phrase that describes them. Thus tormented inwardly, we find that there is conflict between the two sets of desires, so that it takes a certain amount of resolution, plus help from above, to go with what our heart is really wanting, and so be natural as a Christian, doing all that we know of the will of God.

What is the cure for this conflict? Psalm 86:11, as we saw, asks God to "unite my heart to fear your name." The psalmist is asking God to advance the process of integration so that all of our energies will come together, to fear the Lord. Fearing the Lord has nothing to do with panic and alarm; it has everything to do with reverence, and response, and obedience to God's revealed will. When God unites our heart to fear his name, that fear includes a humble, honest response of love to the God whose love to us is measured by Calvary, as the psalmist's measure of the love of God would have been the exodus. Appreciating God's love as one seeks to resist the urgings of indwelling sin is the way to maintain and increase our spiritual health.

This links up with Paul's admonition in his letter to the church at Galatia. "Walk by the Spirit, and you will not gratify the desires of the flesh" (Gal. 5:16). That is a statement of certain fact, but this walk will not be easy. Paul warns us in the next verse that there will be a fight. "For the desires of the flesh are against the Spirit, and the desires of the Spirit are against the flesh, for these are opposed to each other, to keep you from doing the things you want to do" (Gal. 5:17).

This is why conformity to the will of God is never perfect in this life. Even if the performance outwardly regarded seems perfect, the motivation, the state, and desire of one's heart is never as strong in its God-centeredness, never as passionate in its purpose of bringing God honor and glory, as it should be and will be in heaven when God's work of grace is finished in us. So inwardly there is always an element of battle against lethargy and distraction. We accuse ourselves of not being zealous enough for the Lord, and we are right to do so because none of us is as zealous for the Lord as we should be. So we need to keep asking the Lord to *unite my heart more fully, to fear your name more thoroughly*. That is how Christians progress in sanctification all through this life.

In the same passage, Paul goes on, in verses 19–25, to provide a full-scale self-test for spiritual health, almost in check sheet form. First, in verses 19–21, he lists the desires of the flesh: sexual immorality, impurity, sensuality, idolatry, sorcery, enmity, strife, jealousy, fits of anger, rivalries, dissensions, divisions, envy, drunkenness, and orgies. Many readers pass over this list quickly glancing first at "sexual immorality" and last at "orgies," and then rating themselves as not much involved with these "works of the flesh." But in the midsection, Paul lists common sins, some of them sins specifically of the mind and heart: enmity, jealousy, fits of anger, rivalries, dissensions, envy. Who has not on occasion been enmeshed in these? These "soft sins" also reveal the state of the heart from which they pour, and wise Christians will take an honest look inside and ferret out their presence.

But the fruit of the Spirit is also present in the heart of the true believer. This is the same Spirit who is presiding over the work of grace within us and by whose power we are to walk daily in God's presence. Paul lists his ninefold fruit, and thus gives us a further self-test for health. The Spirit's fruit too includes "soft" realities, attitudes that are quantitatively unmeasurable, yet their presence or absence in our hearts are true health indicators. A wise Christians holds his or her life to this ninefold fruit and regularly asks, to what extent do my heart and life overflow with love, joy, peace, patience, kindness, goodness, faithfulness, gentleness, and self-control? How would the person who knows me best answer that question?

J. I. has been directed to take regular walks for his health, ideally every day, and Paul's "walk in the Spirit" can be construed as God calling us to a constant spiritual "health walk." The picture of walking is itself instructive. Walking is a purposeful steady activity; it is one foot in front of another. You go on, and you go on. You may not feel that you're moving very fast, but you get to your destination. Walking spiritually often feels exactly like that—but you get to your destination. Charles Wesley's prayer, expressed in one of his hymns, was that he might "closely walk with thee to heaven." This is God's picture of every Christian's life; in and through the Spirit, it is a walk, indeed a walk home with the good Lord himself.

Habits

Principle Two: Holiness of life is the fruit of habits in the heart. A common proverb says:

> Sow an action; reap a habit.
> Sow a habit; reap a character.
> Sow a character; reap a destiny.

There is great wisdom in this pronouncement. Your habits, increasingly, are you; all our habits, increasingly, are us. In the regenerate heart, as we have seen, certain habits are inbred and instinctive. If you are a Christian, you will habitually desire to please the Lord, to glorify the Lord, to show proper gratitude for the Lord's love, to show proper reverence for the Lord's greatness. You will in addition want to please God by obedience, in wisdom. You will also want to praise and pray because that is one of the habitual urgings which is implanted in you in the new birth. The Spirit comes into your heart and pulses, as we might say, so that you instinctively desire all of this and more.

Earlier in Galatians Paul wrote, "God sent forth his Son, born of woman, born under the law, to redeem those who were under the law, . . . so that we might receive adoption as sons. And because you are sons, God has sent the Spirit of his Son into our hearts, crying, 'Abba! Father!' So you are no longer a slave, but a son, and if a son, then an heir through God" (Gal. 4:4–7). "You are sons," says Paul. Becoming God's child is what happens when you put faith in Jesus. With justification (pardon and acceptance) has come adoption and inheritor status. And God has sent his Spirit into your heart, to prompt you to address God henceforth as "Abba," which means father in an intimate sense. The analogy is the young child who doesn't need to be told that Daddy and Mommy are there to speak to. The child just comes to them and starts talking. It is the most natural thing in the world; in a normal healthy family it happens, we could say, by instinct. In a spiritual sense, theologians label this intimate approach to God "filial instinct," the instinct of the child who raises her arms to her daddy knowing that he will pick her up and love her and take care of her and give her all that is good for her. It is a Christian paradox that while we approach God with reverence and awe, we also come to him with all the instinctive confidence with which the small child runs to her daddy. Holiness is the fruit of this filial instinct, expressed now in God-pleasing habits of heart and life that reproduce in us the moral profile of our elder brother in the Father's family, our holy kinsman-redeemer, Jesus Christ our Lord.

These nine habits that Paul called the "fruit of the Spirit" (singular, "fruit," not "fruits"), this love, joy, peace, patience, kindness, goodness, faithfulness, gentleness, and self-control, are nine facets of Christlikeness. They are so important as essentials of spiritual health, that we shall spend a few moments now explaining their nature.

Note first that each of them is a fixed habit of behaving as distinct from a passing mood or a fitful gust of feeling. They are aspects of character, life-habits that persist in place of external incentives, or shall we say temptations, to behave differently. Thus, love persists in the face of active hostility; joy, in face of grounds for bitterness; peace, in face of traumatic troubles; patience in face of impatience and panicky pressures; and so on. Each of these behavior patterns involves a willingness to swim against the stream of unthinking impulse, as did the Lord Jesus before us.

Note second, that they are expressions of conviction, shaped by knowledge of God's love to us and will for us. As they are not natural virtues, so they are not supernatural endowments wrought in us over our heads, so to speak, that is, while our heads are still empty of this knowledge. The fruit of the Spirit is the outcome of learning and obeying the gospel, consciously trusting Christ as Savior and Master, and resolutely repenting of our sins. Now look at these qualities separately.

Love: Love (*agapē*) is the habit of seeking some form of greatness for the other party, laboring to do what is truly good for that person. It is the way of love always to do its best for the beloved one. When we worship God it is love seeking to show him to be already great in our estimation, and to encourage others to acknowledge his greatness. When we love our neighbor, which is a further instinct of the regenerate heart, we seek to discern and to meet our neighbor's real need. Thus, love aims and works to make the neighbor, the loved one, great, whether or not this love is recognized and returned. Paul profiles the fundamentals of neighbor-love in 1 Corinthians 13.

Joy: Joy is a habit that, like the rest of the fruit, matures into an active attitude. Joy is a discipline—a delightful discipline—of rejoicing, which begins with simply thinking over the things that God has done for us, the commitment that God has made to us, and the service that God renders to us. To this kind of meditative thinking on God's kindness, joy is the natural reaction. But joy begins with a disciplined habit of *thinking* of these things until one is freshly thrilled by them. Then one's rejoicing finds natural expression in smiling, singing, and sharing and as has truly (and picturesquely) been said, joy then proves to be like jam: the more you try to spread it, the more it sticks to you. Joy in the Lord can coexist in the Christian's heart even with grief at unhappy things; "sorrowful, yet always rejoicing" (2 Cor. 6:10) is a Spirit-induced state of mind, incomprehensible to the world but well-known among God's saints.

Peace: One of the great gifts that our Lord has given us is objective, relational peace between us and our God through the achievement at Calvary. Subjective, personal peace flows from the *habit* of never forgetting the cross, but constantly remembering what our Lord went through in order to bring us pardon for sin and justification through faith. As we hold the cross before our minds, brooding on it (as is the good habit of many devout Christians, a habit regularly reinforced at the Lord's Table) the outcome is not morbidity, but peace—knowing peace with God, enjoying the peace of God, and becoming a center of peace, a peacemaker and peace-bringer, as we move around among the strife-torn. "Blessed are the peacemakers," says the Lord Jesus, "for they shall be called sons of God" (Matt. 5:9). The peace of God produces pleasure, praise, and patience under God's hand of providence; those privileged to know and share it are key people in every community of which they are part.

Patience: Patience, as we have just said, is a habit of mind and heart that grows out of inner peace. Patience trusts God to be at work even in the frustrating events of life, whether it is engorged traffic or crying babies or implacable vendettas or a seemingly unending series of personal disasters. Patience thinks before speaking, aiming to avoid offending. Patience wills the self to see the world from someone else's perspective—and to walk with that person through their world. Patience is rooted in hope because "if we hope for what we do not see, we wait for it with patience" (Rom. 8:25). Patience takes the long view; unfazed by short-term setbacks, it will carry on unruffled instead of giving up in despair. Patience accepts God's timing and responds to others in a way that reflects the patience God has toward us. "With the Lord one day is as a thousand years, and a thousand years as one day. The Lord . . . is patient toward you, not wishing that any should perish, but that all should reach repentance" (2 Peter 3:8–9). Patience sees today in the perspective of eternity—and so can laugh.

Kindness: Kindness is a habit that softens the atmosphere. It is an outgoing of neighbor-love that becomes instinctive, and is often unnoticed even by the person who practices it; yet voices and actions and even thoughts surrounding acts of kindness impart this softening toward others as if it were a benevolent virus, a happy infection that eases everything for everyone. The bewildered "sheep" of Matthew 25:31–40 could hardly remember when they visited the prison, fed the hungry, welcomed a stranger, and they had no idea that Christ valued these acts of kindness so much that he considered them as done to himself. Kindness is like that. It is a selfless form of thinking that sees a need and meets it, almost by reflex, with no thought of reward. Like the other fruit of the Spirit, kindness comes by receiving and then imitating the kindness of God, as the apostle Paul wrote to the church at Ephesus,

"Be kind to one another, tenderhearted, forgiving one another, as God in Christ forgave you" (Eph. 4:32).

Goodness: Goodness and kindness run into each other and so are often confused. Yet goodness has a quality of moral discernment about it that naked kindness might lack. Goodness thinks beyond the present and evaluates what is best in the long term. Kindness spends its strength handing out boatloads of fish to the hungry. Goodness both feeds the hungry and then helps them set up a microenterprise of fishing. Goodness discerns what is good and what is evil disguised as good. Goodness, we might say, is kindness well-soaked in wisdom. Like the other qualities that make up the ninefold fruit of the Spirit, goodness is a habit or disposition modeled after God's own character. When Moses asked God to show him his glory, God responded, "I will make all my goodness pass before you" (Exod. 33:19). Later when David composed Psalm 23, reflecting on a life guided and guarded by his shepherd, he said, "Surely goodness and mercy shall follow me all the days of my life" (v. 6). Because of the goodness of God's character, the goodness with which he deals with us and in which he wraps our lives, healthy people of God can truly be described as, in the best sense of the word, "good."

Faithfulness: Faithfulness doesn't quit. The book of Hosea pictures God's faithfulness with unforgettable poignancy. God tells Hosea to marry a prostitute named Gomer who (predictably) continued to practice her craft bearing a number of children not fathered by Hosea. Years later when Gomer, having long left Hosea, has as it seems become another man's sick and destitute slave, God commands Hosea to buy her and take her home once again as his wife, saying to her, "I will betroth you to me in faithfulness. And you shall know the LORD" (Hos. 2:20). Throughout the book, Gomer is a living symbol of Israel's unfaithfulness to God, and Hosea is a symbol of God's faithfulness to his people—so much so that at some points it is difficult to separate Hosea's words to Gomer from God's words to Israel. Hosea, in ways far past human expectation, has absorbed into his own character the sacrificial faithfulness of God. Most of us are not called to make Hosea's kind of sacrifice. But to the extent that we develop the habit of faithfulness, whether it is in keeping appointments, keeping bills paid when due, or keeping marriage vows, we begin to mirror, even partially, the character of our God who is faithful always.

Gentleness: We rarely see gentleness in a corporate boardroom, but small children, especially babies, seem to draw gentleness from within us. A favorite desk photo of Carolyn's shows a burly car mechanic, shoulders hunched protectively forward, calloused hands willed to a soft cradle, head sloping downward as his eyes meet those of the newborn son in his arms. A healthy Christ-follower is gentle to the core. Gentleness in the Bible is not the opposite of strength; it is not wimpishness, as modern usage might suggest; it is, rather, strength under control, harnessed to love and serve. Gentleness is all the more real because every time it is practiced, gentleness is a freely made choice that is backed by strength. Isaiah, in foretelling the coming of Jesus describes him in shepherd terms: "He will tend his flock like a shepherd; he will gather the lambs in his arms; he will carry them in his bosom, and gently lead those that are with young" (Isa. 40:11). This is a *strong* shepherd! He climbs rocky mountains looking for pastures, he carries recalcitrant lambs, he leads. But he notices those who need help, and those who are hungry, and those who require protection. It is his gentleness that notices, and cares. So it is with healthy Christians. People who follow their strong shepherd grow constantly in gentleness.

Self-control: An uncontrolled self is a deadly force. It wills to defy or ignore God and tries to take the place of God—as Eve, our foremother and Adam after her, discovered through encounter with the serpent. Idolizing, exalting, celebrating, and indulging oneself as one's god is the root cause of all the shame, folly, decadence, and moral blindness that mark modern Western culture so ruinously. When Jesus declared that the two greatest commands are that we must love God with all of our heart, soul, strength, and mind, and love our neighbor as much as we love ourselves, both of these commands attacked this human idolatry of self in a way that shows us how we are to transcend and overcome it. If we direct our whole being toward love of God, and if we give as much value to our neighbor as to ourselves, if not indeed more, the project of gaining control of self is well under way, and the fruit of the Spirit includes the habit of behaving in this fashion. As with gentleness, self-control operates from a position of strength. A strong understanding of oneself, a strong sense of selfhood, even of self-worth (under God's governing), is entirely proper and even necessary for fruitful life in Christ. And a self that knows itself and has embraced self-denial and given itself to God's control can become a powerful force for good. Indeed, this is the kind of gift that God asks of us through the apostle Paul: "I appeal to you therefore, brothers, by the mercies of God, to present your bodies [your whole selves] as a living sacrifice, holy and acceptable to God, which is your spiritual worship" (Rom. 12:1). This path leads deeper and deeper into the grace of self-control.

All nine aspects of the fruit of the Spirit, as we noted above, are in essence habits of reaction: habits of benevolent reaction to awkward people and difficult situations, habits of glad reaction toward God in light of his love. These reactions to other people and oneself are not determined by the way people are behaving toward us, but by what we know of the God who made us, loves us, and has saved us. All nine are from one point of view responsive love to God in various expressions. "We love because he first loved us" (1 John 4:19).

Here, then, is the diagram, the blueprint, the outline, the profile, the checklist of the habits that make up the kind of holiness that constitutes true spiritual health.

Heart

Principle Three: Habits of living are the fruit of desires in the heart. Here we dig more deeply into the realities of Christian motivation. At surface level we have covered this point already, but there is more to be said. Repetition forms habits. We sometimes hear euphemistically that this or that person "has a habit." These poor souls are the druggies, the gamblers, and the drunks. They have formed their habits of life by repetition, and now they are in the grip of them. They have repeatedly indulged certain cravings of the heart, and these cravings now control them. The habits they have acquired are self-destructive; they dissociate aspects of their personhood with increasing depth and sharpness—and so increase, rather than heal, the inner disintegration that is sin's legacy to us all. Those in the grip of these habits become increasingly untrustworthy and unreliable, and the waste of their human potential becomes increasingly obvious and tragic. This is the negation of spiritual health from every point of view.

These unhappy folk are in the grip of a desire that grows, as long-term, other things being equal, all desires do grow, by being gratified; subsiding temporarily, perhaps, they are desires to which we yield and which come back all the stronger next time. The addictions we mentioned, and others like them—smoking, gluttony, sex, thieving, and so on—often begin with casual desire, perhaps only the desire not to be left out of what one's friends are doing, but through being indulged the desire becomes compulsive, and strong enough to take over large areas, frequently indeed the central areas, of people's lives. As the desire for a repeat fix feeds the habit, so the habit feeds the desire, and the person slips further and further under the power of both.

Now the point we would make here is that a comparable, though very different, process goes on in every healthy Christian life. As the heart's *desire* to know and love and please and serve and exalt and glorify the Father and the Son more and more finds expression in our behavior, and comes to command more and more of our creativity, our imagination, and our inventiveness, so the *desire* itself grows stronger, with the result that the habits of life that it generates becomes more and more deeply ingrained in us. This aspect of the God-ordained pattern of life in Christ and in the Holy Spirit is not always appreciated as it should be. But when the New Testament writers call for growth and increase in the distinguishing life-qualities of born-again Christian people, it seems clear that this is the essence of what they mean.

To understand this, we must first note that desire does not always take the same psychological form. The spectrum that includes the young man's constant desire for sexual relief, the child's recurring desire for ice cream, the scholar's intense desire to solve an academic problem and publish the solution in a convincing form, and the overworked teacher's frantic desire for a vacation, is broad indeed. Desire is sometimes passionate, sometimes calm, sometimes physical, sometimes intellectual, sometimes panicky and hysterical, sometimes free from emotional overtones altogether. What constitutes it as desire is not its feeling-tone and emotional temperature, nor its moral quality, whether virtuous and noble or vicious and degrading, nor its comparative strength or weakness, but just the fact that it invades our thinking and tries, with or without success, to exercise some control over our planning so as to ensure its own gratification. Though we may resist its pull in our actual behaving we cannot get it out of our minds, at least not by simply saying "go away." The deep desires of non-Christians are like that—they nag, as we say—and the deep desires of Christians are like that too.

Twenty years ago John Piper startled the evangelical world with his book *Desiring God*,[1] in which he advocated what he called Christian Hedonism. Some who knew that in moral philosophy hedonism is the secular view that gaining pleasure is the natural, necessary, right, and proper goal of life and motive for action, and who knew too that in New Testament morality self-denial and cross-bearing, self-control, and self-surrender are central found Piper's phrase paradoxical. But what Piper means is impeccable. He is pointing to the principle that God is most glorified when he is most enjoyed by his rational creatures; that, as Jonathan Edwards put it, "when those who see [God's glory] delight in it, God is more glorified than if they only see it;"[2] that, therefore, the famous first answer in the Westminster Shorter Catechism might have been even better than it is, had it read: "Man's chief end is to glorify God *by enjoying* him for ever," in place of "and enjoy him for ever." Equating pleasure with joy, gladness, delight, and the happiness of being gratified and satisfied, Piper aims to stir up in us desire for God in order to induce the condition that pleases and honors God supremely as well as being supremely pleasant, captivating, gladdening, and fulfilling to the Christian heart. Piper is entirely right to insist that we do not desire God enough.

Desiring God is a state of heart that leads us to contemplate God always at work in providence and in grace, and always for our benefit. The phrase signifies a quest for three things. First, desiring God is the mindset that longs for the turning of God's *face* toward us (this imagery points to the closest and most vividly realized intimacy with him). That desire breaks surface at the close of worship services when the pastor prays over the gathered people the same prayer Moses offered for his brother Aaron and his sons:

> The LORD bless you and keep you;
> the LORD make his face to shine upon you and be gracious
> to you;
> the LORD lift up his countenance up on you and give you
> peace.
>
> Numbers 6:24–26

We find echoes of this prayer either as a blessing or a petition throughout the psalms. See for example Psalm 4:6; 25:16; 31:16; 86:16; 119:132, 135. But how seriously do we take the thought? As young children constantly long for magic moments when their parents pick them up, cuddle them, and kiss them, so heart-healthy Christians constantly desire moments when God's face shines on them—that is, so they will say, when God comes very close.

Second, desiring God is a mindset that looks constantly for the tokens of God's *friendship* with us (*friendship* is the noun that best fits the fellowship with the Father and the Son into which we are called). We see this in John's first letter as he defines the connections between himself, his God, and his readers: "so that you too may have fellowship with us; and indeed our fellowship is with the Father and with his Son Jesus Christ" (1 John 1:3). Friendship was the way God defined his fellowship with Abraham (see 2 Chron. 20:7; Isa. 41:8–10; James 2:23), and Jesus defined his fellowship with his disciples in the same unfathomably generous terms when he said, "Greater love has no one than this, that someone lays down his life for his friends. You are my friends if you do what I command you. No longer do I call you servants, for the servant does not know what his master is doing; but I have called you friends, for all that I have heard from my Father I have made known to you" (John 15:13–15). The tokens of this kind of friendship with God are needs relieved and requests met, and heart-healthy Christians treasure them all.

Third, desiring God is a mindset that navigates through life with God's *future* for us, as a compass point focusing on our never-ending expectations and discoveries of how God in grace continually imparts to us a Christlikeness that furthers our glorification and so increases our joy. Paul wrote to the church at Corinth, "And we all, with unveiled face, beholding the glory of the Lord, are being transformed into the same image from one degree of glory to another" (2 Cor. 3:18).

Desiring God hereby comes to appear as a process, indeed a discipline, of *delighting, deleting, denying,* and *dying.* The inward delight that knowledge of this process brings is reflected in John's word of wonder: "See what kind of love the Father has given to us, that we should be called children of God; and so we are. . . . And what we will be has not yet appeared; but we know that when he appears we will be like him, because we shall see him as he is. And everyone who thus hopes in him purifies himself as he is pure" (1 John 3:1–2). The *delighting* is a matter of focusing thoughts on God, reminding ourselves specifically of his good gifts to us already and, with that, of who and what he is and what he has done, is doing, and will do—how he saved us, saves us, and will save us—for the glory with Christ that he has in store for us. Such thoughts will always bring delight and leave us delighted. The *deleting* is a matter of turning our back on all aspects of the ungodly self-service that ensnared us once and seeks now to do so again. The *denying* is a matter of saying no to what the Puritan Richard Baxter called "carnal self" (as distinct from "personal self")[3] in its attempts to evade the call to follow the Lord Jesus totally and without compromise. We must say *no* every day of our lives to the evasions and wrigglings of this carnal self. The *dying* is a matter of recognizing, intellectually and imaginatively, that in God's sight we believers have been crucified, have already died and been buried with Christ (that is, the life we were living previously has ended), and we have been raised up in union with him into a new life replacing the old (see Rom. 6:3–11; Gal. 2:20; 2 Cor. 5:14–17; Col. 2:11–13; 3:1–3). Reminding ourselves that this is the truth about us and keeping ourselves as vividly aware of this as we can, must also be a daily *discipline*. This is the fourfold path for desirers of God to tread, and how far we desire God in our hearts will appear from how diligent we are in the treading of it. For our habits of life, as we said earlier, are the index of the strength of the desires of the heart that produce them.

Paul prayed that the Philippians' love to God and man might "abound more and more, with knowledge and all discernment" (Phil. 1:9), and he presents himself to them as an example of one who "count[s] everything as loss because of the surpassing worth of knowing Christ Jesus my Lord," and whose goal is "that I may know him and the power of his resurrection. . . . I press on toward the goal for the prize of the upward call of God in Christ Jesus" (Phil. 3:8, 10, 14). Also, he prayed that the Colossians might be "filled with the knowledge of [God's] will in all spiritual wisdom and understanding, . . . bearing fruit in every good work, and increasing in the knowledge of God" (Col. 1:9–10), and he directed them thus: "As you received Christ Jesus the Lord, so walk in him, rooted and built up in him and established in the faith, just as you were taught, abounding in thanksgiving" (2:6–7). "Built up" and "established," like "abounding," are present participles in the Greek, signifying a continuous, ongoing process. Peter, having warned his readers against various doctrinal deviations and errors, writes similarly rounding off his second letter by saying to them: "But grow in the grace and knowledge of our Lord and Savior Jesus Christ" (2 Peter 3:18).

What do these verses tell us about the Spirit-given knowledge of the Father and the Son that Peter and Paul have in view?

Three things, it seems. First, this is evidently both cognitive and relational knowledge. It is knowledge about the Father and the Son, and within that cognition, which we may call orthodoxy, it is personal knowledge of both, that is, communion with them. Second, this knowledge evidently brings ability to discern God's will, in a way that otherwise we would not be able to do. (We shall pick up this point in a moment.) Third, this is knowledge in which we are evidently meant to make progress. How is that to happen? If what we have said so far is right, it is to happen through our desiring more and more of God, both cognitively and relationally, and through using appropriate means (primarily prayer, biblical meditation, Christian fellowship, and the Lord's Supper) to gain what we long for. In this we shall be following where holy folk in Scripture itself have led; take these texts for examples:

> Whom have I in heaven but you?
>> And there is nothing on earth that I desire besides
>> you. . . .
> God is the strength of my heart and my portion forever.
>
> Psalm 73:25–26

> I say to the LORD, "You are my Lord;
>> I have no good apart from you." . . .
> The LORD is my chosen portion.
>
> Psalm 16:2, 5

> As a deer pants for flowing streams,
>> so pants my soul for you, O God.
> My soul thirsts for God.
>
> Psalm 42:1

> O God, you are my God; earnestly I seek you;
>> my soul thirsts for you. . . .
> Your steadfast love is better than life.
>
> Psalm 63:1, 3

My soul yearns for you in the night;
    my spirit within me earnestly seeks you.

Isaiah 26:9

"The LORD is my portion," says my soul,
    "therefore I will hope in him."

Lamentations 3:24

To desire and seek God habitually in this way is natural to the regenerate heart and is the root of all real progress in knowing God. Christ's followers can truly be said to "have a habit," but it is a different sort of habit from that of habit-bound druggies and drunks. This habit comes from a different sort of heart, namely, one that has been renewed by God, and is hungry for God, and enjoys adoring and pleasing God more than it enjoys anything else, and wants to know more of God's work and ways and will, in order to worship and serve him better. Which leads us straight to the fourth and final point in our analysis of spiritual health.

Holiness

Principle Four: Holiness of life leads to discernment in the heart. To clarify this, we return to Romans 12:1–2, the verses that stand at this chapter's head. The first thing these verses show us is how holiness becomes a reality in human lives.

The pastoral problem at Rome, as Paul saw it, was that due to fuzziness about some aspects of the gospel, relations between Jewish and non-Jewish believers were tense, with mistrust on both sides. So Paul realized that the letter he was writing to prepare the way for his own planned visit must spell out the whole gospel as he understood it and draw from it true principles of fellowship and cooperation so that the church at Rome would know where he stood, and why, on all that confused and divided them. Hence the layout of Romans, with 12:1 "I appeal to you . . . ," as the transition point from declaring what God did, does, and will do and moving on to directing what Christians should do here and now.

Any thoughtful reader today, having reached the end of Romans 11, might be ruminating somewhat as follows: "What amazing stuff! God is so much more than I had thought, and the sweep of his judgment and his mercy, and his plan of salvation with Jesus at its center, fairly takes my breath away. I had never thought of God's grace working in history, from Adam and Abraham on, the way it is presented here, nor as a believer had I understood my Christian life in terms of being dead and risen in Christ with Christ, and indwelt by the Holy Spirit to make me live so very differently—it's mind-boggling! And seeing how non-Jewish Christians are grafted into Jewish stock and now share the same spiritual root system is amazing too. This Christian faith is big, much bigger and more complex, and much more deeply rooted in world history, than ever I realized, and Jesus Christ, I now see, is center stage and horizon-filling for persons with faith as no other person ever is or could be. I never dreamed that religious truth would be like this. So now what? I know that I don't have to work for my salvation, which has come to me, for good, as a free gift; is there anything, then, that I should now be doing?"

Chapters 12–16 are Paul's answer to that unspoken but deeply felt question. Believers without exception, they tell us, are called to be holy, serving God by neighbor-love in and beyond the church, and the hinge of holiness is 12:1, at which we shall now look in detail. *"I appeal to you therefore, brothers, by the mercies of God . . ."* "Wherefore the 'therefore'?" we ask. Answer: this is an inference from "the mercies of God" as Paul has been expounding them from chapter 3 onward; and just as these mercies in themselves logically require the response Paul is about to specify, so the knowledge and appreciation of these mercies by those who have received them generate a motive of gratitude, leading them to make the response that is required.

"Brothers" in Paul's opening sentence (v. 1) actually means brothers and sisters; the word is an inclusive masculine. All God's adopted children, as those justified by faith truly are (8:14–17),

are each other's spiritual siblings within the divine family, "heirs of God and fellow heirs with Christ" our elder brother (8:17). Adoption is one of the greatest gifts of God's great grace.

"I appeal to you therefore, brothers, by the mercies of God, that you present your bodies. . . ." Not bodies as opposed to souls, or spirits, or hearts for that matter, but whole persons—quite simply, all that you are. The Bible from time to time uses both "body" and "soul" to denote the whole person. Paul's phrase here harks back to the way he spoke of presenting (same verb) ourselves and our body parts to God in 6:13. *"A living sacrifice, holy acceptable to God. . . ."* From the Old Testament we learn that the basic idea of a sacrifice (leaving aside the special role of some offerings in atoning for sin; that is not in view here) is of a gift that expresses responsive gratitude: a gift offered in homage to the God of creation, providence, and grace, at his own command, according to his own specification, and proceeding from a truly God-fearing heart. A study of Leviticus will confirm this. "Holy" (set apart for God) and "acceptable to God" are terms that the Old Testament applies to sacrifices that are offered in the way they should be.

"Which is your spiritual worship" ("reasonable service," as in KJV, is a great thought but a doubtful translation). Real holiness is thankful, responsive, obedient consecration, with adoration of God alongside gratitude at its heart. The Word rendered "spiritual" is not the usual word that points to the Holy Spirit, but one that conveys the thought of something being appropriately rational and intelligent, and done with real understanding.

The second thing these verses show us is how discernment of God's will becomes a reality in holy lives. *"Do not be conformed to this world . . ."* Christian believers, who through their supernatural change of heart and indwelling of the Holy Spirit are radically different from non-Christians around them, must be ready to make this evident by behaving differently.

"But be transformed by the renewal of your mind . . ." The Greek verb rendered as "transformed" yields the English word *metamorphosis*, signifying a real and substantial change in one's personal existence in some way. Being in the present tense, the verb indicates

that the transformation will be an ongoing, continuous, progressive process. "Mind" as we have already seen, is a word with a large and inclusive meaning; it covers all mental processes, all attitudes, all motives, purposes, and plannings. It embraces on the one hand all our power of creative imagination (such as sympathy, identifying with others, skill to practice fine and useful arts, so generating beauty, and ability to express, to perform, act parts and play roles, rise to occasions, and so enrich relationships); and on the other hand it covers all types and lines of analytical thought (such as inferences, calculation, reflections, evaluation, speculations, and guesses). Decision making, which is central to this book, is one of the mind's many joint activities in which our imaginative and analytical powers are united.

"That by testing you may discern what is the will of God, what is good and acceptable and perfect." Here is Paul's punch line! The will of God is the course of action in each situation that God sees as good, pleasing, and complete; the most truly and fully God-glorifying response to each set of needs and possibilities; the most biblical, faithful, and reverent option open to us each time as servants of God and of his Son Jesus Christ. It is this that God wants and helps us to discern and then carry out. We shall make the discernment, says Paul, by testing—that is envisaging and weighing alternatives, and not letting the merely good become the enemy of the best. This means brainwork, which we should do in God's presence, looking to him for light and help; but our reliance on him will not make it any the less brainwork. Discernment of this sort is often hard and demanding, often involves research and consultation to get our facts and principles straight, which takes time and severely tries our patience. Paul is not speaking of a global supernatural disclosure of God's plan for one's whole life, but of a situational perception of what is best to do here and now for God, for others, and for oneself in terms of God's own law and value system, by which his judgments are formed. The Greek word rendered "perfect" means not so much flawless as complete and adequate, covering all angles in the way most satisfactory to God. Our power thus to perceive God's will—our

insight in testing alternatives, that is—will reflect the degree of thoroughness, love, and depth with which we have inventoried our powers of imagination and thought and lovingly consecrated them to God. Should we be lax in this, our discerning of God's will becomes deficient too.

So whenever we seek God's guidance in particular matters, we need to begin by making sure that we are walking with him in Christ, in love and loyalty and full commitment to both him and our neighbor, in the way that we should. Holiness of heart and life, a mind seeking deeper and fuller renewal from God, willingness to think hard in exploring and comparing possible courses of action, and successful discernment of the will of God are four things that go together. Subtract any or all of the first three, and the fourth will suffer.

Perfection, in the sense of flawless Christian maturity in intellectual, moral and spiritual virtues, and in practical wisdom is always an unrealized goal in our present life: we aim at it, but never attain it. Our reach exceeds our grasp. "Lord, I long to be perfect; help my imperfection" must surely be the constant cry of us all. However, the goal of good spiritual health in this life is attainable, and the foregoing pages have, we believe, shown what essentially it involves, with repeated stress on the fact that our grasp of God's will and our consequent decision making are unlikely to be any better than is our overall spiritual condition. So we venture to urge that the way of wisdom for us all is to pause now and institute our own personal health checkup before we go any further.

4

Guided by the Word of God

Your word is a lamp to my feet and a light to my path.

Psalm 119:105

Humor is a funny thing, in more senses than one; for though it may appear in the guise of a shift from seriousness to flippancy, the incongruities that are humor's lifeblood regularly prompt all kinds of weighty questions, often weightier than those being discussed before the humor broke in as light relief. Thus: An American president was famously impassive and taciturn. When news came that he was dead, one wit, so we hear, asked, "How did they know?" Barbed and tasteless as it may be, this joke raises the weightiest question of all: what does it mean to be a human being, alive? With that question, the present chapter must begin.

In broadest terms, adult human life, into which children are to grow, is a compound of three things: discovery, direction setting, and decision making. Each of these involves us in some form of relating, communicating, imagining, and hoping. *Discovery* means the discerning of goodness, truth, and beauty or their opposites in the world order that surrounds us, plus the discerning of love and justice or their opposites in our relationship with other people, plus the realizing of how our responses, positive or negative, creative or destructive, to persons and to situations can achieve or miss goodness, beauty, truth, love, and justice here and now. *Direction setting* means fixing personal goals and embracing purposive action whereby we aim to bring in a future we shall welcome and avoid one we shall not. *Decision making* means the establishing of our various commitments major and minor, some involving change, some confirming continuance, some following our usual habits, some breaking with them, all being positive responses to whoever or whatever is confronting us each moment. The human being has in the past been defined as a tool-making animal. We here are defining ourselves, biblically we believe, as discerning, direction setting, and decision making creatures of God, and seeking to understand ourselves and our lives, first to last, in these terms. Our human life, we are saying, is marked by relationality, resolvings, and responsibilities—either for better or for worse, depending on how we handle ourselves in each circumstance. We know, as we are sure our readers do too, that in today's decadent Western world, aspects of this account of ourselves get dissolved away in the reductionist acids of modern and postmodern philosophy, but trashing any part of what we have just said seems to us a willful evasion of what in our hearts we all know to be our own human reality; so on this basis we shake our heads, roll our eyes, and proceed.

The biblical view of our humanness takes for granted all that we have said so far and goes beyond it. The Bible, and with it the whole Christian church down the ages, tells us that our *discernment* must begin by acknowledging our Creator as present in everything and as both the source of, and the resource for, all that is good; then our *direction setting* must start by establishing the glory of God as our target in every endeavor; and our *decision making* must proceed on the basis that in all that we attempt we are to be guided by God's revealed will. Thus we shall please God by practicing righteousness, and so display in daily life the reality of the divine image and likeness, as we are called to do.

What does it mean to be guided by God's revealed will? To begin an answer to that question, four basic things must be said in sequence: namely, that we are to be guided by the commands of God, the book of God, the law of God, and the mind of God. To say these things as we think they need to be said will occupy us for the rest of this chapter.

Guided by God's Commands

First: We are to be guided by the *commands* of God. Fundamental to Christian faith is the recognition that commands from God are a reality. Christianity views languages as such as a divine gift to our race, given not only so that we might communicate with each other and offer praises and prayers to our Maker, but also, and indeed primarily, so that *he* might communicate with *us*, in both the indicative and the imperative mood—in other words, so that he might tell us both what we *need to know* and what we *need to do*. He is essentially a God who commands his rational creatures. Non-Christian faiths, and the wide range of unorthodox Protestant opinions that we lump together under the name of liberalism, do not usually acknowledge this; whatever they say about God paying attention to our prayers, in which we tell him things, they assume (most of the time, anyway) that God does not use language to tell us things and give us marching orders. Wise souls are thought of in these circles as speaking for God in what they say about him, and in what they tell us to do to get close to him, but God is not believed in any sense to speak for himself, and so beliefs about the specifics of his will for us humans remain blurry. We, however, affirm that God does address us all in the command mode, and we see it as our main task in this book to show just how he does so. As Christianity from the start has taught what is called a divine-command ethic, so now we propose to teach, as one aspect of that ethic, divine-command guidance. This is our agenda.

To start with, historic Christianity, the faith of the continuing orthodox church, rests on the belief that God the Creator has given and kept and will continue to keep promises. Thus, Christianity sees Jesus of Nazareth as the Messiah, the Christ, the fulfillment of God's many promises of a Davidic Savior-King that he gave throughout Old Testament times from Eden on. One who gives and keeps promises is necessarily a language-user, just as every monarch is necessarily a language-user every time he issues a command. God's use of language in stating his promises and commands is the first thing we need to be clear on. Christianity acknowledges Jesus as the world's Savior and Lord on whom we base personal faith and life by trusting promises from and about Jesus as our God-given lifeline. By stating the divine commitment to us who trust Christ, God's promises shape our relationship with him, and that means that those whom God thus takes under his wing are also under his command so that both as our Creator and as our Redeemer he is entitled to say to us, "Now this is what you must and must not do." We (his followers) recognize that and see his commands as linked with his promises to guide all who in every generation live by those promises. But standard Christian belief and piety would both be blown to pieces were faith in God as a promise-giver and promise-keeper negated, for, as we now see, it is this that holds Christianity together as the reality that it is, the frame of faith within which divine commands belong.

Furthermore, Christianity rests on the belief that Jesus of Nazareth is God incarnate, the second Person within the divine unity. He came to save our lost race; he died, rose, reigns, and will reappear. On earth he was a speaker, a teacher, a lawgiver, and a prophet—a language-user, therefore; and central to his remembered utterances are promises and commands that he gave in his Father's name to all who would follow him. By being a language-user he showed that using words to instruct is God's way of communication. He insisted that response to his own words will determine each hearer's destiny, for better or for worse—just as if a man built his house firmly on rock or else on shifting sands at the tide line (Matt. 7:24–27). Jesus said even more directly (and offensively), "The one who rejects me and does not receive my words has a judge; the word that I have spoken will judge him on the last day"

(John 12:48). These and similar statements show that Christianity depends on the divine use of language—fact-and-duty language, promise-and-command language—and on our recognition of that language. As you cannot take the divine Christ out of Christianity, so you cannot eliminate his divine words. If Christ is real, then we may and must affirm that God talks and that denial of this is in truth denial of Christ.

Then, in the third place: Christianity rests on the belief that God through Christ enters into a covenant relationship with his worshippers, in virtue of which the church is right to identify itself as his covenant people. The Christian claim is that the church is the new, true Israel, inheriting in Christ an improved version of the relationship that God through Moses established with Abraham's descendants at Sinai. Now a covenant is made precisely by an exchange of words: in this case, words of promise and command whereby God imposes his covenant, followed by human words of acceptance and pledged loyalty in response. So if God does not use words, his covenant with his people cannot exist, and from this standpoint historic Christianity falls apart. Thus it appears that God's use of language, namely command language within the frame of his promise-giving and covenanting, belongs to the very essence of Christianity and must be acknowledged by all Christ's true disciples.

The Bible displays God as one who commands and humans as required to practice obedience. This presentation starts in Eden, where God, having in effect established his covenant with the first human by the words he had already spoken, "commanded the man, saying" he must not eat fruit from the tree of the knowledge of good and evil (Gen. 2:16–17). Later, God "appeared to Abram and said to him, 'I am God Almighty; walk before me and be blameless, that I may make my covenant between me and you . . . to be God to you and your offspring after you. . . . You shall keep my covenant'" (Gen. 17:1–2, 7, 9). The Ten Commandments, given as part of the covenant-confirmation at Sinai, were and are basic to biblical religion (Exod. 20:1–17; Deuteronomy 5–6; see also Mark 10:17–19; Rom. 13:9). At the close of the book of Ecclesiastes we read: "Fear God and keep his commandments, for this is the whole duty of man" (Eccles. 12:13). Psalm 119 is 176 verses long, and is a sustained meditation on the blessings and joys of people who keep God's commandments. Jesus, risen, is found at the close of Matthew's Gospel giving his disciples marching orders on the basis that all authority has been given him in heaven and on earth: "Go therefore and make disciples of all nations, . . . teaching them to observe all that I have commanded you" (Matt. 28:18–20). Paul adds that "neither circumcision counts for anything nor uncircumcision, but keeping the commandments of God" is what counts (1 Cor. 7:19). How can we know that we belong to Jesus Christ? John suggests this test: "This is the love of God, that we keep his commandments," then quickly adds, "And his commands are not burdensome" (1 John 5:3).

Little stress is laid these days, even in the church, let alone in our supposedly Christian culture, on the reality and authority of God's commands. But the fundamental dimension of being Christian people guided by God is that we labor to learn his commandments as he has revealed them, and to live by them in faithful obedience just as consistently as we possibly can. When, one day, we have to give an account of ourselves to God, it will be important for us to be able to say with truth that we sought to keep all his commandments throughout our Christian lives.

Guided by God's Book

Second: We are to be guided by the *book* of God. The book of God is the Bible; but what is that? It is a composite document consisting of sixty-six separate pieces of writing, four-fifths in Hebrew, one-fifth in Greek, and a tiny bit in Aramaic. In translation it averages between 1,200 and 1,400 pages in most editions. Thirty-nine of the books are called the Old Testament and twenty-seven the New, and the full list, with its two sections, is called the canon. (Catholics espouse twelve additional books in the Old Testament; Greek and Russian Orthodox Bibles include a few more such additions.)

This Old Testament collection took more than a thousand years to write; the New Testament was probably completed within a single generation. All of the books focus on God the Creator and human life in relation to him, viewed in the light of his ongoing purpose for humankind. All of them help to tell and explain the story of how God the Creator became God the Redeemer and how the Son of God, whose human name is Jesus, has become the Savior of the world, the Lord of history, and, with the Father and the Holy Spirit, the object of love, praise, and service without end from the new community, which is the Christian church. The narrative of God's dealings with a people defined by the figures of Adam, Noah, Abraham, Moses, David, and Jesus is the backbone, so to speak, of the Bible, and the prophets' sermons, apostles' letters, psalter (a 150-item hymn-and-prayer book), and wisdom writings are like so many ribs, each needing to be attached to the backbone in the appropriate place. Seeing the Bible this way makes it fairly straightforward to study—but the fact remains that in its totality it is a big book. There is a lot to it, and many who look to the Bible for guidance do not know it very well.

From the days of Christ and the apostles, Christians referred comprehensively to the Old Testament as the Word of God, plus whatever apostolic writings they had, and by the fourth century, virtually everywhere, that meant our full New Testament canon as well. Since then, it has been standard practice for everyone to refer to the entire canon, as such, as the Word of God. By this phrase "Word of God," three thoughts have been expressed. First, all that the Bible teaches is truth from God, coming to us with all his authority. Second, God so overruled the processes whereby the sixty-six books were composed that every generation of the church, and every individual reader, should think of the Bible as a divine product, containing just what God wanted each of us to have so that we might understand his work, his ways, his will, and his worship and live in loving fellowship with him on the basis of this knowledge. Third, when the Holy Spirit opens the spiritually blind eyes of the fallen human heart, people perceive the divine source of the Bible in the same immediate and self-evidencing way in which they perceive the personal divinity of the Lord Jesus Christ. Spirit-taught people find themselves unable to deny either the one or the other. Academic persons sometimes lose their grip on these basic convictions, but they remain central, and rightly so, in the mainstream Christian mind.[1]

A further fact that Christians celebrate is that when people read the Bible, or at least brood on what they know of its teaching, even when they are beginners who do not as yet know the sacred text well, messages from God come through to their hearts in a way that is both startling and encouraging. Bible readers sense again and again that God is speaking significantly to them, "for teaching, for reproof, for correction, and for training in righteousness" (the profitable purposes for which God has given Scripture, according to Paul in 2 Tim. 3:16). Arousing the expectation that this will happen and teaching Christians that each time they turn to Scripture they should have in their heart and mind the prayer "Open my eyes, that I may behold wondrous things out of your law" (Ps. 119:18), are key elements in good discipleship training. Certainly, the closer and more thorough one's acquaintance with the Bible as a whole, the more clearly and fully will one discern its wisdom for living the whole of one's life; but God is gracious and good—he meets people where they are, and often showers beginner Christians with insights for their personal guidance as they take their first hesitant steps in forming the habit of daily Bible reading.

Such experiences, no doubt, were the source from which arose the odd procedure called *Sortes biblicae* in Latin (meaning, chance selections from Scripture): literally, choices by lot. This practice was reverent in intention, and became fairly common, it seems, among eighteenth and nineteenth century pietists (Protestants, that is, who rightly saw one's personal relationship with God as the top priority of their life, and who would go to extreme lengths to keep in step with God all the time). In moments of uncertainty about what to do, these folk would close their eyes, open the Bible at random, put a finger on the page, and hope to find the lead they needed in the verse they had hit. An often-told cautionary tale is of the man whose first hit was "Judas went out and hanged himself," who tried again and whose second hit was "You go and do likewise," and who on the third attempt found his finger pointing to "What you are going to do, do quickly." This story makes the point that, however well meant, this practice of seeking guidance by using the Bible, in effect, as a kind of Ouija board, is superstitious and wrong. God never tells us, nor wants us, to act this way; we are not entitled to expect him to give us personal instruction by some kind of magic method, and to ask him to do so is not reverent at all—rather the reverse. This is emphatically not the way to be guided by the Book.

How then are we to draw from the Bible the guidance we need? Sometimes biblical imperatives and narratives of godly and ungodly conduct speak directly to our own situation and show us directly how we should behave, but more often the decisions we have to make seem circumstantially quite distant from anything we read in the Bible; so how may we find God's guidance in those cases? The clue lies in the point already made, that Scripture contains God's commands, which establish parameters and set limits for all our behavior. As God's promises give direction to all of our hopes, so do God's commands direct us in establishing attitudes and policies with regard to every aspect and department of our life-activities. It is often said that there is no life-problem involving in any way our relationship with God on which the Bible does not speak, at least in principle. We believe that to be a true though challenging statement, not at all an overstatement. We accept Scripture as our rule of practice as well as our rule of faith. Having made these strong all-encompassing statements, our goal to be guided by God's Word now rests on solid footing, but the task before us has barely begun. To learn how to make detailed application of biblical principles to life we have to go further and dig deeper, and that brings us to our next section.

Guided by God's Law

Third: We are to be guided by the *law* of God. What is the law of God? In simplest and broadest terms, it is the entire prescription for Christian living that the book of God yields. In other words, it is the formula God gives for making our personal story fit into his global story, thereby fulfilling the purpose of our creation, that we should glorify our Creator. God's law is the applicatory interpretation of the Bible as a whole. It is the total message—factual and directional, informational and practical—that the Bible presents to us for the guiding of our lives.

In Hebrew the word for law is *torah*, which primarily means not public legislation but domestic instruction, the kind of admonishing, authoritative yet affectionate, that a faithful father gives his children and others in the household of which he is the head. The corresponding word in Greek is *nomos*, which in secular use meant only public legislation, but which had its meaning broadened by being used for *torah* in the Greek translation of the Old Testament, the Septuagint, and which in turn carried this broader meaning throughout the New Testament. God gave Israel his law at Sinai, and much of it deals directly with community rights and duties in the way that public legislation today does. But the basis on which Yahweh spelled out this legal code was that, as Moses reported it to Pharaoh, "Israel is my firstborn son" (Exod. 4:22). God's giving of his commandments was thus a family affair, just as the Solomonic admonitions to "my son" in Proverbs 1–7 are a family affair. And in both cases more is given than bare commandments: the sanctions and undergirdings of the commands are promises, assurances, and guarantees that declare God's covenant commitment to Israel corporately and to each Israelite individually. The verbalizings and modelings of wise life in the wisdom books, and of the faithful, hopeful, praising, praying life in the Psalter, are law also. So the law of God comprises a full-scale philosophy of life for God's people, a comprehensive declaration of how each one is to live in this world as a believer and hoper in God, and more particularly as a sharer in the fellowship of others who also believe and hope in the same way. Later, the apostle Paul, arguing against persons for whom the law meant simply things one must do, spoke of the law in the same narrow sense as they did and contrasted it with the promises of the gospel; but throughout the Old Testament

God's law includes his promises, and law-keeping means being an obedient believer.

The foundation of the *torah* is the decalogue, the ten directive "words" that God, we are told, wrote with his own finger on two stone tablets for Israel's instruction as part of his covenanting action. (See Exod. 20:1–17; 31:18; 32:15–16, 19; 34:1, 27–29; Deut. 9:10; 10:1–5.) This spiritual and moral code (for that is what it is) calls for thoroughgoing loyalty to God and for equally thoroughgoing observance of the claims of one's fellow creatures and fellow members of God's family on one's daily behavior. Since the commandments are not as well known, even among church people, as they should be, we briefly reproduce them here.

> I am the LORD your God. . . .
> You shall have no other gods. . . .
> You shall not make for yourself a carved image. . . . You shall not bow down to them. . . .
> You shall not take the name of the LORD your God in vain. . . .
> Remember the Sabbath day, to keep it holy. . . .
> Honor your father and your mother. . . .
> You shall not murder.
> You shall not commit adultery.
> You shall not steal.
> You shall not bear false witness. . . .
> You shall not covet. . . .
>
> Exodus 20:2–17

We might paraphrase the Decalogue in positive and Christian terms with something like this: "You shall worship your covenant God exclusively and wholeheartedly, according to his own self-revelation, regarding him with consistent reverence and setting aside regular time for rest and worship in his honor; you should respect those who have nurtured you, and labor to sustain the family unit; you must do all you can to safeguard the life, sexual purity, property, reputation, and well-being of all you meet; and, knowing that your God watches over you, you are to be content with what you have." Jesus linked attitude and action in all law-keeping when he told a lawyer who had asked him which was the greatest commandment of the law: "You shall love the Lord your God with all your heart and with all your soul and with all your mind. This is the great and first commandment. And a second is like it: You shall love your neighbor as yourself. On these two commandments depend all the Law and the Prophets" (Matt. 22:37–40, citing Deut. 6:5 and Lev. 19:18). All the specifics of moral and political duty that the Bible spells out are, one way or another, instances or applications of these principles. Here, then, was guidance into godliness for the Israelites—and here is basic guidance for us too.

When Jesus says that the Mosaic legislation and the prophets' exhortations depend on the twin love-commands (the verb "depend" is literally "hang," as when a notice board hangs on a nail or Jesus hung on the cross), he speaks most momentously, and must not be misunderstood. Love in Scripture (*agapē* in the New Testament) is not in essence a feeling (which is often all that the word signifies in modern Western culture) but is rather a resolve of goodwill and a purpose of giving the loved one the best we can, to make the loved one *great* in whatever is the appropriate way. So wholehearted love to God will exalt his greatness by giving adoring praise, grateful thanks, forthright obedience, confident loyalty, and total trust. Psalm 108 illustrates: "My heart is steadfast, O God! I will sing and make melody with all my being!" (The Hebrew says *with my glory*.) "Your steadfast love is great above the heavens. . . . Be exalted, O God, . . . give salvation . . . grant us help. . . . With God we shall do valiantly" (vv. 1, 4, 5, 6, 12, 13).

Wholehearted neighbor-love will match our built-in self-love (a natural disposition before sin ever made it an egoistic excess) and take all possible steps to relieve need, as when the Good Samaritan cared for the mugged Jew and when Christians seize their opportunities to point others to the Savior (see Luke 10:25–37; Acts 16:11–40). Our neighbor, we must remember, is whoever we are with, whether our nearest and dearest or people we hardly know and perhaps wish we didn't know or complete strangers. All the specifics of God's law as taught by Moses and enforced by the prophets should be viewed, so Jesus is telling us, as guidelines that teach loving hearts to express themselves fitly and generously toward both our neighbor and our God.

If we know how God's Spirit makes his Word effective in human lives, it will not surprise us when we read in Psalm 19:7–10:

> The law of the LORD is perfect,
>   reviving the soul;
> the testimony of the LORD is sure,
>   making wise the simple;
> the precepts of the LORD are right,
>   rejoicing the heart;
> the commandment of the LORD is pure,
>   enlightening the eyes;
> the fear of the LORD is clean,
>   enduring forever;
> the rules of the LORD are true,
>   and righteous altogether.
> More to be desired are they than gold,
>   even much fine gold;
> sweeter than honey
>   and drippings of the honeycomb.

God's law, that is, his entire revelation in Scripture viewed as a design and prescription for living in covenant with him, transforms the lives of those who follow it, leading them along the disciple's path of faith, hope, repentance, obedience, and love. Even the psalmist's term "the fear of the LORD" refers to the worship and obedience that comes from taking God's directives seriously. And whatever else changed when Jesus died and rose and the new covenant replaced the old, the inner reality of these virtues—graces, as the Puritans called them—did not. We should have this understanding clear in our minds as we meditate on Psalm 19, and especially as we move on to what Luther called "the little Bible," Psalm 119, where all but one of the 176 verses celebrate the law of God as a source and means of unbounded blessing and benefit. The writer of this remarkable composition loves God's law, cherishes it in his heart, turns it over in his mind, commits it to his memory, and, come hell or high water, resolves to live by it, seeking and expecting to find God through it, for as long as life shall last. In this, we urge, he remains a model for us all.

What it means to live by God's law is made clear by Jesus's reply to the Pharisees' test question, "Is it lawful to divorce one's wife for any cause?" Jesus's words were, "Have you not read that he who created them from the beginning made them male and female, and said, 'Therefore a man shall leave his father and mother and hold fast to his wife, and the two shall become one flesh'? So they are no longer two but one flesh. What therefore God has joined together, let not man separate" (Matt. 19:4–6). There are two points to note here. First, Jesus quotes the marginal observation of the human writer of Genesis as what the Creator "said." Had he forgotten the context? Surely not; this is evidence, rather, that for Jesus (as of course for his opponents, and for all Jews and Christians until modern times) the text of Scripture, as such, is as truly God's utterance and message as it is man's utterance and message; it is the testimony of God himself, given in the form of the testimony of his chosen writer. Second, Jesus answers the question by transcending it, simply reminding his interrogators that God's ideal for marriage is permanence and that this must therefore always be the goal.[2] He does this on the basis of what he finds written in Scripture. Thus he models living by the light, and under the authority, of God's law.

The law of God, then, as we meet it in Scripture, is first and foremost a law of *loyalty* and *love* toward the God of grace, with whom all believers are in covenant. Legalism is no part of this picture. Legalism (that is, looking to law-keeping to secure a status with God) was the basic perversity of the Pharisees, which Jesus was constantly challenging. Rooted in the pride and unbelief of the fallen human heart, legalism is always the besetting sin of religious people who do not know the grace of their Creator and Judge, the merciful God who for Jesus's sake "justifies the ungodly" through faith (Rom. 4:5). Legalism is thus a spiritual blind alley, which we mention only in order to dismiss it from view. One big thing, however, is still to be said about the law, namely that it is, in the words of James, "the law of liberty" (James 1:25; 2:12)—that is, the path of *freedom*. Think for a moment what this means.

Freedom exists when not only have we been freed *from* whatever oppressed us, but are also now enjoying the state of dignity, happiness, fulfillment, and contentment that we were freed *for*. Freedom is thus two-sided. So it is when it appears today as a political ideology; so it was when God freed Israel from Egyptian captivity for *shalom* (peace and prosperity) in the Promised Land. The same two-sidedness was implicit when the Lord Jesus Christ told those around him, "If you abide in my word, you are truly my disciples, and you will know the truth, and the truth will set you free" (John 8:31–32), just as it is implicit when Paul tells believers, "For freedom Christ has set us free; stand firm therefore. . . ." (Gal. 5:1). Jesus explains that the freedom he gives his followers as they engage with his Word is freedom from sin's dominion for life as a child of God, at home with one's Father (John 8:34–36). So freedom is a supreme gift, inasmuch as it covers both our forgiveness and acceptance (justification, adoption, and freedom from final condemnation) and also the anchoring of us in the life of enjoying, serving, and pleasing our heavenly Father. The gift thus changes both our status and our state in relation to God. Constant batterings from circumstances outwardly and fears and temptations inwardly make the life of freedom a constant struggle for us, as anchored boats are tossed and made to strain at their cables by stormy seas. But our anchor holds, our freedom remains, and our deep joy and contentment in the knowledge of being limitlessly loved by the Father, the Son, and the Holy Spirit continue within us as we labor to hold steady. This is a quality of life that only believers know.

James warns us that it is possible to miss this fullness of freedom by not paying enough attention to the pattern of freedom by faith and in obedience that the law paints. "If anyone is a hearer of the word and not a doer, he is like a man who looks intently at his natural face in a mirror. For he looks at himself and goes away and at once forgets what he was like. But the one who looks into the perfect law, the law of liberty, and perseveres, being no hearer who forgets but a doer who acts, he will be blessed in his doing" (James 1:23–25). Being a doer of God's Word—that is, in James's understanding, one who trusts, obeys, and worships Jesus Christ the Lord—changes us. It makes us what Paul calls "slaves of righteousness" (Rom. 6:18–19; see the whole section, vv. 15–23). But this is the reality of our freedom and of our blessing from God, and Christians rejoice in it as such.

Being unable to forget that Paul told Christians, "you are not under law but under grace" (Rom. 6:14), often keeps believers from being able to take seriously our thesis that God's law as we have analyzed it, including in itself the promises that undergird its directives, is to be our primary life-guide, giving us both our ideals to pursue and our restrictions to observe as we labor to glorify and please the God who loves and has saved us. But in those words from Romans it is clear that Paul is talking specifically about the law viewed as a system of salvation, a source supposedly of status and strength—which it never was, and in a fallen world never could be. By contrast, however, he speaks of the law as we are speaking of it when he describes himself as "not being outside the law of God but under the law of Christ" (1 Cor. 9:21), and his statement reveals a relationship that is a fixed point for all believers at all times in every age. The law of Christ as a rule and way of life is a transhistorical, transcultural, transdenominational, international, intergenerational reality; whoever we are, and wherever and whenever we live, we who believe in Christ are under the law of Christ and must act accordingly.

So the moral and spiritual fundamentals of true religion never change. As God the Father and Jesus Christ the Lord do not change, so orthodoxy and orthopraxy (right belief and right practice) are always essentially the same. What was morally right and good yesterday remains morally right and good today, and what was morally wrong in the past does not become morally right in the present. True law-keeping, which has always started in the heart with God-honoring motivation, must do so still. True love according to God's law continues to be a matter of keeping God's commandments (1 John 5:3) out of loyalty to him and goodwill to our neighbor. True righteousness was and always will be a matter of avoiding all forms of known evil and all that is demonstrably less than the best for furthering God's goals and his glory, and of doing what is fitting and fair as we deal with other people. True holiness remains a compound of willed separation and devotion to God, single-minded zeal in his service, and passionate care not to lapse from integrity and purity at anytime, plus humble straightforward acceptance of whatever pains and hardships may come our way as we seek to follow Christ our Lord. Living by God's law takes us into, and keeps us in, this world of unchangeables, and living by God's law, understood as has been stated, will never cease to be the basic form of divine guidance in our lives.

One further point now needs to be made.

Guided by God's Mind

We are to be guided by the *mind* of God. How, we ask, does this point take us on beyond the last one? Is not the law of God itself a full and precise expression of his mind? Yes—and no. "Here's another fine mess you've gotten us into," griped comedian Oliver Hardy over and over to his dim-witted peer Stan Laurel. Life is full of "fine messes," and knowing what God wishes us to do in messy situations is often difficult. Messy situations are those in which there are no ideal answers, but whatever we do has sad side effects and some disagreeable risks and consequences. Many have heard of the Irishman who answered the motorist's request for guidance by saying, "If I was going to Dublin I wouldn't start from here." This parallels what we regularly feel in messy situations of all kinds, where the most we can do is make the best of a bad job, for the honor of God and the good of neighbors, all of whom we are seeking to love in the way described earlier. What is required of us in such messes is not to go hunting for Bible texts that speak directly to our circumstances (there are not likely to be any), but we are to practice prayerfully the art of applicatory thinking, using logic before the Lord to determine by the light of biblical principles the course that promises the most good and the least evil. This is the *casuistry* of which we spoke earlier. We are not very good at this, and often have to acknowledge, when we look back on difficult decisions that we made as best we could, that we did not, after all, manage to discern the mind of God, that is, the better decision that Scripture shows we might have made. It is always the best decision that circumstances allow that expresses the mind of God. How to apply Scripture in "fine messes" so as to see our way, God helping us, to the best decision each time is the theme of this final section of being guided by the Word of God.

Our first move toward rightly applying Scripture is to grasp the old-fashioned distinction between *moral* and *positive* law. *Positive* as a quality of laws carries a meaning quite distinct from what the word means in everyday speech (affirmative, emphatic, trustful, confident, hopeful, and so on). Here it signifies laws enacted as means to end, whose binding force stems entirely from the legislator's decision, and which can be changed at the legislator's will as circumstances may require. Examples are the speed limits on the roads, the year-by-year level of income tax, and the powers given to the police, all of which are conceived as means to community well-being. Positive laws have sanctions attached to them, and must be observed under penalty for disobedience as long as they are in force.

There is much positive law in the Bible, marking the progress of God's redemptive plan. Before Israel reached the Promised Land, God had already supplemented the Decalogue with his political law, which he gave to regulate community life in the forthcoming Israelite theocracy. (Theocracy is government in which God is the named ruler and his law is the governmental law.) The books of Exodus and Deuteronomy record this God-given civil legislation in great detail. More detailed still was the blueprint, also given in the wilderness, for the nation's religious observance, namely the building of the tabernacle, the place of sacrifices, the establishing of priesthood, upkeep, and sacrificial rituals. Exodus and Leviticus provide the details. The writer of Hebrews explains that these things were all "types" (advance patterns of entities, agents and acts that would come later in God's economy and have greater significance), pointing forward to Christ, and they were all superseded through his ministry. Christ, the divine-human priest-king, effectively did away with theocracy by bringing in the nongeographical, nonnational, eternally real faith-relationship to himself that is called the kingdom of God, and he ended the era of Old Testament priesthood and sacrifice by his own atoning death. Outwardly, both the theocracy and the sacrificial system ceased to be when the Romans obliterated Jerusalem in AD 70. In actuality, however, both had already lost their significance through the action of the Lord Jesus fulfilling and replacing them. Jesus Christ, the "antitype," fulfilled these prophetic patterns and established a new and better order of worship and community in that form of the kingdom which, following the New Testament, we call the church. Thus God changed his positive law for Israel to the whole world's advantage.

Typical too were the lists in Leviticus of creatures and conditions causing "uncleanness" that had to be purged away. What this ritual uncleanness typified was the spiritual defilement caused by all breaches of God's law, all of which made lawbreakers abhorrent in God's sight. Instituting rules about typical defilement appears to have been God's educational strategy for inducing throughout Israel an indelible awareness that there is such a thing as the alienating defilement of sin that separates humans from God. This, be it said, is a truth that everyone everywhere needs to face up to and that we fallen human beings are all slow to learn. By Jesus's day, after many centuries of living with these typical purity laws, this lesson, we may suppose, had been sufficiently mastered; at all events, Jesus, insisting that it is sin and only sin that defiles, explicitly canceled the category of defiling foodstuffs. ("Thus he declared all foods clean," Mark 7:19.) This dispelled the whole concept of some created things and some physical states having defiling effects in themselves; the New Testament is entirely free of the idea, and Paul censures the notion that some foods are off limits, even though he had been brought up to follow precisely all of the Kosher rules (1 Tim. 4:3–4). Here, once more, we see God's positive law repealed by God's own action.

Clarity about the temporary nature of the Old Testament's political and ritual laws clears our way through various uncertainties. Thus, for example, there are unhappy families in which for whatever reason Christian parents' offspring are totally out of control and have become a danger to others. Deuteronomy 21:18–21 says that a son who is rebellious, gluttonous, and a drunkard is to be taken by his parents to the elders of the community for death by stoning. Even when this is seen to have been a permissive rather than a mandatory enactment, a last resort in a migratory theocratic community with no prisons or police, knowledge that God once legislated this can cause Christian parents sleepless nights as they wonder what they should do about (say) a son who is a drunk, a drug addict, wildly selfish, sexually licentious, and a layabout at home, paying them no regard save to bully them into giving him endless money to spend. Knowing that God's ancient political law is no longer in force can be stabilizing to them as they try to work out what form "tough love" should take in their invidious situation. If they see reason to turn their son over to the civil authorities for a jail term, or drug rehab, or restitution for harm he has caused, it will be as a responsible act of neighbor-love, not a superstitious deference to the God-givenness of the book of Deuteronomy. So, too, it will ease the embarrassment that some women may feel about their menstrual cycle and some men about their nocturnal emissions of semen to know that the divine law that once tagged these things as defilements, needing ceremonial purging (Leviticus 15), is no longer in force. They will, however, like the rest of us, benefit from the reminder that worship is only acceptable when we approach God with hands and hearts made clean by confessing our sins and receiving his forgiveness through our Lord Jesus Christ. And they will benefit from remembering that the moral law, which directly reflects God's own moral character, stands firm and never changes. Sin is the Bible name for breaches of it, and it is a fixed point that no sin is ever permissible or justifiable in the mind of God.

Our second move toward wisely applying Scripture is to grasp the *true wavelength* and *inner unity* of the moral law. Often God's law is thought of as a series of separate commands, and because it is the nature of the human mind to concentrate on one thing at a time, we easily slip into pursuing one virtue, or practicing one imperative, at the expense of others. The truth, however, is not only that all our doings should express love to God and neighbor, as we saw Jesus insisting, but also that Jesus himself, the embodiment of all the virtues, must be our model, for he is God's law incarnate. Law-keeping is in truth imitation of Christ, and vice versa: the two are one. The implications are far-reaching. To start with, we now see that the law is not telling us simply to do this or that, but rather to aim at being a certain type of person who behaves in a certain way. Ingenious Bible teachers have expressed this by saying that as all the promises of God to Christians analyze as beatitudes (so many assurances of blessings to come) so all the commands of God to Christians analyze as "be-attitudes" (so many calls for Christlike character), that blend of virtues that are all to be expressed in Christlike behavior. Within this frame, the question "What would Jesus do?" becomes pertinent over and over again. And now we also see that imitating Christ means more than merely aping him as comedians do when they impersonate politicians; for as the qualities of vivid imagination and sometimes breathtaking ingenuity and creativity appeared in Jesus's dealings with the many people, and many sorts of people, whom his heart was loving all along, so we need to ask him to enable us to show the same qualities as we deal with others on his behalf.

For this we shall need a strong sense of who we are in Christ as our life, and with Christ as our Lord; and with that we shall need a strong awareness of the greatness of God's grace in saving us and a strong passion to honor him for doing so. So we shall need a strong realization of the deceptions and distractions issuing from the world, the flesh, and the devil designed to keep us from consistent Christlikeness; and so too we shall need a strong sensitivity to the indwelling Holy Spirit whom we must trust to make us see on a moment-by-moment basis what to say and do in order to be Jesus-like in each developing situation.

This, and nothing less than this, is the true wavelength and unified thrust of the moral law of God.

Nor is Christian law-keeping an individualistic affair. John Wesley said that there is nothing more un-Christian than a solitary Christian, and we part company with the mind of God if we try to be Christlike on our own. Because none of us is omniscient and omnicompetent, we need each other's help to discern the best course of action according to the fullness of the moral law, and we all should find it as natural as it is necessary to ask our fellow pilgrims such questions as: "What do you think God's law requires me to do in this situation?" "How can I most faithfully witness to Christ, give help to the needy one(s), and glorify God as I follow up on this opportunity?" "Do you think the standards of God's law are really an obstacle to accepting this proposal?" Whatever answers we may receive, it will be wholly in line with the mind of God that we should have asked.

Our third move toward rightly applying Scripture to our lives now comes into prominence. It is to grasp the principle of *cultural adjustment*, sometimes (dangerously!) referred to as *cultural adaptation*. Adaptation ordinarily involves changing the substance of something to make it fit into a new framework. What we have in view, however, is an adjustment of form that leaves the substance (the principle) intact: as will shortly appear.

In the Scriptures every bit of moral teaching, like every bit of doctrinal instruction, is given within a frame of reference, a context that is both situation-specific and culture-specific. Cultures change, as do situations, and in order to apply biblical teaching correctly to ourselves we must first make sure that we are understanding it within its own situational and cultural context; otherwise, we are likely to find that we have first misunderstood and then misapplied it. We have already made the point that the substance of biblical teaching is transcultural. But its form is situationally and culturally conditioned, and so our task is to unshell it from the situational and cultural casing in which we find it embedded in the biblical text in order then to apply it to our own more or less different circumstances; sometimes, indeed, with details changed in order that the principle may stay the same.

Here is an everyday example. Five New Testament letters end with the writer telling his readers to greet each other "with a holy kiss" (Rom. 16:16; 1 Cor. 16:20; 2 Cor. 13:12; 1 Thess. 5:26; 1 Peter 5:14). The ritual kiss is still a familiar formality among priests and monks in Eastern Orthodoxy, but acting on these words in a Western church would create red faces, averted eyes, acute embarrassment, and perhaps worse. The holy kiss in biblical days was a nonsexual expression of mutual welcome, goodwill, love, trust, and offering your service to the person being kissed. But our culture is such that kissing means only one thing, at least in popular estimate. A twenty-first-century kiss on the lips would disrupt worship and not carry Paul's and Peter's intended meaning at all. Half a century ago, J. B. Phillips in his paraphrase, *Letters to Young Churches*, saw the problem and substituted "a hearty handshake all round" for the holy kiss, because this seemed to him to be the modern gesture that carried the meaning that was required. So this paraphrase told us to do something different from what the apostles prescribed in order to keep observing the moral principle that the apostles taught, namely, that gestures of goodwill involving the whole congregation should regularly be made, family-style. Does Phillips's rendering guide today's Bible readers according to the mind of God? Quite likely, though some congregations might substitute with equal fitness the "holy hug."

Another example, taken from something rather different: the second commandment forbade the Israelites to construct an image to worship. What was forbidden was precisely what they did when they adored the golden calf as the god "who brought you up out of the land of Egypt" (Exod. 32:1–6, 19–20): that is, they demeaned God by picturing him as part of his own animal creation. Today's stock-in-trade of unbiblical speculations about God is what corresponds: mental images have taken the place of metal ones. The principle underlying the prohibition is that our notions about God must match the fullness of his self-revelation, and not go a step beyond it, or idolatry results. Moderns with nonbiblical conceptions of God are as much idolaters as were the ancient Israelites on the plain below Mount Sinai: this continuity underlies all the cultural changes that have taken place in the world over the past three thousand and more years, and needs to be clearly discerned. All who begin, "My idea of God is . . ." or "I prefer to think of God as . . ." are ordinarily breaking the second commandment already, before they finish their sentence. We have to realize that lack of a firm grasp of the principle of cultural adjustment must sooner or later frustrate our desire to be guided by Scripture according to the mind of God.

Now to our fourth move, our last directive on discerning God's guidance through rightly applying the principles of Scripture. Move four is to grasp the principle of *double effect*, or *unintended and undesired consequences*. This principle covers all those cases in which doing what we discern that we ought to do carries the risk, sometimes indeed the certainty, of unwelcome side effects. They may not be unforeseen, but they are no part of our intention, and we wish we were not so placed that we cannot do the right thing without triggering the unhappy fallout. Since it would clearly be disobedience not to do it, we go ahead, asking God to take care of the entire outcome and, in the startling phrase that Oswald Chambers uses, we "smilingly wash our hands of the consequences"—if we can! What we are doing is actually choosing the lesser evil in situations where not doing what one should because one fears the fallout would actually be choosing the greater evil.

Where some evil is unavoidable, choosing the lesser evil is always the right thing to do. But such choices can be, and often are, harrowing and heartwrenching to the last degree. An old film, *The Cruel Sea*, illustrated this. In this movie set during World War II, the captain of a destroyer escorting a convoy across the Atlantic has to decide whether to head at speed through the icy waters where desperate seamen, their ship sunk by a U-boat, are struggling, so that he can drop a depth charge that might destroy the U-boat as it lies on the sea floor waiting to attack the rest of the convoy. This is a course of action which is certain to kill some of the swimmers who are desperately hoping to be picked up. The alternative of course, is to stop and rescue as many of the swimmers as possible and leave the U-boat free to torpedo other ships another day. The captain goes ahead, ignores the swimmers, and drops the depth-charge, whether successfully or not he never knows; and he says afterwards that there are times when all we can do is guess at our best choice of action and then get down on our knees and ask God's mercy. We along with our readers know that feeling: the realization, namely, that we shall cause others grievous pain whatever we choose to do linked with uncertainty as to whether what we have chosen really is the best option. When we look back at what we did and what came of it, the feeling recurs, and we are left wondering. With reason, then, will our thanks be more heartfelt that the blood of Christ cleanses from all sin and that Christians live precisely by being forgiven.

For a milder example of this dilemma, think of a Christian father who loves his children and has taken to heart Paul's injunction against provoking one's offspring to anger (Eph. 6:4). He is facing up to his teenage son's declared conviction that his entire happiness depends on pursuing what his parents see as a patently unhealthy and potentially ruinous relationship with another individual. What is he to do? Inaction, as so often, is easiest, but would that be choosing the lesser evil, behaving as a father should, and so doing the best he can for his son? But if out of love for his son he acts to try to curb the relationship from further development, he can expect to make the boy furiously angry, and what will the fruit of that be? The pain is great in such cases, which in our fallen world are far from uncommon. The most we who seek God's guidance can hope for is to be sustained by the knowledge that in good faith, according to what light we had, we have acted according to the mind of God, who always wills that we choose what appears as the plainest duty and/or the least evil, who never wills that we allow ourselves to sin, and whom we must ever trust to look after the consequences of our attempts to honor and obey him. But the scars of agonizing situations like these stay with us for life.

Progress Notes

It is now time to pull the threads together. What has this chapter shown us? We have seen, first, that Holy Scripture, the inspired Word of God, has been given by God to the church, the body of Christ, and to every Christian as part of that body in order to give guidance for all of life in the way that a maker's manual guides one through all that is involved in using and caring for a complex piece of apparatus—a car, a computer, a two-seater aircraft, a fax machine, or whatever. There is a wise warning in the familiar one-liner, "If all else fails, read the instructions." Neglect of the handbook's directives can lead to costly misuses, malfunctions, and need for repairs; so too neglect by God's sheep of God's own handbook for living is bound to lead to unfruitful wanderings offtrack and making continual messes as we move through life under our Shepherd's care. Though our gracious Lord restores those who have slipped when they repent, it is clearly better to let Scripture teach us how not to slip in the first place.

We have seen, second, that the canonical Scriptures, our God-given guidebook for living, set before us God's commands, prohibitions, provisions, and promises within a frame of father-to-family admonition that the Bible itself calls law. Every Christian should repeatedly read and constantly study the Scriptures in a lifelong quest for ever deeper understanding of God's law in this broad sense—for all the basic guidance into godliness that we need is set before us here. As we are taught to search all the Scriptures for pointers to Jesus Christ and the knowledge of his grace, so we should search all the Scriptures for their teaching, both by explanation and by example, on the way to live as a child of God.

We have seen, third, that though biblical interpretation is complex, as we would expect when the book comprises sixty-six separate books written over a period of more than a thousand years, many problems of how its various teachings apply to us as Christians today are resolved from within the canonical corpus. Bible teaching for Christian living is remarkably coherent and clear, as well as remarkably searching and humbling, once we learn to follow out these inner links. It is as we do this that we are truly being guided by the mind of God set forth in his Word.

And we have seen, fourth, that living in our fallen world is never so straightforward that true and authentic guidance from God guarantees an easy passage through the problems, as if all decisions about the right and the wrong thing to do are black and white and, if rightly made, will take us along a level and pain-free path. On the contrary, following God's guidance with loyal tenacity will sooner or later lead us into troubles, sorrows, and hurts that otherwise we might have avoided. It was according to God's mind that our redemption should involve the agony of the cross for our Savior, and it has pleased him to ordain grief and suffering for Jesus's disciples too. As Paul told Asia Minor's first converts, "through many tribulations we must enter the kingdom of God" (Acts 14:22), Paul's own sense of guidance was very clear when he headed for Jerusalem, "constrained by the Spirit, not knowing what will happen to me there, except that the Holy Spirit testifies to me in every city that imprisonment and afflictions await me" (Acts 20:22–23). Similarly God's guidance was very clear to the Lord Jesus in Gethsemane. We who believe can expect to find Gethsemanes await us also. Vitally important in themselves, these perceptions are fundamental to everything further that we are going to say.

5

The Way of Wisdom

Let the wise hear and increase in learning,
  and the one who understands obtain guidance.

Proverbs 1:5

"Never let the good be the enemy of the best" is a wise saying, and it seems particularly appropriate at this juncture in our attempt to train our sights on God's guidance. In the previous chapter we looked at the path of law-keeping, that is, direct submission to the direct commands of the Word of God. Obedience to God as the settled policy of all our living is always the necessary first step toward finding and following his will in particular situations. It narrows our options; for one thing we can know for certain that any path expressly forbidden by the principles of God's law is *not* his will and will *never* be so, and he will *not* guide us in that direction. If we are feeling led that way, it is not God who is doing the leading. Obedience to direct directions from God is the right course as far as it takes us; it is indeed foundational to Christian living, and we will not find any of the details of his will without it. So we borrow from the world of board games the words "Start Here."

But for a believer in Christ to seek God's will through law-keeping alone could all too easily turn one into a grim-faced spiritual accountant, methodically ticking off the dos and don'ts, forever tallying failures against successes, and always feeling oppressed by the shadow of an elusive and as yet unattained perfection of outward performance. Is there some law from God that I do not yet fully understand? Is there some specific implication or application or corollary to obey that I have not yet fully mastered? Though there is a proper place for questions of this kind, formal preoccupation, Pharisee-fashion, with detailed, minute applications of the general principles of God's law is not a full description of the path along which God guides his people. The truth is that a person living and thinking that way is mentally grooved in a style that leaves out of account something vital in our quest for guidance—namely, that gift from the Holy Spirit through the written Word that is creative and humanizing and outward-looking and self-effacing and profoundly perceptive, the gift which is properly named *wisdom*.

In this chapter, we will explore the way of wisdom as the needed completion of what we have said so far about being guided by the Word of God. We serve a wise God who graces all his people to a greater or lesser degree with wisdom, to keep us from falling into foolhardiness (folly, as the Bible calls it) and to open our eyes to dimensions of biblical godliness that without wisdom we should miss. Here, we will explore three topics that together take us over this ground: the *centrality* of wisdom in the Christian life, the *nature* of wisdom in the Word of God, and the *practice* of wisdom in daily decisions.

The Centrality of Wisdom

Seeking to live in wisdom, seeking to be wise in the way that we make our decisions and plan our lives, is one aspect of biblical obedience. Scripture requires us to have this concern. In Paul's letter to the Colossians, a church he had never visited, but to which he sought to teach the same right-mindedness that he taught to all other churches, we find him saying, "Walk in *wisdom* toward outsiders, making the best use of the time." Then he adds some exposition of that thought in the next verse: "Let your speech always be gracious, seasoned with salt, so that you may know how you ought to answer each person" (Col. 4:5–6). The verb "to answer" here simply means, how we respond to what outsiders say, whatever that is. Speech, the way we speak to each other and to those outside our circle, is the great index of whether we are *living* in wisdom. Thus Paul initiates the emphasis on wise thoughts, wise conduct, and wise answers, that will recur over and over throughout this chapter.

"Walk in wisdom" has been rendered "conduct yourselves wisely." That gets the sense but loses the picture. "Walk" is a word Paul regularly uses for "live," as did the Old Testament writers before him. This image of putting one foot in front of another as you move steadily from your starting point toward your destination is in fact a brilliant picture of how human life should be lived, and Paul has already used it in a weighty way. Earlier in the letter he had said, "As you received Christ Jesus the Lord, so *walk* in him, rooted and built up in him and established in the faith, just as you were taught, abounding in thanksgiving" (Col. 2:6–7). Those great words are in truth the central message of Colossians; they establish the frame within which learning to behave wisely in our relation to other people is now being set. Wise behavior is one particular aspect of what it means to walk in Christ.

In the letter to the Ephesians, over and over again, we find Paul picking up and amplifying thoughts that he had already put out in Colossians, and walking in Christ is one of them. So in Ephesians, following admonitions to *walk* worthy of our calling (4:1), in *love* and in *light* (5:2, 8), we find, "Look carefully then how you *walk*, not as unwise [not, that is, in the way that unwise people do] but as *wise* [wise people], making the best use of the time, because the days are evil. Therefore do not be foolish, but understand what the will of the Lord is" (Eph. 5:15–17). Though being foolish is the easiest thing in the world, as the book of Proverbs, to look no further, plainly shows, it must not happen to you!

114

The gospel taught you, says Paul, to "be renewed in the spirit of your minds, and to put on the new self, created after the likeness of God in true righteousness and holiness" (Eph 4:23–24). So, "you must no longer *walk* as the Gentiles do, in the futility of their minds. They are . . . alienated from the life of God because of the ignorance that is in them, due to their hardness of heart" (vv. 17–18). This is not a mere ignorance of moral facts and standards. If that were the case, the problem could be solved by an increase in information. But Paul is talking about the willed ignorance toward God and so toward godliness and so toward decency, which he analyzed in Romans 1:18–31, an ignorance that constantly desensitizes in moral matters and produces the hard—that is, the hardened—state of heart that marked, and still marks, the pagan world. Those who over and over resist God's wisdom inherit the haunting phrase of Romans 1, "God gave them up." Simply put, God gives them what they most want: a life without him. Hard hearts, says Paul, have polluted the moral standards that these Gentiles knew so that the knowledge already encased in their brains did not lead to a life of wisdom. A person who truly walks in wisdom does not merely pause now and then to spout wise words; he or she actually lives a renewed life.

To nail this point down, Paul now gets specific and speaks of a transformation of lives that had formerly been filled with lies, anger, thievery, bitterness, greed, slander, and corrupting talk. Over against these destructive qualities, Paul spells out what a life "renewed in the spirit of your minds" would look like. Here we see habits of: truth-telling, sharing with those in need, speaking encouraging words, honest labor, kindness, compassion, and forgiveness, all of this shaped by a new attitude toward other people that flows from a revolutionized relationship with the living, forgiving God. It is not surprising, then, that Paul ends this full contrast of the two kinds of lives (Eph. 4:25–32) with a summarizing challenge: "Therefore be imitators of God, as beloved children. And *walk* in love, as Christ loved us and gave himself up for us" (5:1–2). Then comes one more defining admonition: "*Walk* as children of light (for the fruit of light is found in all that is good and right and true), and try to discern what is pleasing to the Lord" (5:8–9). Notice the breadth of Paul's three-point thumbnail description of the fruit or evidence of this walking in the light: he specifies it as *all* that is good, right, and true. How does your life and how do all our lives measure up to that? And now, having highlighted this threefold fruit, he moves on to the cautions that we have already cited: "Look carefully then how you *walk, not as unwise but as wise*, making the best use of the time, because the days are evil" (vv. 15–16). He is echoing here what he wrote to the Colossians, but from a different angle. What Paul means by this caution is that there is constant Satanic opposition to wise walking—and we must expect it, and be ready to meet it. The days are evil because of what the evil one is doing in them. Paul will say much more about war with the evil one in Ephesians 6 where he instructs God's people to put on the armor that God provides for us in Christ. Here he simply makes it plain that as far as he is concerned, unwise behavior is Satan scoring points and God being dishonored.

But this passage contains one more phrase of particular interest in our culture where one of the most frequent challenges as we multitask our way through life is "time management." The Greek word Paul uses for "time" means "moment of opportunity," and Paul's thought is that our days and hours are full of moments for advancing God's kingdom and glory, if only we have wisdom enough to see the possibilities and seize these opportunities accordingly. Making the best use of the time is a phrase that to us as well as to the Ephesians is intended to take our minds right up to the axiom that opened this chapter: "Never let the merely good [or the merely possible] be the enemy of the best." We are always to make the *best* use of our time. That is our task. To emphasize this point Paul's very next line is an admonition that takes us to the heart of this chapter: "Do not be foolish, but understand what the will of the Lord is" (Eph. 5:17).

The phrase, "understand what the will of the Lord is," is surely to be linked up with the familiar words of Romans 12:1–2, where Paul, as we saw, opens the final section of the letter by saying: "I appeal to you therefore, brothers, by the mercies of God, to present your bodies as a living sacrifice, holy and acceptable to God, which is your spiritual worship." As we have seen already, what these words call for is a total setting of ourselves apart to serve and please God, as the entire business of our lives, out of gratitude for his grace. This summons leads to the crunch verse: "Do not be conformed to this world [for the days are evil as we have already found Paul saying], but be transformed by the renewal of your mind [that is, by the power of the renewed mind that God fashions in you as you walk with him], that . . . you may . . ." May what? Older translations use the word "prove" here, but those who worked on the *English Standard Version* (ESV), of which J. I. was one, felt they had to amplify that rendering in order to catch the whole thought which no single modern English word covers properly. The old word *prove* pointed to discernment by testing, much as a woman would "prove" the yeast to be sure that it was still alive before using it to make bread dough. *Prove* today, however, has more to do with establishing facts by evidence and argument than with working your way through the alternatives so that you can form a judgment as to what God wants of you behaviorally. But that is the true meaning of the Greek word, which the ESV tries to capture by rendering it as follows: "that by testing you may discern what is the will of God, what is good and acceptable and perfect."

The flow of the thought shows, as we pointed out earlier, that "the will of God" of which Paul speaks here means, not the will of God in general, or the will of God for my whole life, but the will of God in each specific situation in which you and I find ourselves. The same appears to be true in Ephesians 5:17 where Paul says that we are to "understand what the will of the Lord is." In each situation where a decision has to be made and a course of action has to be settled upon, Paul in effect is saying, "May you understand what is the best use that you can make of this opportunity to please God and bring glory to his name. That is what living by wisdom is all about." Do we need help to do this? Yes. Will any form of Pharisaic, mechanical calculations on how to apply God's laws give us the help we need? No. Whence then will come that help? From the indwelling Holy Spirit illuminating and working through our regenerate, renewed powers of mind and heart. Let us explain.

The Christian life, which is a supernatural life from the word go, is a new creation in the heart that begins when we are born again. We have indicated this already. Once we come to know Christ, we are different people from what we were before. This Christian life, the supernatural life which is now our life, is regularly spelled out in the pulpit and in books in terms of tag phrases like: "Be what you are." "Live out what God has wrought in you." "Express your new nature." Or even: "Be natural in Christ." It is indeed natural for those who are born again to live Christianly, and to do the things that according to Scripture born-again Christians do, namely, love and serve God and others with imagination and devotion, with a sense of privilege and a spirit of self-giving, with a self-forgetful humility and a joyful awareness of self-fulfillment. To grow in wisdom and in Christian responsibility (the two overlap) is simply to realize, ever more vividly, that this is how Jesus Christ, our Savior, our Lord, and our life, wants to express himself in the new renewed personhood that he is developing within us. A Christ-centered quest for Christlikeness in all our attitudes and actions is perhaps the best way of describing how we live out the dynamic drives of this supernatural new nature that the Lord has wrought in us and that the Holy Spirit now sustains and energizes.

The New Testament says that seeing this new nature in action will sometimes perplex people around us; they won't understand what we are doing or what it is that makes us tick. When Jesus talked to Nicodemus he said that the work of God's Spirit within a person who is born again is as mysterious as the wind: you hear it and see its effect, but you cannot track it; and those who do not understand what it means to be born again find the Spirit-guided Christian a complete enigma. Jesus says to Nicodemus, "Do not marvel that I say to you ["you" here is plural; Jesus is saying, this means you, Nicodemus, and all your Jewish friends], 'You [all] must be born again.' The wind blows where it wishes, and you hear its sound, but you do not know where it comes from or where it goes. So it is with everyone who is born of the Spirit" (John 3:7–8).

The blowing of the wind makes the sand on the ground whirl and perhaps if it gets stronger it will blow down a lean-to shed, or blow the roof off a house. We hear the wind roar and note its power, but we can neither bring it under control nor predict what it will do next. "Everyone born of the Spirit is like that," says the Lord Jesus. He means that to the observer who is not in on the secret, so to speak, the way that Christians behave is bewildering. They don't know where the Christian is coming from; they don't know where the Christian is going; they don't understand what the Christian is after. So there will often be surprise among people as to why we believers do what we do as we seek to walk in wisdom and make the best use of the time God has given us.

As we can see, however, this is one aspect of what it means to enjoy the reality of Psalm 23:3: "He leads me in paths of righteousness for his name's sake." We have taken that verse almost as a motto verse for this whole book. *Today's New International Version* renders the words, "He guides me along the right paths for his name's sake," a phrasing which points to the dynamism of the Spirit through the written Word moving us to appropriate action. To live by that guidance is to find and follow wisdom, and this is truly central in the Christian life.

The Nature of Wisdom

It is one thing to affirm that wisdom is central to our life in Christ, but quite another to discern what wisdom is. Our task is now to examine the nature of godly wisdom. For this we turn, of course, to Scripture. Wisdom is a pervasive subject in the Word of God, though we would hardly know that from monitoring an ordinary slew of a year's preaching in an ordinary Christian church. We seldom hear of wisdom in the pulpit—which is our loss, for Scripture speaks of it often. We all are called to seek wisdom, and promised that if we sincerely do so we shall find it. God's gift of wisdom is for everyone. You don't have to be clever to be wise; wisdom is not the same thing as cleverness. Wisdom is the ability to apply true principles in a way that produces right living, first and foremost in terms of human values. Wisdom is traveling along the right paths, living in a way that pleases and glorifies God, because you have found the best thing to do for people, others, and yourself too, in each situation. Wisdom is indeed pragmatic, as is often said, but it is humble, honest, realistic, insightful, generous, compassionate, stabilizing, and encouraging also, and the Gospel stories display it vividly as one facet of the human perfection of the Lord Jesus. Wisdom excels in seeing, modeling, and so making known what can be done in particular situations, and should be coveted by all who want to discern and carry out the perfect will of God.

We have already made the point that the Old Testament includes a whole section that we call "wisdom literature": Psalms, Proverbs, Job, Ecclesiastes, and Song of Solomon, which together comprise nearly 10 percent of the Old Testament. What we said earlier about these books was in echo of Oswald Chambers, who affirms that the Psalms teach us how to *pray*, the Proverbs teach us how to *act*, Job teaches us how to *suffer*, the Song teaches us how to *love*, and the book of Ecclesiastes teaches us how to *enjoy*.[1] Chambers is right all the way. Biblical wisdom begins with acknowledging the goodness of the Creator, Israel's God, and of the world he has made, and here Ecclesiastes in particular comes into its own.

The central theme of Ecclesiastes (flanked to be sure by words of trenchant gloom on the emptiness and evil of things "under the sun") really is that we should program ourselves to appreciate and enjoy the simple everyday blessings with which God strews our paths, never mind the big bewildering realities, which, if we allow them to occupy our minds, produce sadness rather than gladness and puzzlement rather than contentment. Life is full of distressing things that would depress us if we let them. But, says Ecclesiastes, having surveyed these things thoroughly and thoughtfully, "I commend *enjoyment*" (8:15 RSV; "joy," ESV; "pleasure," NASB, "mirth," KJV; "enjoyment of life," NIV). Here is a fundamental and far-reaching biblical reality. True wisdom as a medium of God's guidance allows for, even encourages, enjoyment with gratitude to God, though what we are urged to enjoy may be rather different from the more base enjoyments sought by those who are not God's people. Calvin made this point against his favorite theologian, Augustine, who had austerely spoken as if ordinary everyday pleasures should be cut out of our lives.[2] Two hundred fifty years after Calvin, the English preacher Charles Simeon surely got it right when, expounding "All is vanity," he saw Ecclesiastes as teaching "two lessons . . . to enjoy God in everything" and "to enjoy everything in God."[3] That wisdom is about learning to enjoy the enjoyable in an out-of-joint world is indeed part of the bottom line of biblical ethics. But we cannot pursue that here.[4]

We may, however, pause a moment to sharpen our focus on the wisdom books in light of what has just been said. Ecclesiastes, in some ways the most profound of all the wisdom writers, showed us that grateful enjoyment was, is, and always will be a key element in biblical godliness, come what may. Look at the wisdom books again from that perspective, and it becomes easier to see what you are looking at. Song of Songs, to start with, will now focus for you the fidelity-fueled freeness and fervor of wholehearted marital affection between him and her—an enjoyment devised by God that some married couples seem to miss. Job will now focus for you the faithfulness of God, who, after his servant's patient endurance of what seemed a meaningless agony, blessed him more at the end than he had done at the beginning. The Psalms will now focus for you the beyond-words delight that comes to the heart of those who single-mindedly, persistently, and devotedly wait on God, whatever their outward state, and at last find themselves ineffably visited and wonderfully enlivened as God's love and vitality are shed abroad in their soul. And Ecclesiastes itself will now focus for you the spirit of cheerful and contented enterprise that overcomes all forms of disillusionment, frustration, boredom, and disgust by embracing the pleasant simplicities (food, work, friendship, marriage) that God has given us to enjoy "under the sun." With this wisdom digested and internalized, and with the joy in God to which it points highlighted, our discernment of the will and ways of God will become clearer—much clearer, we think—than otherwise it would be.

In the New Testament, the letter of James is a wisdom book echoing in all sorts of ways both the substance and the style of the Old Testament wisdom books and echoing also a great deal of the teaching of Jesus, helping us to realize that among the other things that Jesus was, he was himself a teacher and practitioner of wisdom. James also shows us that, as we have already discovered, the life of wisdom for the Christian is a life of Christlikeness. Living in wisdom is one dimension of what it means to have our Savior as our model.

Scripture speaks of wisdom in many ways, but it will help us to understand the sweep of the concept if we arrange our thoughts about it under the following seven topical headings. First, wisdom is about understanding; second, it is about worship; third, it is about goals and the ends that should be in view in the life we live; fourth, wisdom is about strategies, or means to these ends; fifth, wisdom is about relationships; sixth, wisdom is about self-control; and seventh, wisdom is about humility. Let us elaborate these points.

First, *wisdom is about understanding.* Wisdom, in the book of Proverbs and elsewhere, is as we have seen constantly contrasted with folly. The book of Proverbs devotes its first nine chapters to a general exhortation to seek wisdom as the supreme value of life, since the quest for wisdom is the most important thing that we can ever engage in. These chapters insist on the priority of seeking wisdom as the means of getting understanding of life, and they are worth looking at in some detail. Here are the first words of Proverbs.

> The proverbs of Solomon, son of David, king of Israel:
> To know wisdom and instruction,
> > to understand words of insight,
> to receive instruction in wise dealing,
> > in righteousness, justice, and equity;

> to give prudence to the simple,
>> knowledge and discretion to the youth. . . .
>
>> Proverbs 1:1–4

Having stated what this book is intended to accomplish, the writer says,

> Let the wise hear and increase in learning,
>> and the one who understands obtain guidance,
> to understand a proverb and a saying,
>> the words of the wise and their riddles.
>
>> verses 5–6

Then verse 8 strikes a more personal note:

> Hear, my son, your father's instruction,
>> and forsake not your mother's teaching.

The teaching of wisdom is presented in Proverbs as a parent's instruction to a child. That is, of course, very typical of the Old Testament, but it is very Christian, too. We who are parents are meant, still, to teach wisdom to our children in every way that we can.

In chapter 2, the writer of Proverbs develops further how wisdom is to be gained within the context of family:

> My son, if you receive my words
>> and treasure up my commandments with you,
> making your ear attentive to wisdom
>> and inclining to understanding;
> yes, if you call out for insight
>> and raise your voice [in prayer] for understanding
> if you seek [understanding] like silver
>> and search for it as for hidden treasures,
> then you will understand the fear of the Lord
>> and find the knowledge of God.
>
>> Proverbs 2:1–5

Understanding means specifically knowing how to live as a response to God's revelation. Wisdom includes understanding, but wisdom is larger, for it includes also the prudent doing of what we understand that we should do. In other words, it is *practical*. In some eras and cultures, practical wisdom has been thought of as separate from understanding in a way which might be caricatured as "I don't need no book learnin'; God gives me all the wisdom I need when I need it," but the writer of Proverbs (and therefore God) disagrees. Wisdom for the business of living is gained through the labor of learning to understand; understanding is learned from the book of God and books about the book of God, as well as from live teachers who help us in this. So:

> Blessed is the one who finds wisdom,
>> and the one who gets understanding,
> for the gain from her is better than the gain from silver
>> and her profit better than gold.
> She is more precious than jewels,
>> and nothing you desire can compare with her. . . .
>
> The beginning of wisdom is this: Get wisdom,
>> and whatever you get, get insight.
> Prize her highly, and she will exalt you.
>
> Proverbs 3:13–15; 4:7–8a

Wisdom is personified as a lady, a hostess, inviting us to join her so that we may receive what she has to give.

> Wisdom cries aloud in the street,
>> in the markets she raises her voice;
> at the head of the noisy street she cries out;
>> at the entrance of the city gates she speaks:
> "How long, O simple ones, will you love being simple?
> How long will scoffers delight in their scoffing
>> and fools hate knowledge?
> If you turn at my reproof,

behold, I will pour out my spirit to you;
    I will make my words known to you."

Proverbs 1:20–23

In chapter 8, Lady Wisdom once more lifts up her voice:

"To you, O men, I call,
    and my cry is to the children of man.
O simple ones, learn prudence;
    O fools learn sense.
Hear, for I will speak noble things,
    and from my lips will come what is right."

Proverbs 8:4–6

All through Proverbs wisdom and understanding are the key thoughts. Wisdom in the heart starts in the mind and is thus about thinking and about learning and also about unlearning. One mark of a wise person, according to Proverbs, is that one is willing to accept instruction and correction and to learn to know things better than one does at the moment. The life of wisdom is a life of constant learning: constant evaluating, constant discerning, constant extension of one's understanding. When David declares that his covenant God leads and guides him along the right paths (Ps. 23:3), he means that God does this by getting him to think, and through thinking to understand, and through understanding to gain wisdom—and thus to discern the right path from wrong ones.

Second, *wisdom is about worship* as opposed to the disregard for God which is the mark of the fool both in Proverbs and in the Psalms. Again, the introduction to the book of Proverbs says it all: "The fear of the LORD is the beginning of knowledge, fools despise wisdom and instruction" (Prov. 1:7). Fear, as we have already noted, is a worship-word; it means not panic and alarm, but awe and adoration. If we do not start with the fear of the Lord, then all the knowledge that we manage to accumulate will fall short of the wisdom into which it might have grown—if that knowledge had included an appropriate reverence for God, expressed in a discipline of worship. Fools, on the other hand, don't even try to learn anything; so they end up pathetically ignorant, says the writer, because they have despised wisdom and instruction. "The fear of the LORD is the beginning of wisdom, and the knowledge of the Holy One is insight" (Prov. 9:10). Note that this is said again in Psalm 111:10 and again in Job 28:28. In the Bible, as in ordinary life, repetition is for emphasis! Those who neglect, or refuse, to learn how to honor God will cut themselves off from wisdom, no matter how much information about God they manage to amass. This is a momentous truth, which every one needs to face up to. It is to be feared that many are not as wise as they need to be because they have erred here.

The word *fear* in the phrase "fear of the Lord," as we said, does not imply panic; what it implies is reverence, yet not the sort of reverence that rules out boldness. Christians (along with faithful covenant believers of the Old Testament era) know that through God's grace their sins are forgiven and that they are in God's favor so that they can be bold in invoking him, and looking to him and asking for his teaching and his help. Panicky fear would inhibit all of that. Panic, shaking-in-the-boots fear, is not the sort of fear that the biblical writers are talking about. This fear of the Lord is reverence—with boldness, yes—but reverence linked with awe at God's greatness, and an active, deep concern to obey and please him. That is, incidentally, what the reference to fear and trembling means in Philippians 2:12–13, where Paul directs his readers to "work out [that is, actively express] your own salvation with fear and trembling"—that is, precisely, with awe and reverence. Paul states the reason for the awe and reverence: "for it is God who works in you, both to will and to work for his good pleasure." It is awesome to know that God works in our hearts as we seek to use our minds to think for him, to discern his will, to work out what is the best we can do to advance his kingdom and his praise, and to program ourselves for doing that. Every right thought we manage to think, and every right action we manage to perform, is God's work in us and his gift to us. This realization evokes deep awe and deep gratitude and an ongoing sense of humble dependence on the God who thus confirms to us that he is ours and we are his. This state of mind is at the heart of the human reality labeled "the fear of the Lord."

Worship is the global name for all the approaches to God and all the dealings with God to which wisdom leads us. Worship begins as humble, thankful, self-abandoning trust in, reliance on, and obedience to the God whom we acknowledge as infinitely good and wise. In Proverbs 3:5–8 we find this:

> Trust in the LORD with all your heart,
> and do not lean on your own understanding.
> In all your ways acknowledge him,
> and he will make straight your paths.
> Be not wise in your own eyes;
> fear the LORD, and turn away from evil.
> It will be healing to your flesh
> and refreshment to your bones.

That summons to worship is right at the center of the broader summons to seek wisdom. We are not seeking wisdom as we should if we are not worshipping our wise God, actively practicing "the fear of the Lord" as best we can.

Third, *wisdom is also about goals*, the aims and targets that one sets oneself. We hinted at this earlier. Wisdom teaches us how to set our sights on objectives that are truly worth aiming at. Goal number one (which all the Bible insists on) is that the knowledge of God, the enjoyment of God, the praise of God, and the honor of God should be our constant aim in everything we do, so that we may truly live to his glory. The consequent goals include love, goodwill, and care in all our personal relationships with family, friends, acquaintances, and casual contacts; faithfulness in all business dealings; integrity in all community involvements and all enterprises in which we lead and direct others; and creativity, the quest for order and beauty, in pursuing whatever interests and hobbies we embrace. Wisdom enables us to formulate and focus our goals in our various fields of activity.

In Ecclesiastes 2:13–14a the wise man says, "I saw that there is more gain in wisdom than in folly, as there is more gain in light than in darkness. The wise person has his eyes in his head, but the fool walks in darkness." Part of the implication of "eyes in his head" and "darkness" is that while the wise person sets goals and knows where he or she is going, the fool practices a random kind of living. A fool walks through life as if he were blind. Aimlessness in the most fundamental sense is the sad word that has to be written over the life of a fool. Wise persons, by contrast, have clear purposes and make thoughtful plans. They do not simply drift through life as the fool does.

Fourth, *wisdom has to do with strategies*, that is, the establishing of means to achieve our goals so that we don't slip into pitfalls and places of disaster through imprudences that we could have avoided. Think of the mountain climber whose goal is to get to the top; he has to be very careful about the way he goes or he may fall into a crevasse or lose his footing on a slope or a rock face and come to great grief. The book of Proverbs is from one standpoint a very prudent book, constantly teaching, in one way or another, how to avoid life's pitfalls, so that all the time we are achieving the practice of God-honoring wisdom in all its fullness. This is where willingness to accept advice comes in. Proverbs 10:17 says, "Whoever heeds instruction is on the path to life, but he who rejects reproof leads others astray." The fool (one who has chosen not to walk in God's wisdom nor accept advice and correction from anybody, but to be led by his own mother wit) is going to go astray himself, and he will persuade others to follow him. Everyone has spheres of influence, for better or for worse, and in those spheres of influence others will follow whatever example we set. We are wise to be aware of that—to realize that our way of living and believing will influence others whether or not we intended it so—and therefore to humbly heed advice from others about avoiding pitfalls on our own chosen path. "A wise man listens to advice" (Prov. 12:15). "With those who take advice is wisdom" (13:10). "Listen to advice and accept instruction, that you may gain wisdom in the future" (19:20). We shall have more to say about this in our next chapter.

Fifth, *wisdom is about relationships*, about our thoughts and behavior toward others. This is something to which we have referred already and which the Lord Jesus and the apostles in their teaching underline for us: love and justice and fidelity in our dealings with other people, and the habit of always seeking their good, are matters of priority in the godly life. We need practical wisdom to guide us in living out these virtues, and as with the other aspects of wisdom, Proverbs has some down-to-earth advice for us. For example in Proverbs 14:21 we read: "Whoever despises his neighbor is a sinner, but blessed is he who is generous to the poor." And in Proverbs 25:21–22 (quoted in Romans 12:20 where Paul's theme is overcoming evil with good) we find this: "If your enemy is hungry, give him bread to eat, and if he is thirsty, give him water to drink, for you will heap burning coals on his head [that is, you will prick his conscience by behaving lovingly toward him], and the LORD will reward you." So we see that neighbor-love, even when our neighbor is not behaving lovingly to us, is one of the marks of the wise person, as opposed to the self-centered person. The self-centered person is not and never becomes wise.

Sixth, *wisdom is about self-control.* Being able to master and manage yourself under pressure, not coming apart and "losing it," as we say, is an integral feature of the godly person's mindset, and Paul lists it, as we saw, as one facet of the fruit of the Spirit (Gal. 5:23). Proverbs underlines the prudential value of self-control. Proverbs 25:28 says, "A man without self-control is like a city broken into and left without walls." That is a pathetic image of vulnerability if ever there was one. Proverbs hammers away at the point. "A man of quick temper acts foolishly" (14:17). "He who has a hasty temper exalts folly" (14:29). Proverbs 29:11 reads "A fool gives full vent to his spirit, but a wise man quietly holds it back." Proverbs 29:20 declares: "Do you see a man who is hasty in his words? There is more hope for a fool than for him." Self-restraint is self-control in action; the lack of self-control seen in quick-tempered explosions the moment you see red is a recipe for disaster, a disaster which may well involve others as well as yourself.

Seventh, *wisdom is about humility.* Humility, a brother-virtue to self-control, is the opposite of pigheaded pride. Humility reveals itself in at least two ways: acceptance of things you cannot change, and acceptance of correction in areas of your life where you can change—and where you need to. In Proverbs 17:10 we read, "A rebuke goes deeper into a man of understanding than a hundred blows into a fool." The wise man listens thoughtfully to a rebuke and is grateful for it, rather than resentful, for he knows that he is likely to end up the better for it. As Derek Kidner observes, "Reproof is one of the few things more blessed to receive than to give."[5] Proverbs 25:12 makes the same point: "Like a gold ring or an ornament of gold is a wise reprover to a listening ear," for "the ear that listens to life-giving reproof will dwell among the wise" (15:31). This point like so much of what has preceded makes us aware that wisdom in Proverbs is a moral and spiritual virtue in which almost the whole of genuine godliness is contained.

Our profile of wisdom according to the Scriptures is not complete until we add the point that the Lord Jesus came to this world as wisdom incarnate, wisdom walking and talking, wisdom embodied in a fully human life. In Paul's first letter to the church at Corinth we read: "And because of [God] you are in Christ Jesus, who became to us *wisdom* from God, our righteousness and sanctification and redemption" (1 Cor. 1:30). Christ's embodiment of God's wisdom is further celebrated by Paul in his letter to the Colossians which contains one of the most eloquent Christ-hymns in all of Scripture (see Col. 1:15–20). Shortly after that hymn in chapter 1, we read about "God's mystery, which is Christ, in whom are hidden all the treasures of *wisdom* and knowledge" (Col. 2:2–3). Paul makes it plain to us that the life of wisdom and godliness to which we are called will be a life of Christlikeness, now that Christ has come and modeled wise living in this definitive way for our instruction.

James, wisdom writer of the New Testament, amplifies Proverbs on the subject of wisdom and humility by saying "Who is wise and understanding among you? By his good conduct let him show his works in the meekness of wisdom" (James 3:13). Meekness accepts things the way they come at us; it doesn't quarrel with God when discerning aspects of his providence. Instead, meekness acknowledges that God knows what he is doing and that he makes all things work together for good for those who love him—even if at this present moment things do not appear to be working well at all. A person who is meek accepts the way that God orders things, and such meekness, James says, is a mark of wisdom. As we read further in James 3, we come to verse 17 and find this: "The wisdom from above [that is, the wisdom that God gives, the wisdom of Christlikeness, the wisdom imparted by God's Spirit that we ought to be seeking constantly] is first pure, then peaceable, gentle, open to reason, full of mercy and good fruits, impartial and sincere." To enter into the quest for wisdom, which means, as we now see, the quest for Christlikeness in all these ways is thus to pursue a life of holiness, godliness, and sanctity, marked by prudence, good sense, discretion, purity, meekness, mercy, and thoughtful self-control. In this fashion, God leads us in paths of righteousness—that is, right paths—for his name's sake, in other words, for his own glory as the God who keeps his covenant promises and beautifully blesses his people in doing so.

So now we come to our final question in this chapter: How do we put this understanding of the centrality of wisdom and our insights about the nature of wisdom into practice as we seek to live under God's guidance?

The Practice of Wisdom

The practice of wisdom in daily decisions is an ongoing quest for the best. Three headings will help us cover the breadth of practicing wisdom. We are first to *ask*, then to *assess*, and then to *act*.

First, *we are to ask for wisdom—constantly*. James opens his letter by telling us to do that, and why. The first two verses of his teaching (1:2–3) have to do with suffering. The simplest definition of suffering is not getting what you wanted and hoped for, but getting instead what you did not want and hoped to avoid. As we face the fact that what we most longed for is now ruled out, there are all sorts of ways in which our situations will now cause us to suffer, and in many cases part of that suffering is trying to discover which of a number of paths that remain open to us, is the one least likely to prolong our pain or to cause us or others long-term harm. When a person is dealing with a medical diagnosis of cancer, for example, what that person really wants is for the doctor to rescind the diagnosis and say that it was all a sad mistake, and he or she can now carry on life as planned, moving into further decades of functioning at full schedule with full energy, cancer-free. But most suffering does not have that kind of exit door. Instead, we must make the best we can of a bad job; we must make decisions where the only options open to us are such as we would rather reject. How do we receive God's guidance during such a time?

James says that coping with this kind of problem must start with an attitude shift that may at first seem beyond human capacity. We are to "count it all joy, my brothers, when you meet trials of various kinds" (James 1:2). We must see our suffering as God testing the quality of our faith in order to toughen us up inside, and we must accept the trial as from God for however long it may last, knowing that it is maturing us in ways beyond our power to measure (vv. 3–4). But James knows that being in a situation where one is thus under trial is bewildering, and wisdom to live by his wise words is regularly in short supply; so the next thing he says in verses 5–6 is, "If any of you lacks wisdom [if, that is, you are conscious of being thrown off balance and you can't see what to make of the particular trials you are in and how to count them joy], let him ask God, who gives generously to all without reproach, and it will be given him." He adds, "Ask in faith, with no doubting" that God will answer this prayer, and he warns against the irreverent double-mindedness of the spiritually muddleheaded who ask God for things he has promised without any confidence of receiving them. So, we are to keep asking for wisdom to live to God, and if we do so expectantly it will be given; nothing is more certain than that. The kind of humility that leads to and springs from wisdom will never allow us to say, "Now I know for sure all that God is up to in my life"; rather, it will lead us to learn, as Job did, to praise and thank God for knowing what he is doing in our lives without knowing either the what or the why of it ourselves. So we ask for wisdom in times of trial, wisdom that will enable us to face up to our present situation (even if that situation is cancer, job loss, divorce, or children on the road to ruin) and see what is best for us to do, and enable us also to keep rejoicing in God's gift of present salvation and promise of future glory as we battle through.

Second, *we are to assess by wisdom—painstakingly.* Wisdom calculates. It calculates all of our responsibilities and then works out how to be faithful in handling each of them, because faithfulness to existing obligations belongs to the essence of wisdom. But wisdom also makes appropriate new commitments after careful consideration, because wisdom leads us to live up to the limit of what we can do for God and others. Some commitments automatically accompany the normal Christian life: commitments to our family, church, friends, colleagues, and work, as well as to keep the various promises that we have made. We put wisdom into practice by keeping before our minds a clear-eyed, realistic assessment of our commitments. Such assessments alert us on occasion to circumstances that limit our room to maneuver. For example, a Christian scholar chose not to accept a promotion that would entail a move to a place where his wife would not be able to serve God in the role to which they believed God had called her. Another chose to leave a tenured faculty position because his wife was called to serve a church in another part of the country. A third relocated off the beaten track for the sake of his wife's health. Wise assessment will prioritize some commitments ahead of others. In the decisions of the three scholars above, they saw their commitment to "love [their] wives, as Christ loved the church and gave himself up for her" as higher than personal career advancement (Eph. 5:25). Good decisions cannot be made without wisdom's assessment of priorities, and sometimes that calls for willingness, like John the Baptist, to decrease personally for the increase of another. Wisdom will thus on occasion tap into the truth of John

15:13, that there is no greater love than to lay down one's life for one's friends, and in any case wisdom will operate with a God-first, others-next, self-last mental grid, for that is what the Word of God requires.

A wise assessment will also calculate the consequences of the options that are open and seek to discern which of the possible courses of action would produce the best results not only for self, but for all concerned, and for the cause of God's kingdom and his praise. A wise God-follower will look at these consequences in light of the great double-barreled command: to love God with all our heart, soul, strength, and mind, and our neighbor as ourselves—even when that "neighbor" is someone not to our personal liking. Liking is not the same as loving, and Christians often find themselves called to love people they do not like. Wisdom has to be working out consequences all the time—for God and for everyone else, not just for self.

In making wise choices, we need to be clear on what we say no to, as well as what we say yes to, and in each case why. These yeses and nos are part of Christlike wisdom. When we read the Gospels and watch Jesus in action we see wisdom in his moment-by-moment choices in response to the many demands for his attention. It is amazing and almost unnerving to see how Jesus was able to make out of every situation something creative, ingenious, and genuinely helpful to the people with whom he was dealing. Well may we marvel at the wisdom that was built into his ministry.

When Jesus, God incarnate, walked in human sandals, each time he said yes to one use of his time, he was saying no to some other use. As we trace his actions, we can usually appreciate the priorities underlying his choices on how to use his humanly limited time and energies, and we can discern the loving wisdom that these choices reveal. For example, once when Jesus was busily teaching a mass of people, including a number of hostile Pharisees who were looking for a chance to trip him up with some theological conundrum, a cluster of infatuated parents elbowed their way through the crowd, bringing their young children and even their noisy babies to him so he could "touch them," as if his touch would impart some special magic. His disciples, fulfilling their duty in crowd control, told the parents to leave him alone so that he could continue giving instruction on God's coming kingdom, his own imminent death, signs of the end times, divorce and remarriage, the nature of true prayer, and other matters of similar importance. But Jesus assessed how his time and effort would be best spent and interrupted what the disciples thought was his most important work. He stopped teaching the crowd, scolded his disciples for their mistaken assumption about his and their true priorities, took the children into his lap, and "blessed them laying his hands on them" (Mark 10:13–16; cf. Luke 18:15–17), meanwhile holding them up as illustrations of how by childlike faith and trust we are to enter God's kingdom—the theological topic that is perhaps the most vital of all.

So there is more to this episode than a simple statement on whether children are more important to God than adults, or whether blessing is a more important activity than teaching. Kingdom issues are at stake here, and what we see here is a stunning instance of wise love as Jesus welcomes the parents, blesses their little ones, teaches one lesson to his disciples about caring and another to the crowd about faith, using the children in his arms as an object lesson to make his point. And the example of Jesus's wise love, which we meet constantly in the Gospel stories, must guide us as we seek to calculate how we can make the most and the best, for God and others, of the situations we are in.

Third, *we are to act with wisdom—resolutely.* Some who seek God's guidance get so unnerved by the possibility of making a wrong choice that they become inwardly paralyzed, unable to make a decision, and therefore they take no action at all. Those of us who are tempted in that direction must realize that inaction is itself action. Inaction is simply making the decision that you are going to do—nothing. Sometimes that is the right decision to make, but sometimes, perhaps often, it is a cop-out. Inaction allows fear to rule and prevents us at that moment from contributing anything of significance to God's kingdom. Well has it been said that all that is needed for evil to triumph is for good men to do nothing.

Jesus told a story about three servants who were given their master's money to trade with. The first two took some risks with the money and managed to increase it spectacularly. But the third was afraid to take any risk at all, so he kept it in a handkerchief until his master returned, and then he simply gave it back (Luke 19:11–27; cf. Matt. 25:14–30). Jesus represents the master as very cross with the servant who did nothing with the money that he was given to trade with. Now we, you might say, have been given wisdom to trade with, and it is up to us, with God's help, to do precisely that. We are called to *act* with wisdom, and if, after careful consideration, our decision is to do nothing for the moment, but wait on the Lord, until circumstances change, we must realize that this decision itself is an action which eliminates other choices. Wise action will always be principled, constructive, enterprising, responsible, and calculated as the best thing we can do to please and glorify the Lord in each set of circumstances. It will never be a choice to do nothing because of self-protective fear.

Conclusion

What does all of this add up to? The thrust of the foregoing chapter can be focused as follows. Many Christians are still haunted by the fancy that real guidance from God for the making of each day's decisions is a direct ministry of the Holy Spirit in one's heart that entirely transcends the mental disciplines of analyzing alternatives, applying principles, calculating consequences, weighing priorities, balancing pros and cons, taking and weighing advice, estimating your own capacities and limitations, and engaging in whatever other forms of brainwork prudence in self-commitment is held to require. We emphatically agree that leading us to the best decision is a ministry of the Holy Spirit, first to last, but with equal emphasis we deny that under ordinary circumstances his ministry short-circuits or circumvents any of these sometimes laborious intellectual procedures. On the contrary, they are precisely the means by which the Holy Spirit of

God leads us into seeing clearly what it is right and good to decide and do in each situation.

In the previous chapter, we saw that the basic attitudinal frame for godly decision making, both in its positive, obediential and its negative, restrictive, stay-within-limits aspects, is fixed by the revealed law of God, which tells us his value system and lays out his moral ideal in the broadest terms for the guidance of his human creatures. This chapter has tried to show that Scripture itself points us constantly to our need of the gift of wisdom, that is, the good sense and shrewd judgment that the Spirit makes flow from the goodness of the God-centered, God-taught heart. If we are to implement the ideals of the law and so further the kingdom and glory of God in our daily lives, the best decisions will not be made except as we are guided by what older theology called the virtue of prudence, and there will be no virtue of prudence without the gift of wisdom, just as there will be no gift of wisdom without the down-to-earth realism about the business of living, with all its ups and downs, which we meet in the book of Proverbs, and indeed in all the wisdom writings from start to finish.

We fallen humans excel at self-deception when it comes to decision making. We shut our eyes to inconvenient facts, we naïvely rely on our own imperfectly trained consciences, we make exceptions to rules to favor ourselves, we listen only to people who say what we want to hear, we decide on policies and courses of action in unawareness of our own deep-down motives, ambitions, and rivalries; and so it goes on. In decision making we must ever seek honesty, humility, and prudence, and without the gift of wisdom we shall always miss all three.

Having thus argued that wisdom is a stepping-stone to prudence, we shall now explore the truth that advice is a stepping-stone to wisdom. Are you still with us? Hoping so, we ask you to read on.

6

With a Little Help from Our Friends

Where there is no guidance, a people falls,
but in an abundance of counselors there is safety.

Proverbs 11:14

Let's look back for a moment.

What we have seen thus far is that the God who loves us—the Triune God who in his own being is the Father, the Son, and the Holy Spirit, working in every believer's life as a team to save us from sin and shepherd us home—has promised to guide us along the paths of righteousness, as one aspect of his tripersonal covenant care of us. So in making our decisions, in living with the decisions we have made, and in trying to please this great and glorious God wherever we are and whatever we are doing, we should always look to him for help and strength. Even when our starting point is our wish that we had made different decisions so that we would not be where we are now and even when we cannot change our present circumstances, much as we would like to (how many of us start there!), we can still count on his presence with us, his readiness to show us his way for us, and his power to help us move along it, next step by next step. Slow as we may be to seek his guidance and strength at each bend or intersection of the road, he will not withdraw from us and leave us to our own devices. On the contrary, he has pledged himself to lead and look after us, "for his name's sake," meaning in a way that displays the goodness, mercy, faithfulness, forgiveness, and forbearance by which he defined his love long ago when he proclaimed his name to Moses (Exod. 34:6–7), and this he will most certainly do. God's "name" means his revealed nature, to which he is always true, and when he makes a promise he can be relied on to keep his word. So believers should not think of their quest for guidance as an expanse of black ice where ruinous accidents constantly take place but as the central arena of our real life in which God is poised to be gracious to us, over and over again.

God, however, guides through his appointed means: that is, through direct Bible teaching, to start with; then, through biblically formed wisdom that discerns, digests, and applies biblical principles of action in light of a biblically focused overall view of God and life; and then, as we shall now see, though corroboration and/or correction from fellow members of the body of Christ. Just because we all have flaws and blind spots in our thoughts and outlook that left to ourselves we would never detect, we all need in humility to seek advice from others when we have to make significant decisions. Wisdom itself tells us to let our present thoughts be tested and assessed by theirs and to review our options in light of what they suggest. The world knows that if we are to avoid making mistakes time and time again, we must constantly consult and be advised; that is why so many experienced professionals set up in the business world as consultants, and in the sports world as coaches. It is the same in the Christian life. Advising and mentoring fellow believers is one of the ministries in which Christians should regularly serve each other, and that is what the present chapter will discuss.

Individuality and Individualism

Here, though, we run up against a problem that must be faced squarely. Samuel Johnson, the pontifical compiler of the first English dictionary, once declared that he did not like Scotsmen, and when his buddy Boswell protested that he was a Scotsman himself, Johnson said he recognized that as something Boswell could not help. Similarly, we have to recognize that none of us can help being children of our time, constantly conditioned by the milieu in which we move and the cultural air we breathe every day. And one thing contemporary Western culture does not know how to do, and cannot therefore teach us to do, and indeed actually hinders us from doing, is distinguishing between individuality and individualism. Our culture tells us that developing one's individuality means becoming an individualist—that is, a person consciously detached from external authority and external consensus, thinking one's own thoughts and doing one's own thing in disregard of the patterns that one is expected to fit into. Popular existentialism a generation ago, with its idea that you only become a person by standing apart from the crowd, and popular postmodernism today, with its idea that all claims to assert universal truth are power plays in disguise and that my truth must not be expected to match yours, are products of this mindset, which in fact they serve only to articulate and reinforce.

The bottom line for this way of thinking is that individuality means individualism: isolated, defiant, and seeking in the name of spirituality to explore and express the depths of one's own being all the while refusing in the name of integrity to dance to any tune save one's own. It is a familiar mental mood into which our contemporaries are massaged by the lyrics of pop singers, debunkings of the past by school and university teachers, self-help gurus and their programs on the media, loose talk about freedom, and much else along the same lines. Conditioned by such a culture as ours, it is hard for Christians to learn the humility that should lead them to suspect themselves of insufficiency and therefore to seek advice when they should and value it properly when it has been given. This is our problem.

Individuality and individualism are in fact two very different things, and it is a matter of prime importance for us to grasp that the gospel of Christ forbids the second while fostering the first. How does the gospel individualize? By making us see ourselves here and now as alone before God in the way that we shall be on judgment day; by making us face our sins and follies and what Yeats described as "the foul rag-and-bone shop of the heart," whence all our perversities emerge; and by forming and consolidating within us our personal bond of faith in the Lord Jesus Christ for salvation, so that henceforth we live as forgiven sinners, consciously and conscientiously accountable to the Father and the Son in all that we do, and endlessly giving thanks for the "amazing grace . . . that saved a wretch like me."

So how does the gospel bar the way to individualism? By making and keeping us humbly aware, on the one hand, of our frailties and limitations, which guarantee eccentric lapses if we try to walk alone, and aware too, on the other hand, of God's purpose of fellowship in the body of Christ, in which harmonious helping of each other where help is needed is the rule and constant goal. As self-sufficient pride produces individualistic independence, so humble realism produces mutuality in community, whereby each one seeks to help others along at all points where they see that they can, and each one depends on others to help him or her in just the same way. Asking and accepting advice, giving and receiving counsel, being as open to correction as one is to encouragement, and recognizing that the traffic of this two-way street is essential to the well-being of all, is thus one aspect of faithful discipleship.

But this is very different from the way of our contemporary Western world, individualistic within its institutionalist frame as it is, and that world is constantly seeking, if we may echo J. B. Phillips's happy rendering of Romans 12:2, to "squeeze us into its own mold." As a result, learning to follow this path of fellowship that we are describing, so as not to stray into bypaths of self-sufficient conceit and worldly isolationism as we seek to see and do the will of God, calls for determined effort. Isolationist infection constantly gets into our spiritual system, and has to be detected and unlearned over and over again. For pride is at the heart of all spiritual individualism—pride that proclaims self-sufficiency and hates to act in a way that suggests inadequacy and whispers dependence; and that pride of ours needs to be humbled. It is here that the present chapter, we hope, will give help.

Fellowship and Friendship

But there is some more ground clearing to be done before what we have to say can be properly heard. We spoke of taking advice from within the Christian fellowship to help us make the best decisions. When we used the word "fellowship," what did we mean? For many of us, fellowship is no more than a cup of coffee or tea and a relaxed chat before or after church service or some other Christian meeting. If that is how we think of it, the suggestion that wise counsel will be found through consulting the fellowship will carry little conviction. But fellowship as the New Testament writers envisage it is far more than a casual chat at the refreshment table. The Greek word for it is *koinōnia*, which signifies the act and consequence of sharing what God has given to each of us: I give you what I have to share, you give me what you have to share, and we both end up enriched and encouraged beyond where we were when we started. When we practice this *koinonia* we benefit from it together. Love, respect, goodwill, and a desire to be of service constitute together the motivation of fellowship. Fellowship is the risen life of Christ activating and coordinating the regenerate, who are his body parts; literally and precisely, it is Christ ministering to his people through his people. This grace of Christian fellowship is a supernatural gift operating strictly between those whom Christ has taught to see each other as his brothers and sisters, and therefore ours, in the family of God. Concern that the other person's needs be met and care for that person's well-being shapes the practice of fellowship; the mutuality of seeking to give as well as take and take as well as give is the spirit of fellowship; and being variously enriched—in the present case, in wisdom for decision making—is fellowship's fruit.

Ideally, the congregation to which we belong will be our primary field of fellowship, where our ideas of God's will for us are tested and, if sound, confirmed and where from time to time indications of God's will for us are directly given. When the leadership group (apparently) in the church of Antioch in Syria received God's call to second Paul and Barnabas for missionary service, the whole congregation (apparently) laid their hands on them and sent them off (Acts 13:3). This symbolized their *koinonia* in the decision, and to Paul and Barnabas themselves the gesture must have meant a great deal. Surely the explicit association of the local church with major decisions involving its members ought to be a regular part of its in-house Christian fellowship.

It needs to be frankly acknowledged that the church in the West has been slow to appreciate the strength that comes from drawing on each other's wisdom and insight within the local congregation for personal direction on major decisions. It might well be that congregations in Africa, Asia, and Latin America could lead us into a more corporate (and biblical!) practice at this point than we have yet attained. Part of God's provision for guidance evidently is putting people of different age groups, social, cultural, and racial backgrounds in the same congregation. In their togetherness they then make up the body of Christ in its local manifestation, with the diversity of the body parts on full display. The homogeneous unit principle (like attracts like, or birds of a feather flock together), on which the pioneer church growth leaders laid such stress, may be valid for beginning a church plant, but once a congregation has grown sufficiently in numbers to become self-supporting, adhering to that principle will quench the Spirit and arrest the congregation's qualitative growth into spiritual maturity. God does not want established congregations to consist of people who are all alike any more than he wants us as individuals to limit our close friendships to people just like ourselves. On the contrary, he wants each congregation to contain a wide variety of the human race, and he means us to find that the help we need in discerning his will comes to us through the minds and souls and voices of this wide cross section of Christian believers.

We need people to point out to us all the relevant facts for making our decision, some of which we may have overlooked. We need people to help us make sure we are abreast of all the interests our decision must serve, and to remind us of those whose concerns we may have failed to take into account. We need people who know us well to tell us, with loving honesty, whether we are being realistic about our own abilities and inabilities, and whether we are actually up to the task that we contemplate taking on. We need people to help us explore our own motives, including the self-serving motives that are there but which we are tempted to gloss over. God means us to seek and find much of the help we need here within the fellowship of the living, breathing, many-faceted, multitalented local body of Christ. As it is within the church that God guards and guides us, so we are called to consult the congregation in matters of personal decision that would in any way affect its life and to view it as our corporate, spiritual friend as we do so.

It must be admitted that the practice of *koinonia*, like every other Christian ideal without exception, can be and has been misused and cheapened to the point of absurdity. For example, a young man wrote, lovingly for sure, to a widowed missionary whom he had not yet met to say that God had shown him she should marry him, and he hoped she would gladly follow God's leading. (She did not reply.)[1] Our readers might well be able to tell other stories of nutty advice or proposals or directions given as from God in the name of fellowship. We shall discuss later in this chapter the discernment that is needed to process advice given in good faith. Good faith, however, does not guarantee good sense! So not all well-meant advice will be good advice, particularly when it comes from fellow believers who do not know you well. The advice of close Christian friends, however, is a different matter.

Friendship in Christ is fellowship plus, and it is very precious indeed. Loneliness brings misery; we all need friends! That is a truth about human nature which is doubly true in the Christian life. Friendship grows out of shared interests, attitudes, purposes, and skills, along with temperaments that both parties find stimulating and enriching, so that they love being together to enjoy each other. Christian fellowship, as we have seen, means what has been called "one anothering"—being at the service of one's fellow believers to care for them, share with them, and walk beside them for their good. Christian friendship is all of that, along with the enriching pleasure that comes as the parties draw affection out of each other and refresh each other simply by being natural with each other. There is no friendship without trust in each other, and no deep-level trust without honest transparency with each other. Fellowship is a discipline of sympathy that can be draining, but friendship is an experience of sympathy that is invigorating. Friendship is close and, in intention anyway, permanent; distant and temporary friendship is really a misnomer and a contradiction in terms. Acquaintanceships can be casual and short-term, but not friendships. Fellowship is goodwill shown in the here and now, but friendship adds the desire for continued, ever-deepening connection. The self-giving of Christian fellowship may be one-sided, as in some of Paul's pastoral relationships (see, most strikingly, 2 Cor. 6:11–13; 7:2–3; 12:14–15), but the self-giving of friendship is fully mutual, as with David and Jonathan (see 1 Sam. 18:1–4; 19:1–7; chap. 20; 23:15–16; 2 Sam. 1:26). We may regularly be in fellowship with dozens, maybe hundreds of other believers, but the number of our chosen, cultivated, and cherished friendships will be much smaller because the relationship demands so much more of us, just as it gives so much more to us.

It is right for us to hope and expect that God will guard and guide us through our friends. A godly friend sees us in the light of God's grace and so treats us kindly, magnifying our strengths and making up for our weaknesses. A compassionate friend shares our pain and in so doing lessens our suffering. A joyful friend laughs at us—and with us. A loving friend sees us through the eyes of our holy God, and so confronts us when we need it, pointing us to what is involved in a life worthy of friendship, even the friendship with God that we profess.

But our human *friends* are, well, human. And so we chuckle as we remember that if we drop the *r* from that cozy word, we are left with *fiend*. Our friends lighten our days and challenge us to godliness. But one of the things that we have to be aware of when we think of help from our friends is that their well-meant help is not always marked by well-digested wisdom. Friends can be more fiendish and less truly friendly than they mean to be and certainly more so than we hope to find them, particularly when it comes to discerning the will of God. Yet it is true wisdom for us to turn to them and ask their advice, for all of us easily overlook things and as the epigraph text for this chapter says, "in an abundance of counselors there is safety."

Two far-reaching reminders are now in order, however, before we go further. First, God's way of wisdom for us, when found, may not look wise to outsiders or even to our own friends whose advice we have sought. Does it, for instance, look wise that Christian parents Harold and Jeanette, having raised three children born to them, should then adopt three toddlers from troubled genetic backgrounds and of a different race and at middle age begin again the difficult task of child raising? Or does it look wise for retired missionary Robert to live in frugal independence while donating almost half his income to mission causes that he can no longer serve in person? Or for Mary, a Christian grandmother in an AIDS-striken section of Kenya, to take in her five orphaned grandchildren and attempt to ensure their care and survival by growing vegetables on her tiny plot of land?[2]

Here and elsewhere, brave Christians seek God's wisdom in every case by pursuing a quest for the best. Our line of questions must ever be: "What is the best that I can do for the glory of God? And for the good of others? And for the advancing of God's kingdom? And for a witness to God's truth and power, and to the grace of my Lord Jesus Christ? I must not tempt God by rashness, but equally I must not dishonor him by apathy, laziness, and always taking the course that is easy and comfortable. So, Lord, show me: what is the best I can do for you?" What distills in our heart as we live with these questions may well fail to match the self-protective wisdom of the world and of the worldly, but that will not mean that it is not the wisdom of God.

Second, taking advice from others will not excuse us from hard thinking of our own. What it will do, rather, is set before us options and considerations to think about. It is a mistake to suppose that the way to receive God's guidance is to sit down and wait passively for it, doing nothing until God is felt to "speak." It is only a variant of that mistake to think that advice from one's friends ought to be taken uncritically and without further thought or prayer, just because it has been given. Hard thinking before the Lord is often undervalued when we consider the range of spiritual disciplines, but, as we shall shortly see in the case of Paul, evaluating the advice given us is vital if we are to find and follow the will of God. Bishop Ryle's experience illustrates some of these principles.

Guidance for J. C. Ryle

J. C. Ryle, the Anglican evangelical leader who became Liverpool's first bishop, 1880–1900, was a successful country clergyman in his early sixties when he was offered (as from the Queen through the prime minister, which was and remains the Church of England's way of granting bishoprics and deaneries) the deanship of Salisbury Cathedral.[3] The idea evidently was that this would be an honorific appointment in which Ryle could work out his last days as a minister without having much to do. Deans of cathedrals only had to keep the round of services going in those days, and the rest of their time was their own, as is portrayed in Anthony Trollope's *Barchester Towers*.

But Ryle had no wish to leave his thriving parish in Norwich diocese for Salisbury, where as an evangelical clergyman he would be in a minority of one. Conscious of needing wisdom to respond to this offer, therefore, he consulted his friends, and in a letter to another friend he reported the result. "Flesh and blood were utterly against it [that is, moving to Salisbury] but almost every one of the sixteen men I consulted said, 'You ought certainly to go for the sake of Christ's cause in the Church of England.' So who was I that I could withstand? I prayed for light and signs from God, and this was all I got. If three [of the sixteen] had said 'Refuse,' I would have refused. Cathedral music is not congenial to me. I go into a nest of hornets and shall stand alone." Reluctantly, then, but believing the consensus of his consultants showed this was the right course, Ryle accepted the offer and prepared to move to Salisbury. He announced the move to his congregation, and a solemn send-off was prepared.

Then a telegram from the prime minister summoned him to London on a particular day (April 16, 1880), and Liverpool's member of Parliament met him on the platform, to tell him that before the government went out of office in less than a week they wanted to appoint him first bishop of Liverpool, a new diocese recently carved out of the overlarge diocese of Chester. Realizing what an enormous scope for establishing evangelical ministry citywide and evangelizing Liverpool's half-million people this would present, and being poised to leave his present congregation already, Ryle found it easy to say yes, without further consultation with anyone. The consulting about Salisbury had established in his mind the rightness of being open to a new post "for the sake of Christ's cause in the Church of England," and having led him to that openness God was now giving him a far more influential role than the Salisbury deanship would ever have been. Against the odds, and starting from scratch, inheriting no diocesan institutions or infrastructure at all, he single-handedly established Liverpool as the most robust and significant evangelical diocese in England, which arguably it remains today.

Looking back, it is not hard to see the hand of God in all this. If the difficult decision to go to Salisbury had not been faced and taken, Ryle would not have been in a position to say the immediate yes to the offer of Liverpool that the government required, and if he had not consulted in the first place but simply followed his own inclination, he would never have accepted Salisbury. God's vocational guidance frequently takes a step-by-step form, as here, with lessons on self-denial, humility, and patience being taught through the intermediate steps of the process, and God's overruling wisdom not becoming apparent until the process is complete.

We now turn to Scripture to explore three principles that have already woven their way into our discussion: *seek advice*, *weigh advice*, and *practice prudence*.

Seek Advice

We have not yet done with the book of Proverbs—or, perhaps we had better say, the book of Proverbs has not yet done with us. In addition to its sustained summons to seek wisdom, on which we have reflected already, Proverbs urges repeatedly that the way to wisdom is to take advice from those who are wise already and thus to avoid slipping into the self-sufficient arrogance that marks fools and constitutes their foolishness or folly. So we read:

> The way of a fool is right to his own eyes,
>   but a wise man listens to advice.
>
> Proverbs 12:15

> Where there is no guidance, a people falls,
>   but in an abundance of counselors there is safety.
>
> Proverbs 11:14

> By insolence comes nothing but strife,
>   but with those who take advice is wisdom.
>
> Proverbs 13:10

> Without counsel plans fail,
>   but with many advisors they succeed.
>
> Proverbs 15:22

Listen to advice and accept instruction,
    that you may gain wisdom in the future.

Proverbs 19:20

The tongue of the wise commands knowledge,
    but the mouths of fools pour out folly.

Proverbs 15:2

The more momentous and far-reaching the decision, the more urgently necessary the taking of advice becomes. A man's choice of a wife, or a couple's choice of each other, is a far-reaching decision, needing therefore to be made, as the old Anglican Prayer Book put it, "not unadvisedly, lightly, or wantonly . . . but reverently, discreetly, advisedly, soberly, and in the fear of God"—which means taking advice from people who know both parties well and can tell them, with loving honesty, whether they are really suited to each other long-term, or whether they have unrecognized limitations and skewed motives that would threaten their bonding.

Again, one of the most momentous decisions, with the potential for great harm to a great number of people, is the decision of national leaders to take their country into war. The same was true three thousand years ago; so it should not surprise us when Proverbs declares: "Plans are established by counsel; *by wise guidance wage war*" (20:18).

The principle, then, is clear. Look now at some Bible narratives that illustrate it. Jethro was a priest in the land of Midian, and in Exodus 18 we read how he came to visit the Israelites after they had come out of Egypt. Evidently Jethro had heard how Moses his son-in-law had struck out across the desert leading a horde of people with him. So Jethro gathered up his daughter Zipporah, and his two grandsons, and headed out into the desert to meet Moses. The two men bowed to each other and went through the usual Middle Eastern pleasantries of hospitality and food. Then they sat down in a tent together, and Moses filled Jethro in on all the details that led to the exodus from Egypt. By the end of their catching-up conversation, Jethro is praising the God of his son-in-law, "Blessed be the LORD, who has delivered you out of the hand of the Egyptians and out of the hand of Pharaoh. . . . Now I know that the LORD is greater than all gods. " (Exod. 18:10–11). Jethro offered a burnt offering to the God of Moses, and later Aaron and the elders of the people joined them for dinner.

The next day Moses went to work, and Jethro went with him. It was a tough day for both of them. Here is how it went: "The next day Moses sat to judge the people, and the people stood around Moses from morning till evening. When Moses's father-in-law saw all that he was doing for the people, he said, . . . " 'Why do you sit alone, and all of the people stand around you from morning to evening?' And Moses said to his father-in-law, 'Because the people come to me to inquire of God; when they have a dispute, they come to me and I decide between one person and another, and I make them know the statutes of God and his laws.'"

God had empowered Moses to lead several thousand former slaves out of Egypt and into the wilderness toward a land that would be new to all of them. And, as is typical when any large group of people get together and are under any sort of stress, they developed a huge variety of interpersonal tensions. So Moses, being the hardworking, responsible leader that he was, set himself to solve their problems: He acted as spiritual guide helping them to discern God's will; he served as judge, settling their disputes; and he worked as a teacher, interpreting God's laws to them. It was an all-day job, every day, and the people waited in line to see him. Each evening Moses must have felt exhausted, but that fatigue no doubt blended with a sense of accomplishment and duty and maybe even a smidgen of pride. The people revered him. He was leading his people into righteousness, faithful following of their holy God. Certainly God must be pleased with him! But his father-in-law was not. Here is what happened next.

"Moses' father-in-law said to him, 'What you are doing is not good. You and the people with you will certainly wear yourselves out, for the thing is too heavy for you. You are not able to do it alone. Now obey my voice; I will give you advice, and God be with you!'" So much for in-law tact! Not only was Jethro interfering with the most important task of Moses's life, he was doing so as a relatively new convert, attempting to tell his son-in-law how to do a job that God had been preparing him to do for all of his life. But Moses had himself paved the way for Jethro's interference. What would he expect to happen after his intimate tent conversation about the work of God over the past weeks? He was in effect, even if not in intention, *inviting* his father-in-law to interfere. Under the circumstances interference is what one might expect—and that is precisely what Moses got. Now observe the unsolicited advice that Jethro offered, advice with the term "obey" attached to it.

"You shall represent the people before God and bring their cases to God, and you shall warn them about the statutes and the laws, and make them know the way in which they must walk and what they must do." That was what Moses had been doing all along: no disruption yet. But with the next word out of Jethro's mouth, "Moreover," Moses's datebook was to take a major hit, and his power a major plunge. "Moreover, look for able men from all the people, men who fear God, who are trustworthy and hate a bribe, and place such men over the people as chiefs of thousands, of hundreds, of fifties, and of tens. And let them judge the people at all times. Every great matter they shall bring to you, but any small matter they shall decide themselves. So it will be easier for you, and they will bear the burden with you. If you do this, God will direct you, you will be able to endure, and all this people will go to their place in peace" (Exod. 18:13–23).

Can you delegate? Moses had to learn to delegate. Do you know what to look for in wise leaders for your church? Adhering to Jethro's description of the sort of people Moses was to look for will go a long way toward providing good pastoral care in a church. Do you find it difficult to take advice, especially if it comes in the form of an unsolicited and overbearing order as it did here? Moses, however, was sufficiently humble and clearheaded to accept the wise directive he'd been given. "Moses listened to the voice of his father-in-law and did all that he had said" (v. 24), and his people received better care because of it. Moses and Jethro together provide us an example of advice given, advice taken, and wisdom resulting. Perhaps Solomon had Jethro in mind when he wrote, "A word fitly spoken is like apples of gold in a setting of silver. Like a gold ring or an ornament of gold is a wise reprover to a listening ear" (Prov. 25:11–12).

But not all advice, even from friends, will work out for our ease and comfort. God's ways are far more complex than that—and so is life. Some three hundred years after the time of Moses, kings began to rule over God's people. These kings always surrounded themselves with counselors, some of them wise and good, many foolish and evil. When the great King David (second king in the long line of kings) suffered a momentarily successful coup by his son Absalom, two counselors offered advice to their new king.

Ahithophel had been David's number one counselor, that is, the person he always had by him to consult in cases where decisions had to be made for the kingdom and the people. Ahithophel's reputation was such that the recorder of 2 Samuel comments, "Now in those days the counsel that Ahithophel gave was as if one consulted the word of God; so was all the counsel of Ahithophel esteemed, both by David and by Absalom" (2 Sam. 16:23). But Ahithophel had secretly given allegiance to Absalom. Ahithophel, one supposes, was a man who always looked after himself, and he had decided that Absalom's revolt was likely to succeed; so he transferred to Absalom's side (15:12).

But David had a friend named Hushai, an Archite, who had wormed his way into Absalom's inner circle and presented himself as a man willing to give Absalom advice although actually he hoped to listen in on the battle plan in order to send information back to David (16:16–19). Meanwhile, David, feeling the terrible loss of having his main counselor turn traitor, prayed that Ahithophel might lapse into folly. "O LORD, please turn the counsel of Ahithophel into foolishness" (15:31).

Absalom had already chased David out of Jerusalem and was now occupying it. He asked Ahithophel, as the most respected counselor, what he should do next. Ahithophel said in essence, "Well, you should show everyone that you are in charge here and that your father is powerless to do anything about it. You will make that as plain as possible if you have sex with all of his concubines and make sure everyone knows about it." So Absalom did just that. He set up a tent on the roof of the palace, in clear view of the people, and one by one these hapless women were sent inside. Then Absalom, having (one supposes) rather liked his first experience of Ahithophel's advice, asked again what to do. And Ahithophel, we can assume now wishing a hero's role, said, "Let me choose twelve thousand men, and I will arise and pursue David tonight. I will come upon him while he is weary and discouraged and throw him into a panic, and all the people who are with him will flee. I will strike down only the king, and I will bring all the people back to you as a bride comes home to her husband" (17:1–3). We can almost see Ahithophel's eyes gleam with the intensity of his ambition. And, as verse 14 tells us, it was in fact good advice; had Absalom followed it, David would have been permanently ruined.

Absalom, still David's son, may have gulped a bit when he heard Ahithophel's words and so said something like, "Well that's something to think about, but let's see what Hushai has to say." Hushai, buying time to get a message through to David, dismissed Ahithophel's advice as "not good," following this with a plausible explanation: "You know that your father and his men are mighty men, and that they are enraged, like a bear robbed of her cubs in the field. Besides, your father is expert in war; he will not spend the night with the people. . . . [E]ven now he has hidden himself in one of the pits or in some other place. And as soon as some of the people fall at the first attack, whoever hears it will say, 'There has been a slaughter among the people who follow Absalom.'"

Now Absalom began to think that if he followed Ahithophel's advice, David and his people would defeat Ahithophel's party, and that the victory would raise David's morale and so he himself would be worse off. Recognizing the progress in persuasion he had made, Hushai continued with an alternative battle plan. "My counsel is that all Israel be gathered to you, . . . as the sand by the sea. . . . and that you go to battle in person." In essence Hushai was advising Absalom: Wait. Don't go right away. Make sure that you have an overwhelmingly powerful force to outnumber David and company before you start the battle—and then lead the battle yourself (17:4–14).

Hushai must have known that what he said about David and his men being in a ferocious state of mind was not likely to be true because they had all gone out of Jerusalem with their tails between their legs. David was in deep grief that his beloved son was leading a revolt against him, and he had bowed before the curses of Shimei and felt the sting of stones on his back as he left the city. David was in no mood to fight. Hushai was bluffing, but Absalom bought his story. So Absalom took the wrong advice: Hushai's rather than Ahithophel's. And we are told that when Ahithophel saw that his counsel was not being followed, wounded pride and realistic expectations combined to drive him to suicide. He saddled his donkey, went home to his own city, set his house in order and hanged himself. He couldn't risk what he foresaw for himself if David and his troops were given time to recover and retake Jerusalem, as he thought they were sure to do if given the breathing space Hushai's plan allowed them (17:23).

All of this illustrates the point that while we all need counselors from whom to ask advice, we also need good sense ourselves to evaluate what those counselors say. That truth leads us straight into our next section.

Weigh Advice

Some forty years after King David died and immediately following the death of Solomon, David's son, the people sent a delegation to Rehoboam, son of Solomon, who was next in line to take the throne. First they stated the obvious, "Your father made our yoke heavy," which he did. Solomon had built the famous temple that was to bear his name for the next four hundred years. To do this, he centralized the wealth of a whole nation, with high taxes, forced labor, the skills of artisans, and the gathering of gold and jewels (much given voluntarily). The building, commissioned by

David but built under Solomon had drawn on the resources of every able-bodied citizen and every stockpiled domestic treasury. That was of course very grand for Solomon, but it was pretty rough on Israel. Solomon's subjects had been glad that God was so prospering their king and his kingdom, but they were less than thrilled about the way that they had been mobilized in order to make it happen. So the request to Rehoboam was to make things easier for them. Rehoboam consulted the old men, the circle of counselors with whom Solomon had consulted throughout his life, and they told him to do what the people asked. He should give them a break, take it easy on them. "If you will be a servant to this people today and serve them, and speak good words to them when you answer them, then they will be your servants forever" (1 Kings 12:7).

Before making a decision, however, Rehoboam also consulted the young men whom he had grown up with: dashing young bloods, no doubt, to whom man-management was a closed book, just as it was to Rehoboam himself. They said, No, no, no. You are the king, so swagger. Be big. Make it obvious that you are in charge. Go out and tell them, "My little finger is thicker than my father's thighs. And now, whereas my father laid on you a heavy yoke, I will add to your yoke. My father disciplined you with whips, but I will discipline you with scorpions" (12:10–11). It is as if Rehoboam had said, "My father made it bad for you, and I'll make it worse. I'm the king, you're my subjects, so there. Go home and prepare for further exploitation from your new royal master." Rehoboam was a fool, as his later reign confirmed. He did not adequately weigh the two sets of advice he had received, took the wrong counsel, and headed his country into civil war and eventually two separate nations, which never again united at any point in Jewish history.

In view of these last two stories—the story of Absalom deciding how to war against his father and the story of Rehoboam deciding how to rule his people—we have to ask a question that any careful reader of the texts will raise. Why does bad advice sometimes come to people, as it seems, from the Lord? This was true of Hushai's advice to Absalom and also the advice of the young men to Rehoboam. Hushai's advice got Absalom killed in the battle that resulted from acting on it. The young men's advice brought about a national schism. Both stories have textual clues which show us that God had something to do with each of these events. In 2 Samuel 15:31, we hear David praying *against* his former top counselor: "O LORD, please turn the counsel of Ahitophel into foolishness"—which God evidently did, by letting Absalom conclude there was superior wisdom in what Hushai said. And we read in 1 Kings 12:15, "So the king did not listen to the people [those who had asked Rehoboam to lighten their load], for it was a turn of affairs brought about by the LORD that he might fulfill his word." In each of these stories, things went badly for the person who was looking for advice (with their own flawed motives bedeviling them), and both of them in the outcome received the comeuppance they deserved, but their acting on the bad advice worked toward God's larger purposes. David was duly returned to power. And later, the kingdom was duly split, as God had already declared it would be (see 1 Kings 11:29–39) because of idolatrous worship of the goddess Ashtoreth and the gods Chemosh and Milcom. As ever, God was overruling and his will of events was being done.

What should we learn from these stories? First, that it is certainly right for us as God's people—indeed, as God's children—to seek the best advice from those whom we see as the wisest advisors, to weigh the advice we get as carefully and thoroughly as we can, and to follow what thus appears to us the best course of action; but, second, that right at the outset we need to ask ourselves before the Lord *why* we want the advice we are going to ask for. What is our motive? What is the goal? Is it to advance our own ego at the expense of a family member, maybe a parent, whom we want to put down, as with Absalom? Or at the expense of people whom deep down we despise, and over whom we are happy to ride roughshod, as with Rehoboam?

If our purpose in seeking guidance, and hoping God will show us through advisors the most fruitful course of action, is anything less than God's own glory in our own lives and in the lives of others, it will be no wonder if God leaves us to make misjudgments prompted by our own false motives, misjudgments that will bring home to us the sick and bitter nature of our chosen path. If our professed quest for wisdom boils down to a pursuit of success in self-aggrandizement, as it did with these two men, it deserves to be blasted, and God can be expected one way or another to blast it. As he is constantly active in grace, so he is in judgment. Both Absalom and Rehoboam received wise advice, which they failed to weigh properly—realistically, that is—because a vision of personal grandeur (Absalom leading his army to a huge victory, Rehoboam dragooning cowed Israelites to serve his personal prestige) led them astray. Both of them were puffed up with pride, and we know all too well that pride goes before a fall.

The New Testament adds to this wisdom about weighing advice in two ways. The narrative in Galatians 2:11–14 of Paul rebuking Peter, like the story of Jethro directing Moses, shows how God will use one person to minister to another, and how a person being taught wisdom may have to rethink and change his ways. The new element here, however, is Paul's demand for the consistency of wisdom, that is, the resolve to express one's beliefs in honest, transparent, straightforward action and to ensure that one's actions square with one's beliefs.

Peter had compromised. Following the conversion of Cornelius, recorded in Acts 10, Peter knew that Gentiles have a full and equal place with Jews in God's kingdom; so he could eat at table with non-Jewish believers, ignoring the food laws under which he had lived all his life. But when Jewish Christians arrived from Jerusalem, men of standing one supposes, he stopped doing this. Why? No doubt because he did not wish to risk any kind of confrontation with headquarters. To Paul, however, Peter's action was a devious deception, obscuring a vital Christian truth, and he would not let Peter get away with what he was doing. "I opposed him to his face," says Paul of their encounter (Gal. 2:11). If Peter could eat with Gentiles when Jews were absent, he could and should eat with them when Jews were present. Said Paul, "If you, though a Jew, live like a Gentile and not like a Jew, how can you force the Gentiles to live like Jews?" (2:14). Both Peter and Paul continued as Christian missionaries, and the churches continued to grow full with both Jews and Gentiles; so we can assume that Peter heard, weighed, and acted on Paul's advice—even though he didn't seek it.

The second new lesson is quite different. As we weigh the counsel we are given, we may on rare occasions find that even unanimous advice from God's people may *not* guide us in the direction God is pointing. It takes genuine sensitivity to the people, to our own interior, hidden motives, and to the voice of God's Spirit within to discern God's guidance in so difficult and unusual a circumstance. Late in his ministry, Paul experienced just this kind of conflict, and it is deeply interesting to watch him handling it. In Acts 20:22, we hear Paul confide to the Ephesian elders, "I am going to Jerusalem, constrained by the Spirit, not knowing what will happen to me there, except that the Holy Spirit testifies to me in every city that imprisonment and afflictions await me." From that point on Paul headed toward Jerusalem, giving farewells and receiving dissuasives at every stop. When he "sought out the disciples" at Tyre, "through the Spirit they were telling Paul not to go on to Jerusalem" (21:4). When he arrived at Caesarea, a prophet took Paul's belt and tied up his own hands and feet and said "Thus says the Holy Spirit, 'This is how the Jews at Jerusalem will bind the man who owns this belt'" (21:11). And Luke, who is in Paul's party at this point, writes "When we heard this, we and the people there urged him not to go up to Jerusalem" (21:12).

Still Paul persisted, weighing the advice he heard, but sensing ever more certainly that God himself was sending him to Jerusalem. Luke finally wrote, "And since he would not be persuaded, we ceased and said, 'Let the will of the Lord be done'" (21:14). Luke at least had come to a resigned recognition that God was taking Paul to a place where *none* of his Christian friends would advise him to go. So Paul went to Jerusalem, against their advice, not having accepted it, but not having ignored it either. Processing it had undoubtedly made him surer than ever that God was directing him to Jerusalem, and to Jerusalem he must go. Of course, there was trouble for him, as had been foretold, and that was how he got to Rome—which is where God was sending him all along. In this, God's mysterious plans once again came to light, but only long after Paul had decided to listen to God's voice within *in spite of* advice given by his friends. Their advice had assumed that a key man like Paul should avoid trouble whenever he possibly could. You could call that assumption common sense. But his, as events were to show, was an exceptional case. We shall say more about exceptional cases later. For the moment we simply note that on rare occasions a heart tuned to God will find that he or she must reject even the good advice of godly friends.

Practice Prudence

Prudence is a quality which C. S. Lewis describes as common sense sanctified for the glory of God. In *Mere Christianity*, Lewis speaks of the four cardinal virtues which people like Aristotle had already distilled out from their reflections on life and which in due course became part of the Christian heritage. Prudence is one of the four virtues, along with temperance, justice, and courage or fortitude as Roman Catholics commonly call it, though these would hardly rank as virtues at all if prudence was not their foundation. Lewis expands on this cardinal virtue as follows:

> Prudence means practical common sense, taking the trouble to think out what you are doing and what is likely to come of it. Nowadays, most people hardly think of prudence as one of the "virtues." In fact, because Christ said we could only get into his world by being like children, many Christians have the idea that, provided you are "good," it doesn't matter being a fool. But that is a misunderstanding. In the first place, most children show plenty of "prudence" about doing the things they are really interested in, and think them out quite sensibly. In the second place, as Paul points out, Christ never meant that we were to remain children in *intelligence*: on the contrary, he told us to be not only "as harmless

as doves," but also "as wise as serpents." He wants a child's heart but a grown-up's head. He wants us to be simple, single minded, affectionate and teachable, as good children are, but he also wants every bit of intelligence we have to be alert at its job.[4]

We return to this topic now, as we near the end of this chapter, because, while prudence is an all-time, all-place, all-weather virtue without which we cannot live well in any situation or relationship at all, it is in weighing and evaluating advice from friends, peers, relatives, pastors, professionals, strangers, or whoever, that our prudence is supremely tested, and any lack of prudence on our part will appear most clearly. Prudence is the classical Christian name for the hard thinking that, as we said earlier, the assessing of advice requires. This is, of course, a two-way street: our own advising of others, however good, shrewd, and spiritual in itself, will go for nothing if they lack the prudence to process properly what we say. Deep-level, fully-formed prudence is an absolute necessity for all aspects of the wisdom and discernment that this book commends.

Deep-level prudence involves three things. The first requirement is a clear grasp of the gospel of Christ, with its liberating message of full forgiveness through Christ that begets grateful bond service to him and his Father, who is now our Father too, and therewith an outgoing love to all our fellow humans as well. Prudence cannot grow in a heart that is ruled by any mode of legalism, lawlessness, or lovelessness.

The second requirement is a conscience that functions clearly and consistently in terms of biblical truths and values. Such a conscience will always be countercultural to a degree, and we today in the West need all the time to be inwardly battling the secularism that surrounds us if our consciences are to be well-formed and always in good working order. It is to help us here, where we are all so vulnerable, that God's moral laws are laid out in the Bible at what sometimes feels like laborious length. The seemingly endless contrasts of right and wrong, just and unjust, in the Pentateuch, the prophets, the proverbs, and the psalms are there for a reason, namely, the educating of fallen human consciences up to their full stature, and we must let them all have their way with us to that end.

The third requirement is a resolute realism that insists on finding and facing the true and full facts of every situation regarding which we are called on to take action, pass a judgment, or express an opinion. Being honest with oneself and others in facing facts is far from easy; wishful thinking, rationalized emotions, prejudices and hurts, selective and sometimes deceitful memory, and a desire to be told only what we want to hear easily seep in to muddy our decisions with selfishness. But all facts are God's facts, and any unwillingness to learn and practice the habit of being objective about matters of difficulty or what is felt as a threat will keep us out of the path of godly prudence all our lives.

The bottom line, then, is that there are moral conditions of spiritual discernment. We shall not achieve clarity about God's will for us, either through the clamor of well-meant advisors or through the working of our own thoughtful hearts in times of quiet withdrawal, unless our hearts are set first and foremost on following, obeying, and pleasing the Father and the Son. Basic to true wisdom is an unending quest for holiness—purity of heart and perfection of love to God and men. The writer to the Hebrews warns us that without holiness no one will see the Lord (Heb. 12:14), and we are saying that without holiness no one, however well advised and faithfully admonished, will adequately discern the will of God at any point in his or her life. Holiness, which is fundamental to prudence, must always come first.

7

Modeling

I have given you an example, that you should do just as I have
done to you.

John 13:15

Love one another as I have loved you.

John 15:12

Brothers, join in imitating me, and keep your eyes on those who
walk according to the example you have in us.

Philippians 3:17

People imitate people. That is a natural, universal, creational fact.
Much of the imitating is unconscious. Thus, children learn to talk
by imitation. The newborn's first wails, gurgles, and coos sound
the same all the world over, but as the parents bend over the baby
and coo back, adding simple words and phrases, the child starts
to imitate and in due course becomes a speaker of the parent's
language. By young adulthood these children are likely to have
picked up gestures, inflections, and facial expressions that will

prompt the comment, "Oh, you are so much like your dad" or "so much like your mom." J. I. lived through days when England's two outstanding preachers of the gospel, D. Martyn Lloyd-Jones and John Stott, were both at the zenith of their powers, and he got a good deal of fun from noticing how young admirers, when preaching, imitated the intonation and style and tricks of speech of these two greats. But none of the imitations so far mentioned were or are conscious copying; they are the kind of thing that just happens through ordinary togetherness. Unconscious imitation, or assimilation, if we would rather call it that, takes place much more widely than we realize.

Sometimes however, the purpose of imitation is fully conscious. We find ourselves wanting to be like someone. Is that good or bad? It depends. When a starry-eyed admirer says to a Christian leader, "I want to be a theologian (or preacher, or teacher, or writer) like you; please tell me how," it really is not good. Ambition to be of service in God's kingdom is admirable, but aiming to acquire someone else's spiritual gift and ministry by learning to imitate them is more an ego trip than a path to godly service. The motive is wrong, as one can sometimes make clear to the fan (yes, that is the word that fits) by simply asking, "Why?"

Yet taking people as role models for encouragement, once one knows one's own calling from God, can be very good, for the role model constantly motivates one to do better. Thus, D. M. Lloyd-Jones and Charles Haddon Spurgeon, great evangelists of the nineteenth and twentieth centuries, respectively, both looked to George Whitefield as their ideal and made no secret of the fact. Whitefield was in every way the pioneer and powerhouse of the eighteenth-century revival in Britain—indeed, both sides of the Atlantic—and, from a human standpoint at least, understandably so. His zeal was inexhaustible, his stamina hardly believable; his voice was magnificent, his wholeheartedness in preaching Christ was overwhelming, his power of projecting and applying God's truth was breathtaking, and his love for people overflowed torrentially as he preached. J. I. has enjoyed two role models: Richard Baxter, a seventeenth-century Puritan, and also George Whitefield himself, whose old school J. I. attended. Is it bad to have such figures from the past motivating, encouraging, and admonishing one in the present, forbidding self-satisfaction and calling one to higher aspiration with fuller imitation? Neither of us thinks so; rather, the reverse.

What, you ask, is the relevance of these reflections? Answer: they add a very necessary dimension, and so bring a very necessary enlargement, to our ideas of God's guidance. Let us explain.

God as Guide

Up to now, we have been thinking of God's promised guidance as help in the conscious making of decisions—help through Scripture, help through wisdom, help through friendly advice. Of the inner sense of rightness and peace by which, again and again, God confirms good decisions we have yet to speak. But at this stage we would make the point that there is more to God's guidance of his children than helping us see what to do in particular cases where choosing is called for. Prior to this, God has been guiding us by molding and shaping us, forming and conditioning us, so that we will be inwardly equipped to make right choices, wise and discerning, when the time comes. That fact is to be the focus of this chapter.

Think back to David's great parable with which we started, Psalm 23, where he pictures himself as a sheep in God's flock, joyfully testifying: "He leads me in paths of righteousness." When the shepherd sees one of his sheep wandering, or standing still, puzzled and tempted, poised to start wandering, he will chase, call, and maybe use his crook, as we have seen, to get the animal moving along as part of the flock again. When the sheep is doing that, however, it will have no reason to feel that the shepherd is taking any special notice of it. Yet David's verb, "he leads," comprehensively covers all the regular movement of the flock from pasture to pasture and drinking place to drinking place, no less than it covers the moments of necessary personal attention. If the sheep supposed that the shepherd's eye was off it while it trotted along in the flock, the sheep would be wrong. Similarly, we must understand that God in his sovereign providence is leading and guiding us through each day of our lives, whether that day calls for new, far-reaching decisions or not. And one of the many things he is providentially doing for us is exposing us to influences that will deepen, ripen, and mature us. Setting before us models for imitation is one major mode of his doing this. We may not think of godly people's influence on us as divine guidance—indeed, much of the time we will not be thinking of their influence on us at all—but God-given guidance, guidance at the level of vision, valuation, and, quite simply, virtue is what in truth these saintly souls are to us. God sends them our way in order that we may learn more about godliness through our contact with them.

Psalm 32:8–9, a direct oracle from God, repeats his covenant promise of guidance with a significant emphasis on learning.

> I will instruct you and teach you in the way you should go;
>   I will counsel you with my eye upon you.
> Be not like a horse or mule, without understanding,
>   which must be curbed with bit and bridle,
>   or it will not stay near you.

Here, the shepherd-sheep picture is left behind; schoolroom verbs appear, "instruct," "teach," "counsel," and we are told not to behave like animals that lack understanding, but to learn, and so gain the understanding we need. We ask, "How are we to do this?" In the first place, by ingesting and digesting Holy Scripture, and by distilling wisdom from what we read—practicing, that is, the disciplines with which this book has dealt thus far. But there is more. One further way in which God teaches is, as we said, through the provision of object lessons, mind-expanding and heartwarming models that impact us at different levels, some alerting us to things hitherto taken for granted, some reinforcing priorities that we had already tentatively embraced, and some working by spiritual osmosis, if we may put it so, to make us larger people in

Christ, blessed with more vitality, vision, and virtue than was ours before. Let us open this up.

What Models Do

What is the place of models, and imitations of models, as God guides us into Christian maturity? What can such models do for us anyway? How is rubbing shoulders with godly men and women, in all their variety and with all their God-centered energy, meant to affect us? We offer a threefold answer.

First, *models will enlarge our vision.* They will enable us to grasp more clearly the moral and spiritual ideals which have always been held in high regard among Christians but which we ourselves never really appreciated. Abstract ideals, however noble, rarely come alive in our minds until we see them being lived out. We need to contemplate models in order to realize the full implications of these highest standards. For example, we Christians speak of love, even a special kind of "Christian love." Everybody has some idea of what the word *love* means; but even Bible readers are not likely to appreciate the full significance of love until they have meditated in depth on Jesus's story of the Good Samaritan and on the factual narrative of the Son of God, becoming incarnate, humbling himself to live the life of a poor and insignificant man by human standards, and finally humbling himself further to the ultimate shame and pain of crucifixion.

In Philippians 2:6–11, Paul, perhaps quoting an early hymn, celebrates how the Son did not hang on to equality with God but emptied himself of his dignity and glory and took all those steps down; becoming "obedient to the point of death, even death on a cross. Therefore God . . . exalted him" (2:8–9). But first it was down, and down, and down. All of that was done out of love. As John 3:16 declares, "God so loved the world, that he gave his only Son" to endure it all so that those who believe in him, the sin-bearer, might not perish but have eternal life. Only as we live in light of the love of the Father, and the love of the Son, in the whole work of our redemption, can we begin to see what love means. Only those who can say, with Paul, "the Son of God . . . loved me and gave himself for me" (Gal. 2:20) will ever be able to join him in saying "the love of Christ controls us" (2 Cor. 5:14). This staggering love of Christ is to become our own behavioral standard. But, being spiritually sluggish, we still need close-up models to help us realize what that means. These God in many ways provides. As we link our lives with resolute Christ-followers, we will see in them over and over this Christlike, self-humbling kind of love, and thus our vision of the love we ourselves are to live out will be focused and enlarged and become, shall we say, a little less inadequate than it was.

Second, *models make us realize what could and should be in our lives*. Models show us possibilities that were never in our minds before, possibilities of doing things that are better than we had ever thought. Tennyson wrote, "We needs must love the highest when we see it." For the Christian, at least, that is true. When Christians see God's highest, the vision stays with us. Our conscience operates henceforth in terms of that ideal. It constantly presses on us the question, Are you living up to what you now see to be God's standard for you? You must try to do that. Pacing ourselves alongside a model obliges us to imitation, that is, to an attempt to match the model in our own lives. It must be, in Oswald Chambers's unforgettable phrase, "my utmost for his highest" from now on. J. I. acknowledges that he has been under this constraint ever since, in literary terms, he met Whitefield and Baxter more than sixty years ago, and as he looks back he is grateful for that meeting, which has obliged him to aim higher than he would ever have done had it not taken place. This can work in a spiritually fruitful way—particularly when one of our models is Jesus Christ.

Third, *encountering a model can also help us vocationally*. This is a matter which we will treat more directly in the next chapter, but it merits mention here. For example, many Christians who have become either domestically or cross-culturally significant missionary workers were inspired to do so by the career of some beloved missionary whose written life was read and whose story fired their imagination. Now they reproduce elements of that vision in their own ministry and mission work. Models can thus serve as vocational guides, suggesting goals to us that we would not have imagined had we been left to ourselves.

It should, perhaps, be said explicitly at this point that what we are talking about here is not what the world calls hero worship. Hero worship is precisely what the words say—worshipping the hero, finding and celebrating special excellence in him or her. Hero worship focuses entirely on the persons being admired, sometimes in disregard of their feet of clay, always idealizing them somewhat unrealistically. But when God in his providence brings spiritually outstanding models before us, our minds hone in on the God who enabled them to live and serve with such spiritual authenticity, power and fruitfulness, rather than staying centered on the persons themselves. At least, that is how it is meant to be and how the Holy Spirit within us will cause it to be, unless we obstruct him. And if we allow our appreciation of spiritual models to degenerate into hero worship, so that God's servants rather than God himself take center stage in our minds, we shall frustrate, and so quench and grieve, the Spirit—make no mistake about that. The godliness of our models, which so arrests our attention in the first place, is meant, first and foremost, to help us see more clearly the greatness and goodness of God. Models are given to be signposts rather than shrines.

The New Testament encourages us to imitate models as part of our learning to walk in the way of God. Evangelicals for some reason seem to shy off this subject; we rarely hear sermons about it we rarely read books about it, and when we talk to Christian people; it doesn't often become the topic of conversation. Perhaps this is our way of being careful never to put any human in the place of God. But overcaution in this area may keep us from the God-intended benefit of learning from those who are farther along in their spiritual journey than we, and that could be a major loss.

Of course, the primary model for all Christians is the Lord Jesus Christ, the one who lived the only perfect human life on this earth. He is the model on whom first and foremost we are to fix our eyes. His is the example which has power to transform our lives. His love and his wisdom, his total self-giving and self-humbling in the service of others, his humility, his endurance as he went down and down through Gethsemane, the humiliation of his trials, and finally the agony of his death on the cross—all these are aspects of his earthly life in which he is a model for his followers. So says the New Testament in text after text. Gazing on Jesus runs no risk of keeping us from God, since Jesus *is* God himself, and it confronts us with an absolutely perfect model, inasmuch as Jesus himself is the absolutely perfect human being. No wonder, then, that the New Testament writers lay stress on imitating the Lord Jesus and regard this discipline as a receiving of guidance for life.

Imitation of Christ

Here are some passages that instruct us to model ourselves on Jesus: "Whoever says he abides in him ought to walk in the same way in which he walked" (1 John 2:6). "He walked," of course, does not refer to some literal step-by-step footpath across the landscape of Israel; walking, as we said earlier, is the regular Bible image for living one's life. This passage is instructing us to live our lives the way he did. Not surprisingly one of the priorities in this kind of walk is love. Over and over in this first letter of John we read variations on the theme, "We love [one another] because he first loved us" (1 John 4:19; see also 1 John 2:7–10; 3:1–3, 23–24; 4:7–12, 16–19; 5:2). In John 15:12 the same point is made; here the Savior says to his disciples, "This is my commandment, that you love one another as I have loved you." His prophetic example of what that kind of love would entail follows in the next verse. "Greater love has no one than this, that someone lays down his life for his friends" (v. 13). Jesus was about to do that very thing; these words were among his final teachings to his disciples before he walked to the cross. He had already demonstrated the radicalism of this kind of love, through pantomime, as he knelt before his disciples one by one and washed their feet (John 13). When he had finished, over the stunned silence of eleven of them and Peter's strenuous objection, he stood and taught them all the meaning of his gesture: "If I then, your Lord and Teacher, have washed your feet, you also ought to wash one another's feet. For I have given you *an example*, that you also should do just as I have done to you. Truly, truly, I say to you, a servant is not greater than his master.... If you know these things, blessed are you if you do them" (John 13:14–16). This is Jesus talking about the radicalism of real love.

In Ephesians 5:1–2, we find Paul saying, "Be imitators of God ... and walk in love, as Christ loved us and gave himself up for us, a fragrant offering and sacrifice to God." Christ's sacrifice of himself was quite literal; he died on our behalf. If we follow him as our model, we must be prepared to put self-interest aside in any number of ways any number of times. The order will always have to be *God* first, *others* second, *self* last. And this is not just a word for the good times. In 1 Peter, a letter of encouragement written to churches who were soon to enter into persecution, the same challenge to model the self-sacrificing love of Jesus appears emphatically at the end of 1 Peter 2:21, "Christ also suffered for you, leaving you an example, so that you might follow in his steps." Peter tells his readers to prepare for the fact that though they were doing good, they were likely to find themselves suffering for it, suffering, that is, for their Christian discipleship in this time of coming persecution. After calling on them to follow in the steps of Jesus, Peter reminds them what Jesus's own experience was: "He committed no sin, neither was deceit found in his mouth. When he was reviled, he did not revile in return; when he suffered, he did not threaten, but continued entrusting himself to him who judges justly" (vv. 22–23). Those were challenging words to probably new converts about to face undeserved violence: there must be no deceit, no bitter talk, no threats, just sustained trust in God that he will pass just judgment on the enemies by his own means and in his own time. Modeling Jesus involves the unflinching practice of this trust.

Working up similarly to a climactic charge to imitate Christ's fortitude in the face of the fiercest and deadliest opposition is the extended exhortation to faith and faithfulness that fills Hebrews 11 and 12. It begins with a roll call of heroes of faith during and after Old Testament times—Abel, Enoch, Noah, Abraham, Isaac, Jacob, Joseph, Moses, Rahab, Gideon, Barak, Samson, Jephthah, David, Samuel, "the prophets," unnamed "women," and others. For readers with a Jewish background, mention of these names and events would have triggered lifelong memories of stories told and retold as parents created in the earliest years of their children's lives a sense of belonging to the people of God and a confidence in God's marvelous protective guidance of his people through history's ups and downs. These men and women of Hebrews 11 are our models too, every single one of them, living by faith and enduring what came their way as they did so. None was perfect. As we read their stories spread out through the Old Testament, we see their failures, weaknesses, and sins. But we also see their great acts of faith and how God guided them to greatness through that faith.

But now the writer steps out of history and addresses his readers directly in the present, speaking as though these heroes still live— which in fact, of course, by God's grace, they really do: "Therefore," he writes, "since we are surrounded by so great a cloud of witnesses, let us also lay aside every weight, and sin which clings so closely, and let us run with endurance the race that is set before us, *looking to Jesus, the founder and perfecter of our faith, who for the joy that was set before him, endured the cross, despising the shame, and is seated at the right hand of the throne of God*" (Heb 12:1–2). This is the climax, to which the tour of the heroes' gallery was, it now appears, simply the preliminary. Jesus, centrally and definitively, is the one whose faithful hoping must be the model for his followers. Jesus, suffering patiently in expectation of joy to follow, is the supreme example of unyieldingness triumphant, on whom hard pressed Christians must ever fix their gaze. "Looking to Jesus." The Greek verbal form conveys the thought of concentrating one's vision on something so that one is looking at it with full intensity and not looking directly at anything else. "Consider him . . ." the writer continues. He, above all others, is the model; we, his latter-day disciples, are to walk in his steps at all times.

That imperative and the example Christ has set both belong to our guidance from God.

We round off this section by pointing out that Jesus himself taught, quite explicitly, that discipleship to him, across the board and in every respect, was to be conceived as modeling oneself on the Lord himself. This was his meaning when he said, "Take my yoke upon you, and learn from me. . . ." (Matt 11:29). The picture is of two oxen pulling a cart or plow, one of them a veteran, the other a youngster in training. A wooden yoke fastened over both their necks links them side by side. The young ox, paired with the veteran, learns to pull by imitating the other; indeed its only choice for comfort in this twosome is to keep in step with the older partner. In the disciple's case, pairing with Jesus and learning from Jesus will be a lifelong business. The Savior's invitation to it is compassionate. "Come to me, all who labor and are heavy laden, and I will give you rest. Take my yoke upon you, and learn from me, for I am gentle and lowly in heart, and you will find rest for your souls. For my yoke is easy, and my burden is light" (vv. 28–30). Modeling Christ, as part of the larger process of being modeled by Christ, is thus of the essence of the Christian life and of the divine-guidance process. Christians learn to live *in* Christ, to follow and fulfill the example that Christ has set us, and to recognize that this—only this—is the way of our maturation, namely, through imitation of him. It is by this means, in the first instance, that we are led in paths of righteousness, namely, by consciously keeping in step with our divine-human leader with whom we are inseparably yoked. The image is truly awesome, but very clarifying and very supportive.

Imitation of Leaders

Paul calls on the people he pastors to imitate Christ, as we saw. "Walk in love, as Christ loved us. . . ." (Eph. 5:2). But he does not stop there. Writing to the Philippians, he first tells them to imitate Christ: "Have this mind among yourselves, which is yours in Christ

Jesus, who . . . humbled himself. . . ." (Phil. 2:5–8). But a little later he says: "Brothers, join in imitating *me* (Phil. 3:17). He includes with himself other believers who are mature in faith adding at once: "And keep your eyes on those who walk according to the example you have in us." The *us* is Paul and Timothy, who are writing the letter together. Paul's principle here is double-barreled: it is, first, that, following Christ and under Christ, many "walk according to the example" that Paul set in following the example that Jesus set and all of these are benchmark people on whom it is proper to model oneself; and, second, that all Christians should take note of these people and make imitation of their virtues a deliberate project in their lives.

Peter exhorts the stated leaders of Christian congregations (elders he calls them) saying, "Shepherd the flock of God that is among you" (1 Peter 5:2). This points to a responsible kind of leadership that has the well-being of the flock in mind. Under Christ, "the chief Shepherd" (v. 4), leaders of churches are to exercise shepherdlike qualities toward the people in their care. A shepherd sees the big picture and guards the whole flock, but a shepherd also cares for individual sheep—as our Lord Jesus effectively underlined in his parable of the shepherd who left ninety-nine of his flock, then at great personal inconvenience and with much effort went off looking for and finding one recalcitrant sheep who had strayed away; whereupon, he placed it lovingly on his shoulders for a free ride home (Luke 15:3–7).

Human shepherds of God's people are to extend this same kind of wise, compassionate, self-sacrificing, Christ-following care to "the flock of God that is among you." (Note who is the owner of this flock.) Peter continues his charge to undershepherds by challenging them to take a hard-eyed look at their motives and their manner. Leaders in the church are to exercise "oversight, not under compulsion, but willingly, as God would have you; not for shameful gain, but eagerly; not domineering over those in your charge, but being examples to the flock" (1 Peter 5:2–3). Not drivers or organizers or teachers or visionaries, we note, though leaders will also be some and perhaps all of those, but *examples*. Here it is pertinent to point out that in God's church everybody is a leader to somebody—parents to children, siblings to siblings, seniors to juniors, the strong to the weak, friends to friends, encouragers to the discouraged, one disciple to another—and all of us, therefore, have leadership responsibilities that we must take seriously. We should expect God to use us his maturing followers as models to somebody and thus to live our lives accordingly. What a daunting assignment, and what a rewarding one. Peter finishes his admonition with a glimpse of the future when the Great Shepherd gathers us all to himself, the stated and the informal leaders together: "And when the chief Shepherd appears, you will receive the unfading crown of glory," a joyful prospect indeed!—and one that, please God, will include us all.

Reverting to Paul, we may be surprised to see how much he makes of the modeling motif. He commands a congregation to imitate him. "I urge you, then, be imitators of me" (1 Cor. 4:16). "Be imitators of me, as I am of Christ" (11:1). He commands a colleague: "Set the believers an example in speech, in conduct, in love, in faith, in purity" (1 Tim. 4:12). He reminds a congregation of the example he has set them: "You yourselves know how you ought to imitate us. . . . We worked night and day, that we might not be a burden to any of you. It was not because we do not have that right, but to give you in ourselves an example to imitate" (2 Thess. 3:7–9). He reminds them joyfully how they have already been following examples given: "You became imitators of us and of the Lord. . . . You, brothers, became imitators of the churches of God in Christ Jesus that are in Judea" (1 Thess. 1:6, 2:14).

We should not, however, be surprised at Paul's emphasis. Paul saw his church planting and pastoral leadership in family terms: from one standpoint he was the father and mother of his converts (see 1 Cor. 4:14–15; Gal. 4:19; Philemon 10); from another standpoint, he and they were brothers in Christ; and the family in God's intention is a prime area for setting and following examples—for modeling, in other words—as we noted above. This was doubly so in the ancient world, as it is in a good deal of Asia today. In the modern West, much of this aspect of family life has dissolved away, but our obligations to each other in the church remain unchanged, and one aspect of the love and care that we owe to each other in Christ is setting each other good examples, just as Paul did to the churches he founded long ago. Paul's presentation, indeed projection, of himself as an example to follow was not any form of egocentricity or tyranny; rather, it was ministry, plain and straightforward, and the responsibility of ministry to each other remains real in a way that our secular culture cannot comprehend.

But what if a leader of God's people turns bad? It happens. We cringe when we see one of our own as newspaper fodder for some stupid statement or some shameful deed. We are chilled to our heart when a Christian icon's immorality is exposed. We hurt when we read of a national leader who names Christ on Sunday but on Monday squanders the funds of his country on personal luxury while his nation's children die of hunger and disease. The Old Testament shows us an instance of this as it tells us how the prophet Jeremiah confronted Jehoiakim, the younger son of a great and godly king, for this kind of egoistic malfeasance. Jehoahaz (Shallum) had reigned as king of Judah briefly in 609 BC. His father had been the good king Josiah who during a reign of more than thirty years instituted godly reform, led the people to return to God, and eventually died honorably of battle wounds (2 Chonicles 34–35). Within weeks Jehoiakim was following his brother to the throne, where after eleven years he reaped the epitaph all too common among the kings of Judah and Israel: "He did what was evil in the sight of the LORD his God" (2 Chron. 36:5). Jehoiakim was firmly in the saddle when Jeremiah addressed to him the following message from God:

> Woe to him who builds his house by unrighteousness,
>   and his upper rooms by injustice,
> who makes his neighbor serve him for nothing
>   and does not give him his wages,
> who says, "I will build myself a great house
>   with spacious upper rooms." . . .

Do you think you are a king
    because you compete in cedar?
Did not your father eat and drink
    and do justice and righteousness?
      Then it was well with him.
He judged the cause of the poor and needy;
    then it was well.
Is not this to know me?
    declares the LORD.
But you have eyes and heart
    only for your dishonest gain,
for shedding innocent blood,
    and for practicing oppression and violence. . . .

With the burial of a donkey he [Jehoiakim] shall be
    buried,
    dragged and dumped beyond the gates of Jerusalem. . . .

The wind shall shepherd all your shepherds,
    and your lovers shall go into captivity;
then you will be ashamed and confounded
    because of your evil.

Jeremiah 22:13–17, 19, 22

Scripture blames the eventual exile of both Israel and Judah on the irreligion, immorality, and untrustworthy double-dealing of their kings; bad examples have great power to corrupt. The ripple effect of personal influence, for good or ill, is incalculable in advance; one can only say that it is likely to exceed our anticipations. Nor did Jehoiakim's callous depravity injure only himself. The prophet warns that his underlings in government ("your shepherds"), having taken their cue from their master, will receive retribution too ("The wind shall shepherd all your shepherds"). As good examples have great power to inspire, so when a Christian public figure is publicly disgraced the negative fallout may well be huge. So we need to walk warily—very warily indeed.

Conclusions

Pulling together the threads of this chapter, we may now make three closing points. First, the guidance that God gives to his covenant children is not exhausted by the help he provides for our decision making, nor by his protecting and preserving ministry that restores us if we slip or stray. It extends to the forming of our characters, out of which our decisions are made, and to the formative influences shaping us into the persons we become. This is the providential aspect of the work of God in the personal sanctification of each believer. It complements the faith-and-obedience aspect of personal response to God's words of promise and command, which often is all we think of when sanctification is under discussion. In older evangelical parlance, the language of guidance was used comprehensively to cover God's eliciting of faithful obedience from us within the often enigmatic and daunting frame of providentially ordered circumstances (of which more will be said later in this book). One example is the close of Charles Wesley's hymn, "Jesus, My Strength, My Hope" which runs as follows (emphasis added):

> I rest upon Thy Word,
>   The promise is for me;
> My succor and salvation, Lord,
>   Shall surely come from Thee:
> But let me still abide,
>   Nor from my hope remove,
> Till thou my patient spirit *guide*
>   Into thy perfect love.

The present book was conceived in terms of the older, broader usage of guidance language, and we shall keep the older, broader conception explicitly before our minds as we move into our final chapters.

Second, imitation is natural to humans, and God's work of sanctifying grace in each Christian life includes, as we said above, the provision of models and imitations. The first and most perfect of these is our Lord Jesus Christ himself. Wisdom would seem to direct that in order to receive the full sanctifying benefit of contemplating this model, we should read and reread the Gospels, where we watch the perfect person living, working, speaking, reacting, relating, caring, rejoicing, praying, and enduring. Constant reading of the Gospels will allow the perfection of Christ's character to have its full influence on the shaping of ours. It is to be feared that some evangelical Christians, in their very proper zeal for reading the whole Bible, fail to read the Gospels as frequently as wisdom would prompt them to do. The letters of Paul and John, and the Psalms, should also be read frequently as well, for here too are models of godly inner life, life with God, that are given to shape us and guide us in godliness; not so much by the doctrines that they teach or imply as by their attitudes to God—praise, thanks, petition, celebration, complaint, submission—in the circumstances of their lives. The old dictum, that you become like what you look at, applies directly here.

Third, our purpose of consciously conforming ourselves to good and godly models should teach us to learn from the examples of both faithful Bible characters and faithful persons in the congregation. As the personal impact of live actors on the stage has a quality that surpasses the impact of actors on the screen, so the impact of live Christians with whom one rubs shoulders will exceed the impact of Christians about whom we read in books; yet wisdom directs us to expose ourselves to the influence of both, and the habit of reading Christian biography, as well as Scripture, is as much to be encouraged as is the habit of associating with the liveliest and ripest Christians that we know. Does God guide us by leading us to form these habits? And can imitation, which has been cynically described as the sincerest form of flattery, also be described as a major means of guidance and of grace? We believe that the answer to both questions is yes, and it is in this confidence that we proceed.

8

Guided Life Commitments

> The LORD took me from following the flock, and the LORD said
> to me, "Go, prophesy to my people Israel."
>
> Amos 7:15

Our life, from one standpoint, is a long string of decisions. Some
are small-scale, short-term, and of little or no consequence. What
we decide to wear, what we choose from the restaurant menu,
which seats we book at the theater are decisions that in the long
run, other things being equal, make no difference and so do not
matter. But some decisions are far-reaching, and we know before
we make them that they will be; these are decisions, for instance,
about education, career, marriage, location, church affiliation, or
adoption of children. Understandably, we face the making of such
decisions with some angst.

It is true, of course, that we can never be sure what is going to
come of our decision making. What feels like major decisions may,
after all, have no effect, and apparently trivial decisions may prove
momentous. Small-seeming decisions do sometimes turn out in
God's providence to have life-changing consequences—decisions
such as accepting an invitation to the party where you first met

Mr. or Ms. X, or attending a conference that led to an unexpected career opportunity, or turning to the day's set Scripture passage and finding in it light from God, shining directly on a knotty personal problem. Such events bring joy; they are precious reminders of the guardian grace and covenant care of the God we serve. And then it is also true that unanticipated circumstances will suddenly negate long-term decisions that were carefully, even laboriously, made before the Lord, so that one has to start all over again. At such times we need to remind ourselves that God does all things well and that he knows what he is doing with us when we don't. In the present chapter, however, we leave these realities on one side. Our concern at the moment is with the making of decisions that we expect to be life-shaping hinge-points on which we think our future will turn. We hope that what we have to say will go some way to relieving the tension and anxiety that the making of such decisions can bring.

We shall describe such decisions as vocational, and the guidance of God in relation to them as vocational guidance. We do so because the language of vocation is so deeply embedded in today's Christian usage, where it reflects the idea that any life-strategy decision, correctly reached, is in fact being made in direct response to a "call" from God to engage in that form of service. (*Vocatio* is Latin for "call.") Hence people committing themselves to pastoral ministry or monastic life are often said simply to "have a vocation." Though neither the Hebrew nor the Greek words for "call" are used in Scripture in quite this way, the language of "being called" to a particular walk of life (to minister, or to marry, or to relocate, or to change jobs, or whatever) is firmly established in the Christian church; and among evangelicals, at any rate, it determines expectation of experiences to a remarkable extent— not always helpfully, as we shall soon see. We note in passing that the world has borrowed Christian vocational phraseology and watered it down; in secular usage, vocational guidance has nothing to do with God and ordinarily relates simply to employment; and since many jobs today are short-term, it rarely rises to the point of offering any form of life-strategy. But in Christianity the thought of vocation as a personal, life-embracing mandate from God continues in unabated strength. We shall discuss it with full recognition that this is so.

Vocational Guidance: Its Nature

In the Bible we read of spectacular encounters with God that left the persons concerned in no doubt at all that the Almighty was insisting on changing the direction of their lives. Moses was confronted by a burning bush and a voice that ordered him to leave the relative comfort of quietly tending his father-in-law's sheep and return to Egypt (where he was wanted for murder) to convey an unwelcome message to Pharaoh and to lead a ragtag Israel out of the country to an unknown Promised Land (Exodus 3). Christ met Saul on the Damascus road when the latter was on his way to torture and kill Christians, and turned him into Paul, Christianity's most outstanding pioneer missionary and theologian (Acts 9; 22; 26). Gideon, the farmer's son, was commissioned out of the blue to deliver Israel from the Midianites (Judges 6). Countryman Amos, preaching in sophisticated Bethel and now told to leave, testified: "I was a herdsman and a dresser of sycamore figs. But the LORD took me from following the flock, and the LORD said to me, 'Go, prophesy to my people Israel'" (Amos 7:14–15; cf. Jer. 1:4–8; Ezekiel 2–3). We speak of each of these transforming encounters as a divine *call*, and the word fits. They remain, however, exceptional events, recorded in detail because of the significance of the ministry that followed, and there is nothing to suggest that they are set down in Scripture in order to establish a universal pattern.

In the late nineteenth and early twentieth centuries, however, it became common among evangelicals to expect something of this startling kind whenever far-reaching decisions had to be made, particularly with regard to career and marriage. People hoped and prayed for, and expected, some sort of supernatural indication from God as to what they should do, and in its absence they felt obliged to say, "Well, I haven't received my guidance yet." What kind of indication was being looked for? At the very least, a powerful feeling of "rightness" in connection with one of the options, or possibilities, between which one was trying to decide. But was their expectation of guidance by distinctive feeling, or vision, or voice, in such cases really warranted? Moses, Paul, Gideon, and Amos were being directed to forms of service that they themselves never would have dreamed. Therefore, only through a conscious encounter could God communicate to them the task he had in store for them. Decisions about whether, or to whom, to commit oneself in marriage or whether to offer for the pastorate, at home or abroad, hardly come in that category. Expecting special, supernatural direction for these and similar decisions was surely a mistake. We do not question that a settled sense of rightness and peace ordinarily accompanies a right decision as distinct from a wrong one; our point is simply that in many decisions of great consequence it is still unwarranted to expect, and in effect demand, some form of direct, informative encounter with God. That is what "supernatural" refers to here.

Certainly, the fallout from the mistake, if mistake it was, has been decidedly unhappy: bewilderment, depression, guilt, inaction, desperate dependence on inner urges, random decisions at the end of the day—all because no supernatural indication of this kind of desire has been given. The root of the mistake, it appears, was twofold: (1) an underlying mistrust of Christian reasoning, as not in itself a sufficiently spiritual activity, and (2) an undue reliance on significant gusts of emotion, whether euphoric or gloomy, to show how one stood with God in relation to this or that particular problem. What was needed was a recognition that this almost superstitious preoccupation with how or what one felt, so far from being a sign of deep spirituality, was an eccentricity, a somewhat zany spin-off from the romantic movement in Western culture; and what was also needed was a recovery of confidence in Christian reason, even without the icing of supernatural signs on the cake of cogent, biblically based thinking. Such a recovery would be a return to the way of making vocational decisions that had pertained in the Protestant world for three centuries, before the latter-day infection of "feelingitis" set in. Such a recovery would not be anything new; on the contrary, it would be a restoring of the tried and true after a period of unsuccessful experiment with something else. It is important that we recognize this.

From the mid-sixteenth to the mid-nineteenth century, Protestant teachers did not discuss career choices as such, but from their approaches to recruiting future clergy, they clearly agreed that career choices should be made in terms of two questions—first, what options do your circumstances allow? And, second, which of these options are you best fitted for in terms of interest and ability? Then, of course, many, perhaps most, young people were hemmed in by family considerations plus the iron railings of social stratification—whereas, hundreds of career options lie open today. Then, too, in the matter of holy matrimony, most marriages were arranged, more or less peremptorily, by parents; whereas, today couples make their own decisions on such matters.

Yet the way to pray about these matters has not really changed. With regard to a career, the proper prayer is: "Give me clarity as to what line of work I can happily follow for life, should the form of employment with which I start last for life." And with regard to marriage, the proper prayer is: "Give me clarity as to whom I can loyally and wholeheartedly love for life, assuming many years together before death brings about a parting." The answer to both prayers will be, precisely, the clarity that is asked for, and the sign of its attainment will be an inner peace that says in effect, "You need not churn over this matter in your mind any more; now you *know*, so you can proceed." Through weighing pros and cons before the Lord, along perhaps with prudently taking advice, the person who prayed has now gained rational clarity from the Lord, and that is the conclusion of the matter.

A further limitation on evangelical thinking about vocation at the turn of the nineteenth and twentieth centuries was the idea that there are just four really worthwhile vocations for men: missionary, pastor, physician, or teacher—and just four for women: missionary, teacher, nurse, or the wife of a man committed to one of the men's halo-ringed four as listed above. We should be glad that this way of thinking has become a thing of the past and has thus cleared the road for the truer insight that honest, faithful, honorable work of any sort, done as best one can and as helpfully to others as possible, glorifies God. So a believer may see his or her work as hallowed, whether that work involves handing fast food out of a window, cleaning offices late at night, bartering at the stock market, caring for children, plowing a field, balancing accounts, repairing a car, or (even) composing a manuscript. God gives his people all kinds of skills and interests and opportunities, and he receives their praise not only in verbal form, but in the form of all kinds of work well done in his name. What turns work, which might otherwise become drudgery, into a vocation is not the nature of the work itself, but the fact that it is done for the glory of the Lord.

Let us be quite clear about this. Work means, precisely, useful, creative employment in the service of God and others—just that. Skills are involved in work, but salary may or may not accompany it. A lot of our work is unsalaried. Homemaking is a case in point; yet homemaking fulfills a crucially important calling from God at the most significant time of a child's life. Homemaking parents serve God and others in a profound way by caring for their children and by creating a home in which the entire family receives physical, emotional, and spiritual nurture. Homemaking as a call from God is sometimes overlooked, as are the para-homemaking aspects, as we may call them, of church life. Carolyn has enjoyed observing a distinguished scholar occasionally spending Sunday mornings playing with toddlers in the church nursery and an elder digging out the church's cesspool because he would not ask someone else to do something unpleasant that he was unwilling to do himself. We need to get our minds off the equation that vocation and career equals profession and status and earnings. The reality of vocation extends far wider than that. All Christian voluntary work is vocational.

In saying all this, we would not lose sight of the fact that the four haloed professions are indeed precious in God's kingdom because of their outstanding potential for doing good to others.

On the contrary, we do ourselves highlight them as options to be considered by all whose interests and skills might incline them to one or the other, and we urge all pastors and youth leaders to see it as part of their responsibility to do the same. ("Fostering vocations" is what this aspect of ministry has traditionally been called.) Our point is simply that the holy four are not the only ways of living that count for God. But it remains, as true as ever it was, that these four are of high value in themselves, and that recruiting young people to their ranks is signal service of God. For the young person or an older person with career-change in mind, the question boils down to this: what is it that I can do well and happily, and among the things I can do well and happily, which will be the best for the honor of God, the extension of his kingdom, the benefit of my neighbor, and, through all these, my own job satisfaction? Facing this question prayerfully, the God-guided Christian's mind may well find itself settling in one direction, and this may properly be seen as the call of God, whether to one of the five-star four or elsewhere. The question should, indeed, be kept before us until this happens. God's faithfulness as our shepherd guarantees that he will continue his guiding care whenever a decision has to be made.

The criteria for making vocational choices have to do with following God-given information, interests, and skills on the one hand, and God-given responsibilities on the other. When, for instance, you are responsible for the welfare of others in your family, you have to make sure that the work that you choose enables you to fulfill those responsibilities. Parents of young children are rightly giving highest consideration to their children's welfare when they opt, as they sometimes do, for a second or third choice vocation because they cannot pay for both family food and their own education at the same time. Or they may choose a job near grandparents or good schools even though it means lower pay or less prestige. Or they may decide not to accept a promotion because it would mean interrupting their teenager's sports opportunities. Likewise, adult children will consider the well-being of their aging parents and, perhaps, reject a move to another state or refuse a job that allows no time for doctor's appointments and errands with their parent. Family members of people with special needs make lifelong career adjustments in order to provide for their children or siblings or parents in ways that few less-encumbered people could begin to understand. Yet Scripture ascribes real dignity to those kinds of sacrifices. "But if anyone does not provide for his relatives, and especially for members of his household, he has denied the faith and is worse than an unbeliever" (1 Tim 5:8). Christians who have honored these family responsibilities will often be the first to testify of their joy in God's redeeming work, even though outsiders might see principled choices as vocational sacrifices.

Vocational Guidance: Its Elements

The reality of vocational guidance, we now see, comes down to choices and decisions which are either wise or foolish, either godly or ungodly, and God guides us by teaching us to make appropriate decisions. He guides us vocationally through the means of our thinking, our consulting, our reflecting, our praying, our allowing him to convince us that this, rather than that, is the way that we should be going. Throughout that process God prepares us for decision, directs us in decision, and nudges us for any necessary course correction after decision. He is our shepherd leading his sheep, yet watching over them as he does so, and keeping them secure under his care. Bursting the bounds of our illustration for the moment, we should remind ourselves that it is the Triune God (Father, Son, and Holy Spirit) who is our Shepherd, who sets us on track, and he keeps us on track until journey's end. In doing this, God works through means, and the aim of this part of the chapter is to map the means he uses. The central decisions are the vocational decisions, the big, long-term, life-shaping commitments that God prompts us to make, but flanking these are the *preparatory* and *triggering* means that precede and the *sustaining* and *course-correcting* means that follow. For examples of all these, we propose to focus our attention on three Bible characters: Moses, Nehemiah, and Paul.

Let's first introduce them.

Moses was a man with terrific gifts, who yet was deeply tempted to diffidence, and who had a furious temper that he could not always control. A flawed man? Certainly. We all are. But a great man in God's kingdom, nonetheless.

Nehemiah was a wonderfully resourceful person. We guess that he was tempted constantly to bull-at-a-gate self-reliance, and that when in his memoir he tells us, as he frequently does, that he prayed and got others praying too before any action was taken, he is acknowledging this fact and testifying that God enabled him to overcome temptation again and again on this point. "Pray before you act" is a crucial and universal rule of spiritual health.

Paul was by nature a visionary, a pioneer, an opportunist, and a little ball of fire, long before the Lord got hold of him. He was tempted, so you find as you read his story, to a boldness that verged on foolhardiness. God, it seems, sometimes had to hold him back from doing silly things. (Look at Acts 19:30–31.)

Our temptations often arise out of our greatest strengths. Where we are strong, there Satan seeks to make us weak through being off our guard, relaxing our watchfulness, and lapsing into self-reliance without quite realizing what we are doing. Again and again we, the people of God, fail in this way. Wisdom says, "No, no, learn a different habit," but we turn a deaf ear. We can *never* trust ourselves, never. All three of these characters we are to study will give us warning here.

Preparation for Service

We start by noting how, long-term, God in his providence prepared these men for the vocational tasks he had in store for them. A few words from the Bible crystallize the preparation in each case. First, Moses "refused to be called the son of Pharaoh's daughter" (Heb. 11:24). Found as a baby in a bulrush basket, Moses had become Pharaoh's daughter's foster child. He was brought up in the palace, rubbing shoulders with royalty, speaking Egyptian, learning Egyptian wisdom, and accepted as an Egyptian grandee. But, having presumably learned Israel's faith and his own identity from his mother, who had brought him up as Pharaoh's daughter's hired nursemaid, he maintained contact with his birth family, he felt outrage at Israel's enslavement, in a fury he killed an Egyptian for beating up on an Israelite, and as a result, top person though he was, he had to flee the country. All of this prepared Moses for his mission of publicly defying Pharaoh and spending forty grueling years as Israel's leader.

Second, Nehemiah tells us, "I was cupbearer to the king" (Neh. 1:11). Nehemiah was a Jewish alien at the Persian court—really a high-class slave. The cupbearer's position was high-risk employment, for the cupbearer's job began with sampling the food and drink that were prepared for each royal banquet, so that if it were poisoned (a not unknown ploy) he, rather than the monarch, would be the victim. We can see why the Persian king would recruit a non-Persian for this post. But the cupbearer's position was also one of privilege; kings regularly used their cupbearers as confidants and counselors. Artaxerxes's attitude to his cupbearer was no exception; clearly he liked and trusted Nehemiah, appreciating his loyalty and admiring his ability, and the warmth of their relationship was God's preparing of the way for Nehemiah's mission as restorer of Jerusalem.

Third, Paul told the Jerusalem mob: "'I am a Jew, born in Tarsus in Cilicia, but brought up in this city, educated at the feet of Gamaliel according to the strict manner of the law of our fathers, being zealous for God'" (Acts 22:3). A Roman citizen by birth (v. 28) as well as "a Hebrew of Hebrews . . . a Pharisee" (Phil. 3:5), Paul was providentially equipped for unitive ministry in cross-cultural, Jewish/Graeco-Roman/pagan evangelism, for developing Christian theology into a full-scale philosophy of history with Christ as the center, and for writing nearly a quarter of the New Testament. To be sure, he started as a ferocious persecutor of the church, a Christian-killer in the most literal sense, but he came to see even this as providentially overruled preparation for the ministry he was to have. "Formerly I was a blasphemer, persecutor, and insolent opponent. But I received mercy because I had acted ignorantly in unbelief. . . . I received mercy for this reason, that in me, as the foremost, Jesus Christ might display his perfect patience as an example to those who were to believe in him for eternal life" (1 Tim. 1:13, 16). Thus God prepared Paul for the spectacular leadership role that he was to fulfill.

God's long-term preparation of us for service to come remains a reality, though in the nature of the case, we often do not recognize this preparation for what it is until the ministry itself becomes apparent. Prior to that, significant events in God's plan for us will seem simply bewildering. The dashing down of Moses's dream of championing the Israelites when he had to become a refugee from Egypt, and the official authorizing of Paul to clear Damascus of Christians (Acts 9:1–2), looked at the time like the exact opposite of what was to come. J. I. recalls how when at age seven a road accident permanently damaged his skull, blighting his boyhood; yet eleven years later, since the injury unfitted him for military service during the Second World War, he was able to go to school at Oxford, where he became a Christian. His life changed completely, and he began moving into a ministry that continues to this day. When the place of seemingly purposeless and damaging events in God's plan of blessing becomes plain, this revelation brings joy; and it belongs to the life of faith to be sure that such events are preparation for fruitfulness in God's good plan, even though one cannot yet see how.

The Triggering of Commitment

Commonly, if not invariably, God orchestrates circumstances that bring to a head the issue of life commitment to a vocational task. The divine purpose evidently is that the memory of this decisive moment may keep vivid in the committed person's mind the reality of his or her vocation. God dealt so with Moses, confronting him with the burning bush and the command to return to Egypt in an encounter that clearly he could never forget.

God dealt so with Nehemiah, when the king said to him: "Why is your face sad, seeing you are not sick? This is nothing but sadness of the heart" (Neh. 2:2). Nehemiah, a passionately patriotic and God-fearing Jew, had been fasting and praying since he heard the bad news of leveled walls and low morale in Jerusalem. Believing, what his friends had evidently told him, that he himself had what it would take to set Jerusalem on its feet, he had started to pray that God would "grant [his servant] mercy in the sight of this man" (Neh. 1:11)—in other words, that King Artaxerxes would actually send him to Jerusalem. But he could not raise the subject himself, and he and his friends had prayed in these terms for three months, during which nothing had happened. Now, however, in one sense out of the blue, the king's words were opening the door to actually fulfilling the prayed-for request. Since it was officially death to appear less than joyful in the king's presence, Nehemiah's heart must have been very heavily jolted at the king's form of words, but he prayed and plunged in and straightaway found himself authorized to go and rebuild Jerusalem, just as he had longed to do. That moment when the king's words put him on the spot must surely have stayed in Nehemiah's memory all his life. God also dealt in this way with Paul. We may be quite certain that Paul never forgot what had happened to him on the Damascus road.

The Sustaining of the Committed

Within the present cosmic order, or maybe we should say disorder, where the world and the devil are set against God and all his ways, vocational tasks are invariably a tussle. The ministries of Moses, Nehemiah, and Paul, to look no further, are set forth in Scripture as panoramas of almost unimaginable strains and pains. Hardship and discouragement due to constant challenges to their authority, including and policy from lower down in the pecking order, and malicious demolishings of what they have labored to build up are the recurring themes.

Moses had to endure direct challenges from Nadab and Abihu (Leviticus 10), from Korah, Dathan, and Abiram (Numbers 16), and even from Aaron his brother and Miriam his older sister (Numbers 12), plus endless grumbling from the mass of the people, to whom he was constrained to say at the end of his life: "You are a stubborn people. Remember and do not forget how you provoked the LORD your God to wrath in the wilderness. From the day you came out of the land of Egypt until you came to this place, you have been rebellious against the LORD" (Deut. 9:6–7).

Nehemiah rebuilt Jerusalem's wall against constant opposition from Sanballat, Tobiah, and Geshem, and when he left the city much of the moral and spiritual order that he had established collapsed, so that it had to be set straight again by forceful action when he returned for his second spell as governor (Neh. 13:4–31).

Paul, goaded, lifts the veil on his own track record as follows:

Five times I received at the hands of the Jews the forty lashes less one. Three times I was beaten with rods. Once I was stoned. Three times I was shipwrecked; a night and a day I was adrift at sea; on frequent journeys, in danger from rivers, danger from robbers, danger from my own people, danger from Gentiles, danger in the city, danger in the wilderness, danger at sea, danger from false brothers, in toil and hardship, through many a sleepless night, in hunger and thirst, often without food, in cold and exposure. And, apart from other things, there is the daily pressure on me of my anxiety for all the churches.

2 Corinthians 11:24–28

Yet God sustained them. The burden of leadership did not break Moses's health. "Moses was 120 years old when he died. His eye was undimmed, and his vigor unabated" (Deut. 34:7). Nehemiah ends his memoirs with the humble yet quietly confident prayer, "Remember me, O my God, for good" (Neh. 13:31). Paul declares, toward the end of his last letter, "The Lord will rescue me from every evil deed and bring me safely into his heavenly kingdom" (2 Tim. 4:18). The last word is always upbeat, peaceful, and hopeful. God does not abandon his faithful servants.

Courage and Corrections

There are, however, times when, within an ongoing vocational commitment, God takes action to adjust and improve what we are doing, and at such times we need rational flexibility, a willingness to make changes when we are given good reason to do so. Stubborn unwillingness to change at such times, however we might rationalize it to ourselves, would be pride corrupting God's call.

Moses, as we have already seen, accepted course correction, via his father-in-law Jethro, to help him decentralize public administration within the Israelite community. After a day of watching Moses at work settling disputes among the people, Jethro warned him, "You and the people with you will certainly wear yourselves out, for the thing is too heavy for you. You are not able to do it alone" (Exod. 18:18). Then Jethro laid out a plan whereby Moses could delegate all minor responsibilities and still maintain responsible spiritual oversight of the people as a body. Moses was wise enough to see that this was a good plan, and to accept it accordingly, and humble enough to accept it even from the hand of his father-in-law.

Paul experienced a more momentous course correction on his second missionary journey. In Acts 16:6 we find him and Timothy moving along a main road running west through southern Asia Minor, "having been forbidden by the Holy Spirit [how, we are not told] to speak the word in Asia" (southeast Asia Minor, the Roman province of Asia). They followed the road round the coast northward till they reached Mysia (northern Asia Minor) and thence "attempted to go into Bithynia [northeast Asia Minor], but the Spirit of Jesus did not allow them" (v. 7). So they followed the road to its end in Troas, a western-facing seaport, wondering no doubt what God had in mind for them. That night Paul saw a vision of a Macedonian, a Greek, saying, "Come over to Macedonia and help us" (v. 9). They did so, and the gospel came to Europe—an altogether more significant advance than evangelizing Asia Minor would have been.

Course corrections of this kind affirm and extend the original vocation, rather than disrupt it, and we must always be open to find that God has in mind something better than we knew.

Conclusions

Who are the Christians whom God leads to make long-term vocational commitments? In his intention, just about all of us, though the commitments themselves will vary and some Christians, alas, will turn a deaf ear to God at this point.

How may we become clear as to what long-term commitments God is calling us to make? By considering what our circumstances allow, and, within *that* frame, what our interests and skills suggest to us, and, within that frame, what in our hearts we would most like to do for God and for others, out of gratitude for Calvary, and love for people, and a desire to make a difference for God in the world.

How do we sustain a long-term vocational commitment, once we have made it? By putting our heart into fulfilling it as it stands, and by reviewing it from time to time before God, asking him to show us if there is anything in our conceiving or handling of the task that he wants us to change. Perhaps there will be, as with Moses and Paul; perhaps not, as apparently with Nehemiah.

Should we regard a sense of personal inadequacy as reason for not taking on a vocational task that has our heart? Not necessarily; if we have some of the qualities needed for fulfilling the role, it may be that we should trust God to supply the rest as needed. In face of uncertainty here, we are likely to be helped by taking advice from persons who know us well.

When should we consider ourselves set free from a long-term obligation that we have assumed? When circumstances no longer allow us to fulfill it. But until that happens, we should understand our obligation as having the nature of a vow to God, and so as continuing to stand.

Carolyn tells of a pivotal guidance event that seems even more mysterious to her now than at the time, yet it included many of the principles of vocational guidance that we have explored in this chapter.

Like many of her era in the rural farm country of southern Ohio, college was not a widely assumed goal for her as a high school student. No one in her family had ever gone to college; few of her friends or neighbors intended to. Yet John Reno, a Christian teacher in her public school, suggested to her that she might consider such an option. He even provided a small extra class of three students (while he monitored a large study hall at the same time) in order to grant some semblance of college preparation in mathematics. He mentioned that she might consider a Christian college, perhaps a place called Wheaton.

Carolyn dutifully went to her county library a dozen miles away and began to study their shelf copies of college catalogues. There she discovered materials from several dozen Christian colleges in various parts of the country. As she looked at the educational backgrounds of their faculty members, she noticed a common thread: many had done undergraduate work at Wheaton. She then studied Wheaton's catalogue, found it less colorful than most, and far more expensive than her summer job savings could support.

She applied anyway. By now she was beginning to sense what she thought might be the call of God to this mysterious school that she had never seen. Cost loomed high as an obstacle. She applied to the Kettering foundation for a science scholarship—and received one that would cover half of a year of college expenses, but in the interest of economic use of funds the scholarship committee stipulated that she must attend a state-funded school in Ohio.

Was God now leading in some other direction? Had God through circumstances closed the door to her first choice and opened the door to an even better way? Why this continued nagging pull toward a school she'd never even seen? Age eighteen is young to make such important decisions, but Carolyn reviewed her research, her motives, her thoughts—and she prayed. Two weeks before classes were to begin, she told her employer that she hoped to work for another year before going to school in order to earn funds. Then she wrote a letter to Wheaton postponing her entrance for one year and (dreading the pain of dropping the letter into the mailbox) left it standing on her dresser for a few days. Was she foolish to turn down a university education due to begin in two weeks, in exchange for a (possible) education at Wheaton now more than a year away? Was this God's guidance or personal foolishness? Hard to say—at the time.

In the few days that the postponement letter to Wheaton rested on her dresser, the representative from the scholarship called. "Was she set to go to school? Where should he send the payment?" Carolyn expressed her thanks and apologies, and told him of her resolve to go to Wheaton later. He said, "Wait, let me see what I can do." Two weeks later she was on a train to Wheaton, her grandfather's trunk packed with school necessities, scholarship in hand.

It was a small decision—really. Thousands of eighteen-year-olds make a similar decision every year. Only with hindsight, can Carolyn see how God-guided was that whole process. From her God-given intelligence, to the example of her hardworking family, to the advice of her Christian teacher, to her library research, to the kindness of a scholarship representative, to the considered reasoning about the kind of person that she wanted to become, to the nudging inner pull to a place she'd never been—God guided it all. The impact of that decision was momentous. But that's another story.

9

Situation Ethics

So I said to them, "Let any who have gold take it off." So they gave it to me, and I threw it into the fire, and out came this calf.

Aaron, Exodus 32:24

I am satisfied that when the Almighty wants me to do, or not to do, a particular thing, he finds a way of letting me know it.

Abraham Lincoln

Because I could.

Bill Clinton

Forty years ago, during the dismal decade that Britain now recalls as the Swinging Sixties, a novel account of Christian behavior calling itself situation ethics went up like a rocket on both sides of the Atlantic. Situation ethics offered guidance about guidance; it affirmed that in determining how to act toward other people, one's guiding star should be the maxim that "love trumps law." According to situation ethics, the rules and restrictions that the Bible sets out as God-given are at best rules of thumb, generalizations that tell us what actions neighbor-love will require more often than not—but there will be justified exceptions, and we must always be on the lookout for them. Those who espoused situation ethics saw love as the whole of what God commands and the law of Moses, which with adjustments reflecting the move from Old to New Testament conditions is also the law of Christ, as a provisional pointer only. These rules should not be seen as divine mandates on how to fulfill the law of love, but rather as human footnotes, embodying the verdict of experience as to what love requires in most cases, yet not closing the door to other possibilities from time to time. Presenters of situation ethics commonly assumed that fulfilling the second table of the law (neighbor-love) was in and of itself fulfillment of the first table (honoring God); so the theory reinforced the de-Christianized drift of those times—the drift of which, arguably, it was itself a product.

It was not, then, a happy development; rather the reverse. In the secularized, self-indulgent sixties, which had already started swinging vigorously, this view of ethics encouraged people to think of love—Christian love!—as gratifying other people, from their infancy to their old age, by giving them whatever they said or showed that they wanted. It led people to make exceptions in their own favor, particularly in sexual matters. In various forms of sexual encounters, they were able to persuade themselves that they were acting lovingly, and break the rules accordingly. Thus situation ethics contributed to the emotional immaturity, behavioral immorality, and intellectual incoherence that have become the hallmark of the present era.

Situation ethics was a form of what was once known as utilitarianism and is now called consequentialism. This is the view that one discerns the right thing to do *entirely* by calculating consequences. If we choose the course that will lead to most good (pleasure, profit, privilege, progress, or whatever) and will do least harm, we have done what we should. Bible-believers, who take seriously God's specifying what pleases him and what does not, have not found it hard to see the holes in this idea. They see that law and love belong together, that law is love's eyes, that love for

God and humankind is the law's heart, and that the conjunction remains a nonnegotiable of Christianity. So Bible-believers have never welcomed situation ethics, and that is one reason why little is heard of it among evangelicals.

But situation ethics leaves us with the question, highlighted and sharpened up: How should Christians pick their way on a day-to-day basis through the bewildering complex of static and shifting circumstances, of personal, societal, and cultural pressures, of competing claims and rival options that surround us? We have spoken about this in general terms, but more, we think, needs to be said. Hence this chapter.

The Doctrine of Situations

There are three things that we need to understand about our life-situations. First, they are a field of *God's sovereignty*. What does that mean? It means that the living God, who created the entire universe and actively upholds it in being (otherwise it would vanish away, and so would we as part of it), knows everything that has been and now is and foreknows everything that will be just because, in a way that totally passes our understanding, he plans and decides and controls everything that takes place. From inside (and we are all insiders at this point) the cosmos appears as a huge interlocking system of cause and effect, the working of which scientists can examine, map out, and within limits predict because the processes all operate with what appears as built-in regularity. But Christians know what science can never find out, namely, that all the processes of nature are willed and sustained directly by the Creator, every moment, down to the smallest detail, as also are the free-flowing thoughts that run through our minds, and the dreams that befuddle us while we sleep, and the self-determined, accountable decisions about what we will and will not do that we make in a steady stream throughout our waking hours. Let us say it clearly: all the regularities of nature, including the functioning of our own minds and bodies, are as they are because God wills and keeps them so. Nothing would be as it is—nothing, indeed, would exist at all—were it not for the active will of God.

Some time back J. I. learned that a teen was referring to him as "J.I.P., O.O.C." Enquiry revealed that O.O.C meant "out of control," and that this was intended as a compliment. J. I. did not know quite what to make of that, and since the idioms of teen talk change constantly, he imagines it is now a thing of the past anyway. But it made him recall an old hymn on walking with Jesus: "Take time to be holy, / Be calm in thy soul; / Each thought and each temper / Beneath his control." And, beyond this, it brought to mind words from Psalm 139: "O LORD, you have searched me and known me! . . . You discern my thoughts from afar. . . . Even before a word is on my tongue, behold, O LORD, you know it altogether. You hem me in, behind and before, and lay your hand upon me" (vv. 1, 2, 4, 5). And he would not have it any other way. To be totally in the hand of God, not only in grace but also in providence, which is where he is, is where he wants to be. Carolyn concurs. And we hope all our readers are with us on this.

To affirm God's sovereignty over everything around us, within us, happening to us, and issuing from us takes nothing from our certainty (which Scripture confirms) that all our thoughts, words, and deeds, including all our motives, purposes, attitudes, and reactions, are truly our own, not forced upon us from outside but coming out from within us, so that we are in truth responsible subjects, open to assessment both by other people and by our own consciences, and finally by God himself. Rather it adds to our certainty that, as our continued existence and all our living really involve God, so God really involves himself in an overruling way, somehow (just how, no creature can conceive), in all our circumstances, motives, actions, relationships, experiences, joys, pains, pleasures, griefs, and ventures, which form the situational reality of our daily lives. This rock-bottom fact is the launchpad from which true wisdom takes off in all its flights of thought.

Second, situations are a field of *Satan's endeavor*. The first situation we meet in the Bible is in Eden, where the serpent tempted and deceived Eve, and through the disobedience that resulted ruined our race. The New Testament tells us that the serpent was the devil, the malevolent destroyer, whose name (Satan) means adversary, who is man's permanent adversary because he is God's permanent adversary, who is always laboring to thwart God's plans and wreck his work, and whose attentions we shall be constantly receiving as long as we are in this world. In the New Testament, we learn about Satan as Christ's adversary (Luke 4:1–13; Matt. 16:23; John 14:30), as the church's adversary (1 Peter 5:8; Rev. 2:10; chap. 12), as each Christian's adversary (Luke 22:31–32; Eph. 6:10–18), and as the world's captor, keeping people from truth, faith, spiritual life, and personal well-being (Luke 13:16; 2 Cor. 4:4; Eph. 2:2; 2 Tim. 2:26; 1 John 3:8; 5:19). In just about every life-situation, therefore, we must reckon with the fact that Satan is present to lead us astray, if he can. So we need always to remember Jesus's words to the disciples who slept in Gethsemane: "Watch [stay alert and on guard] and pray that you may not enter into temptation" (Matt. 26:41). The clause in the Lord's Prayer, "lead us not into temptation," undoubtedly refers to this need to be always on guard, as we shall see in a moment.

Third, situations are a field of *personal responsibility*. As we have tried to show in previous chapters, God calls us to live our lives in wisdom, and that means living in a thoughtful rather than a thoughtless manner. To do this successfully requires careful application of principles and discerning of priorities, careful balancing of short-term and long-term considerations, and within that frame, careful calculation in particular of the likely consequences relationally of different courses of action. Now we see that we need to test our reasoning, step-by-step, to make sure that Satan is not one way or another fooling us into letting the good be the enemy of the best, or into being imposed on by bad that he has dressed up as good, as happened so tragically to Eve in Eden. Deception, we must remember, is Satan's regular ploy. Going over the various considerations in prayer to our heavenly Father and asking him to help us see which course of action will most effectively advance his glory and his kingdom will often lead us to true clarity of discernment and decision. Let it be burned into our consciences that the moment thoughtlessness enters in, Satan begins to score heavily, and we are immediately at risk. It is to be expected that he will have us on the mat very shortly.

Self-deception and Satanic Seduction

The principle that in every situation we are to seek the best among competing options, which involves following the rules of wisdom for judging between alternatives, has been fully covered already and need not be discussed again. But we need to say more about how sin in our heart and Satan in our ear constantly combine to allure us into making, over and over, the same basic mistake. J. I. once read on the back of a matchbox the following bit of wit: "Experience is a wonderful thing. It enables you to recognize your mistake when you make it again." Well, what we are to discuss now is an error into which Christians all too frequently slip. It is the mistake of inferring—from the fact that circumstances, which God providentially orders, make a particular line of action *possible* and from the fact that we are being *urged* to follow it—that it will be all right with God if we make this move. What we have here is really two mistakes for the price of one. The first is to be guided by circumstances without referring to God's revealed truth. The second is to treat human urging as divine encouragement to act in a certain way, again without referring to revelation. The end product is wrong move after wrong move.

What happens is that two unhappy things combine in a kind of pincers movement that temporarily squeezes our conscience into silence. The first is deceiving thoughts that Satan injects directly into the mind. We see him doing this to Eve in the Eden story, as the serpent speaks to her; doing it again as he tempts Jesus during the forty days in the desert at the start of the Savior's ministry; and doing it once more as he turns Paul's thorn in the flesh (some form of disabling pain) into a reason for the apostle to feel hopelessness about his own future ministry, thus establishing it as "a messenger of Satan," sent to prompt the despairing thoughts Satan wanted

Paul to think. The second factor is the deceitful working of our own self-serving imagination which, driven by the pride that constantly seeks some form of personal distinction, tells us how responding to others' urgings by doing what they want us to do will give us status, win us admiration, and so suffuse our egos with a glow of achievement. We see this in a classic biblical instance as we watch Aaron making the golden calf.

Aaron, Moses's eloquent older brother and colleague, Israel's first high priest, is a shadowy figure in the Bible story and was, we guess, an equally elusive person in real life: a supporter rather than a leader, one whose thoughts regularly reflected what the last person to talk to him had said rather than anchoring themselves in the firmness of abiding truth. We see him backing Moses both in the latter's finest hour of God-honoring challenge to Pharaoh and at his low point of dishonoring God by his petulance at Meribah (Num. 20:6–13). We see him backing Miriam, their older sister, in her arrogant demand to share Moses's leadership, which led to the temporary leprosy she suffered that Aaron begged Moses to ask God to heal (Numbers 12). And in the calf affair we first see Aaron acting as the people's cat's-paw (or should we say, stooge?), letting himself be dragooned into promoting idolatry when they said to him, "Up, make us gods" (Exod. 32:1), after which we hear him excusing himself to his brother in the lamest way imaginable—"I threw it [the people's proffered gold] into the fire, and out came this calf" (v. 24)—as if the calf had constructed itself while Aaron's back was turned! Pliability and undiscerning compliance with people who put pressure on him were clearly Aaron's weaknesses, and they betrayed him into at least the following modes of what we may call misguidance, or (to use the usual word) misguidedness:

(1) Entertaining *self-serving rather than God-serving motivation*. Aaron's heart, like everyone else's, was infected with original sin, the essence of which (so Christian thinkers unanimously affirm) is *pride*. It has been said that there are four types of pride: pride of face, pride of race, price of place, and pride of grace, and the last is the worst. However that may be, Aaron's defect was clearly pride of place: he wanted to retain respect for himself as second-in-

command, and was prepared to give the people what they wanted, even if it was the wrong thing for them to want, rather than risk losing their respect by saying no.

(2) Embracing *man-made rather than God-taught religion*. Though Moses had not yet come down the mountain to announce the first and second tables of the Ten Commandments, from Israel's history it should have been clear to Aaron (and, we are sure, actually was) that God is not to be demeaned by being worshipped in the form of an idol—even a bull-calf, a symbol of brute strength. However, to oblige the people Aaron pandered to their superstition rather than trying to correct it—and disgraced himself by coming up with an idol to order.

(3) Excusing himself with a *self-justifying rather than self-humbling explanation*. Pride in all its forms, particularly pride of place, makes it always difficult, and sometimes insuperably hard, for people to face themselves and admit that they are astray, or mistaken and wrong, or ignorant or naïve, or at fault and blame-worthy, and they wriggle verbally in order to avoid having to do that. So here Aaron talks to his brother in a self-affirming rather than God-fearing way, as if the calf was somehow an unhappy accident for which he was not really responsible, and for which he could not really be blamed. ("You know the people, that they are set on evil" [v. 22].) No response from Moses to Aaron is recorded, and we may guess—even hope!—that at that moment he was too disgusted with Aaron to trust himself to say anything. Disgust would certainly have been appropriate; no one can quarrel with that!

What we see in Aaron is self-deception on the grand scale, a conscience "hardened" at least temporarily into insensitivity and moral dishonesty "by the deceitfulness of sin" (Heb. 3:13), and pride warding off a sense of guilt by assuring Aaron's heart that for him to have done what he did in his situation was all right and that everything was going to be all right for the future. Nothing explicit is said of Satan, but we may be sure that he was actively on the scene, now backing Aaron's corrupt conscience after first encouraging Aaron's lapse.

From this cautionary example of a malformed situational ethic leading to misguided behavior, we turn for contrast to a story of right reasoning about the situation resulting in a triumphantly right response to pressure, namely, Jesus's temptation in the desert.

About the story, some things must be said at the outset as a basis for our treatment of it. First, it is Jesus's own story, as told to the disciples. We would not know anything about it had it not come from his own lips. Second, Matthew and Luke narrate the second and third temptations in a different order. While the personal theological interests of each evangelist may explain his choice of order, we guess that Jesus told the story more than once, and on different occasions followed both orders himself. Third, the wording of all three temptations makes them appear as both personal and Messianic: relating, that is, both to the Savior's person-to-person obedience to the Father as the divine Son that he eternally was and to his role and destiny as "the man born to be king" (Dorothy L. Sayers's haunting phrase) in the salvific kingdom of God, where "Son of God" as a title meant Messiah. Satan cleverly frames each temptation so that it embraces both elements of Jesus's identity inseparably. Fourth, Jesus's story is an interpretation and as such leaves some questions open and unanswerable. Did the devil "come" to him visibly and "say" things to him audibly? Or was it that he found in his mind thoughts of what he might do and discerned their devilish source from their content, as we have to do in our own temptations? We assume the latter, but in fact nobody knows.

We take the temptations in Luke's order, noting first that Luke ends his story by telling us that Satan "departed from him until an opportune time" (Luke 4:13): that is, "until the next opportunity came" (NLT). Temptation was a recurring reality in Jesus's experience, as it is also in ours.

First temptation: the situation is hunger in the desert, and the Satanic suggestion is to relieve it by making loaves out of stones. Jesus's kingdom could then be founded on supernaturally supplying bodily needs, according to this miraculous model. Jesus's procedure was to discern the wrongness of this suggestion by reference to what he knew of his Father's will and then to rebut it from Scripture—specifically, by affirming the text from which he was resolved to take his guidance on the point, Deuteronomy 8:3, "Man does not live by bread alone."

Second temptation: the situation is an envisioning of all the world's kingdoms together, and the suggestion is to receive them all from Satan's hands at the price of worshipping him. (We take it that, quite apart from the fact that Satan is a liar and has no power to give what he promises, the suggestion is essentially of world conquest by godless means.) In the same way as before, Jesus discerns the wrongness of this suggestion for him as Son of God in both senses and cites the text from which he will draw his guidance—"It is the LORD your God you shall fear. Him you shall serve" (Deut. 6:13).

Third temptation: the situation is Jesus certainly in imagination, maybe in fact, standing on the pinnacle of the temple and being encouraged to throw himself down from there and get up unhurt from the flagstones more than a hundred feet below—in other words to establish an identity for himself, as man and Messiah, as a superhuman wonder-man, something like Batman, and to base his kingdom on his superhuman powers. This, too, Jesus sees as a distraction from his true calling, which was to bring in the spiritually authentic kingdom of God through spiritually authentic discipleship to himself as the God-sent Savior-King. Satan, observing that Jesus has hitherto looked to Scripture for his guidance, now quotes Scripture himself to support his suggestion: he misapplies a promise of the Father's protection in time of trouble (Ps. 91:11–12) as if it were a divinely provided safety net for the Batman act. But Jesus trumps Satan's ace and demolishes the temptation by counterquoting Deuteronomy 6:16: "You shall not put the LORD your God to the test." That is: you shall not provoke the Father by trying him out, creating a situation that puts him on the spot as if he were your servant rather than you his.

In each of these temptations, Satan eggs Jesus on to break the bounds, and Jesus avoids being deceived in his heart and derailed in his ministry by keeping in mind what he knows already of the Father's declared will. Thus, at the point where Adam and Eve fell, Jesus remained upright. Thoughtlessness such as theirs would have ruined him; thoughtfulness like his would have kept them from sin. Desire, by throttling thought, opens the door to deception. "Each person is tempted when he is lured and enticed by his own desire. . . . Desire when it has conceived gives birth to sin. . . . Do not be deceived, my beloved brothers" (James 1:14–16). Satan foments and exploits desire; that is how his deceiving is regularly done. Know his tactics, then, and do not let desire stop your thinking! It is through thoughtlessness, induced by desire, that we fall.

The mix of triumph and tragedy that was David's career gives instructive confirmation of what we are saying. Spiritual triumph through difficult times is the first part of David's story, and twice in particular David refused point-blank to conclude that he should do what he could do, just because he kept in mind what he knew of God's revealed will. He knew that God had rejected King Saul and that he himself had been anointed to take Saul's place; and he knew that Saul was chasing him with an armed force, seeking his life; so he was living as a fugitive, trying to keep out of Saul's way. One day, however, when David and his men were hiding in the recesses of a cave, Saul entered that cave alone. David's men said in effect: "This is God in action! He has given you the means of fulfilling his plan! Kill Saul now!" But David would not do it, because Saul was the Lord's anointed (1 Samuel 24). Shortcuts that are immoral in their own right are never the will of God. Not long after, a virtual rerun of this incident took place (1 Samuel 26). David and Abishai found themselves standing over Saul's sleeping body, surrounded by Saul's army, also sleeping. Abishai whispered: "God has given your enemy into your hand this day"—let me kill him for you! But David again said no, for the same reason as before: "Who can put out his hand against the LORD's anointed and be guiltless?" (vv. 8–9). So far, so good; David escaped the temptation to do what was in his power to do, because he remembered the boundaries God had set. Circumstances may indeed give us obvious opportunities to break God's rules, but it is never God's will that we should do that. In due course, Saul was killed in battle and David became king. He had practiced obedient restraint, and avoided self-deception, and God honored him for it.

But in the case of Bathsheba and Uriah (2 Samuel 11–12) it was a different story. This was a tragedy in which David did what he realized he could and might reasonably expect to get away with. Lust stifled thought, as lust always does, and blanketed conscience; David gave no thought to the fact that he was breaking God's commandments, and, as we saw earlier, effectively broke the whole series from the sixth to the tenth before he was finished; he deceived himself by assuming that since he was king, what he was doing was all right, for this is how kings behave; and his conscience slept soundly until Nathan came a year later to wake it up. From then on, David's career went downhill. It is a sad story, luridly revealing the misguidedness that self-satisfied self-deception can lead to, even in the best of men and women.

Situational Guidance

While the situation ethics of half a century ago ruined itself by opposing love to law, it rendered service as a reminder that our situation must always be our focus as we seek God's guidance, whether in general terms (What should I be doing with my life? What sort of career should I plan and fit myself to follow? How should I prepare to be a change agent for God?) or under specific pressures (How should I handle this crisis? Should I propose marriage to this person? What ought I to do to repair this friendship?). Taking stock of the situation as a whole is the necessary first step. Let us round off this chapter by pulling together the threads of our discussion to point up the full series of steps that should be taken if we would be led to situational decisions that are wise and right.

First, *survey the situation*, collecting all the facts that we see our decision must take account of and being ready to collect more should subsequent developments make that necessary.

Second, *separate the questions that the situation raises.* We may feel our need of guidance on more than one issue in our situation, but guidance questions have to be worked through one at a time. As in algebra too many undefined qualities make it impossible to work out an equation, so it is in relation to God's guidance of us in a particular situation. We may well need others' help to sort out which uncertainty we should seek to resolve first.

Third, *search the Scriptures with regard to the situation,* looking for the principles and examples that apply. Here we may find help in consulting those who know the Bible better than we do.

Fourth, *suspect yourself in relation to the situation.* Over and above our built-in temperamental weaknesses that may make us too impulsive or too negative in assessing possible courses of action, Satan will constantly play on our pride, our fears, our greed, our anger, our inner hurts, our passion to conform and our unwillingness to stand out, our overall slackness and thoughtlessness as disciples, and any other quality that gives him a handle so as to lead us into foolish decisions. "Take counsel from at least two people whose relationship with God you respect, preferably those who are *not* your buddies."[1] Always be on the watch for Satan's deployment of any of these devices for blinding us to our heavenly Father's will.

Fifth, *supplicate humbly about the situation.* We should lay everything before God in as good order as we can manage, asking him to make us realistic, clearheaded, and purehearted in seeing how we are to glorify him. We should ask that when we think and decide rightly, he will give us inward peace to confirm to us that we are indeed on track. We may well find that clarity of insight increases slowly, as when mist rolls away, so that we can see the landscape which at first was hidden from us. Repeated spells of supplication will need to take place as we move toward a definite determination of God's will for us.

Sixth, *spend unhurried time in deciding how to handle the situation.* Discerning and planning are processes that always take time, and second and third thoughts often exceed first thoughts in wisdom. The expectation that guidance will be given instantaneously, as soon as we ask for it, is unbiblical and superstitious. What is true is that God will make his will clear to us by the time we have to commit ourselves in decisive decisions; but that is something rather different.

Seventh, *submit absolutely to God in relation to the situation and with it to all other situations.* Throughout the process of discernment, make it clear to yourself and to him that it is his will and glory, and that alone, that you seek. Look to God to guide you by the rational means we have discussed, and do not expect him to guide you by inward impressions that go beyond your present knowledge; and if he does (as sometimes, when we are seeking guidance by rational means, he really does), check what you think he has given you with the respected nonbuddies to whom you appealed before, and only act on the impression when it has both their support and the inner-peace confirmation of which we spoke a moment ago.

Here then, you have the biblical situation ethic. The Good Shepherd loves and cares for his flock; the Father is faithful to all who look to him to guard and guide them; those who truly seek divine guidance in each situation as it arises will surely receive it. We who write believe ourselves to have verified that. We invite our readers now to discover it too.

10

Guarded and Guided
by the Holy Spirit

Come, gracious Spirit, heavenly Dove,
With light and comfort from above;
Be thou our guardian, thou our guide,
O'er every thought and step preside.

Simon Browne (1680–1732)

As pearls start to be formed when a bit of grit gets inside mollusk shells, so this book has grown out of the concern we feel for the many—we find that there are many—who have hang-ups about guidance and who fear irrevocable spiritual loss should they get their guidance wrong. In hope of helping we have tried to establish at least the following truths.

First, God's guidance is a promised part of his covenant care for his own adopted children.

Second, if like silly sheep we wander off track in our decision making and commitments, God, who is our heavenly Shepherd and Triune Lord, the Father, the Son, and the Holy Spirit, pledged to love us forever and bring us to glory, will take action to restore us to the fullness of life, hope, and fellowship, as we knew it before.

Third, God guides us by means of the Bible's teaching, the exercise of wisdom, and the counsel of fellow believers, plus insights and ideals sparked within us by the examples of faithful folk past and present, and supremely by the virtues shown in the way that the Lord Jesus lived.

Fourth, when it comes to making a long-term, life-shaping decision, God calls us to wait on him with prayerful thought and thoughtful prayer until he settles our minds and hearts on a particular commitment, positive or negative, as the way he wants us to go and gives us inner peace at the prospect.

Elsewhere, under the heading "A Biblical Approach to Guidance" in an earlier book, J. I. had already written along the same lines as follows:

1. Live with the question of "What is the best I can do for my God?"
2. Note the instructions of Scripture; the summons to love God and others, the limits set and the obligations established by the Law, the call for energetic action (Eccles. 9:10; 1 Cor. 15:58), and the drilling in wisdom to enable one to make the best choice among behavioral options.
3. Follow the examples of godliness in Scripture, most of all, imitate the love and humility of Jesus himself. When that is what we are doing, we cannot go far wrong.
4. Let wisdom judge the best course of action: don't be a spiritual lone ranger; when you think you see God's will, have your perception checked. Draw on the wisdom of those who are wiser than you are; take advice.
5. Take note of any nudges from God that come your way—any special concerns for ministry and service, any restlessness of heart which might indicate that something needs to be changed.

6. Cherish the divine peace which, as Paul says, will garrison (guard, keep safe and steady) the hearts of those who are in God's will.

7. Observe the limits set by circumstances to what is possible, and when it is clear that those limits cannot be changed, accept them as from God.

8. Be prepared for God's guidance on a particular issue not to appear until the time comes for decision about it, and expect God to guide you one step at a time; for that is how he usually does it.

9. Be prepared to find God directing you to something you thought you would not like, and teaching you to like it!

10. Never forget that if you make a bad decision, it is not the end of everything: God forgives and restores. . . . The Lord is my shepherd; he leads me. What a relief it is to know that.[1]

In both those summary statements and in the present book up to this point, there remains a gap waiting to be filled. In foregoing pages, we have spoken at length of the Triune God as our guardian and our guide, and we have focused attention on both the Father and the Lord Jesus, whom we know as the Good Shepherd. But we have not yet highlighted the ministry of the Holy Spirit in guarding and guiding us. That is what we must now do, for the Spirit's ministry here is vital.

Introducing the Holy Spirit

The Holy Spirit shaped creation; he gave revelation and caused the Bible to be written; he renews hearts and transforms lives; he assures Christians of their eternal salvation, and he equips them to serve the Savior to whom he unites them. You will note that we are saying "he," not "it." The Spirit who in the Old Testament represents himself as merely a divine force, potent but not personal, appears in the New Testament as a Helper and Counselor who speaks and teaches, who can be grieved and lied to, and who intercedes passionately for Christians on a regular basis. These things could only be said of a person, one who is as truly personal as are the Father and the Son.

The Spirit is the Third Person within the unity of the God-head; that is why he is called "Holy," as the Father and the Son are (see John 6:69; 17:11). "Holy" is the Bible word that points to the God-ness of God, to all that sets him apart from, and above, and sometimes against us, to all the greatness and purity, all the awesomeness and occasional fearsomeness, with which the Triune Yahweh confronts us. Holiness has been described as the attribute of all God's attributes, the distinctive quality of all that God is and does. So the church's habit of referring to God as "the Holy Trinity" is natural, right, and proper. Now the Holy Spirit is the executive agent of the holy Father and the holy Son in all the ongoing divine works of providence and grace. And as the Scriptures associate divine love primarily with the Father and the Son, so they associate divine power primarily with the Spirit. They link the Spirit particularly with the output of divine energy and movement, change and transformation.

It was Augustine who articulated what the New Testament everywhere implies, namely, that in all the acts of God all three persons of the Trinity are involved, expressing their unity in what we might call combined operations. And the New Testament reveals that in all these united activities there is a set pattern serving a single purpose, namely, the Father's resolve to glorify the Son, first in creation and then in redemption, "that all may honor the Son just as they honor the Father" (John 5:23). So, in the order of creation, "all things were created through him and for him. . . . And in him all things hold together" (Col. 1:16–17). And in the order of redemption, the incarnate Son, living, dying, rising, and reigning, is eternally the mediating means of all the blessings, first to last, that make up our salvation and constitute the church. "He is the head of the body, the church. He is . . . the firstborn from the dead, that in everything he might be preeminent" (v. 18).

This is supremely clear in the book of Revelation, where, whatever else is of uncertain interpretation, the designated glory of Jesus

Christ as the church's Savior, Lord, Mediator, and Lover is perfectly explicit (see 1:5–7, 13–18; chaps. 2–3; 5:5–14; chap. 7; 14:1–5; 19:6–16, 21:22–22:5, 12–13, 16, 20–21). It is the Father's will that the Son be "highly exalted" and bear "the name [Lord] that is above every name" (Phil. 2:9–10). So it belongs to the eternal plan that Jesus Christ should fill the horizon of his people's thought about what is ultimately real and ultimately important and ultimately authoritative for shaping their lives. It was within the frame of this divine purpose that the exalted Lord poured out the Holy Spirit at Pentecost, following his ascension, so that the Spirit might begin the enhanced ministry that he had pictured and promised before his passion. It will be helpful to glance at this ministry now, as it is set before us in its universal aspect, applying to all Christians, in the pages of the Gospel of John. (John, who clearly has a special interest in the Spirit's ministry, also reports words of Jesus about the Spirit that apply specifically to the apostles, but these we leave aside for the moment.) Here are the key passages:

The Spirit descended on Jesus at his baptism in the visible form of a dove fluttering down and settling on him. One purpose of this anointing, if that is the right word for it, was to mark Jesus as the one who would in due course baptize with the Spirit (that is, initiate people into Holy Spirit life). The Spirit-bearer would thus become the Spirit-giver (John 1:32–33).

The Spirit brings people into the kingdom of God by a work in them that Jesus described as being born again (i.e., born anew, or perhaps born from above), in a manner that involves faith in Jesus himself as the God-given Savior (3:3–15).

The Spirit in people's lives will generate true worship of the Father (real worship that accords with God's truth), so making them into the kind of worshippers that the Father seeks (4:23–24).

The Spirit will so work in those who came to Christ for the quenching of spiritual thirst that "rivers of living water" will flow out of their heart. Here we have a clear allusion to Ezekiel 47:1–12, the Christian being pictured as a temple in which God dwells, and in this image a clear portrayal of overflowing joy, peace, hope, and love. This would become a matter of personal experience, John explains, only after Jesus had been glorified (7:37–39; see 17:5).

The Spirit will be given by the Father and the Son to Christ's disciples to live within them as their Helper-Counselor-Supporter-Comforter-Encourager (no one English word renders the full meaning of *paraklētos* in the Greek). The Spirit will stay with them permanently, and through his coming Christ and the Father will also come to indwell them permanently (14:16–17, 23).

The Spirit's ministry will be consistently and exclusively Christ-centered. "He will glorify me, for he will take what is mine and declare it to you" (16:14). He will call attention to Christ, not to himself. It is the Spirit's way to keep out of our direct view, like a shy child hiding behind a door. Think of his ministry as floodlight ministry: the floodlight, hid in a niche in the wall, is trained on what the observer is meant to see while remaining itself out of sight. Or think of it this way: Christ stands before us, addressing us, calling us to himself, while the Spirit stands behind us shining his light over our shoulder so that we see Christ and know him to be real, and at the same time the Spirit whispers into the ear of our heart his own echo of the words that Christ speaks to us: *Do you hear him saying, "Come to me . . . learn from me . . . you will find rest . . ."? Go to him; he is saying these things to you.* This is the formula, not only for personal conversion, but for our entire Christian life. Recognizing, approaching, trusting, loving, adoring, and serving the Lord Jesus is the essence of that life. Jesus Christ, not the Spirit, is our constant focus; but it is precisely through the Spirit that we are enabled to focus on him.

We may multiply the illustrations. The Spirit, as we said, is the floodlight, or the searchlight, picking out and illuminating the Lord Jesus for us; also, he is the contact lens that enables us to see him clearly; also he is the matchmaker, drawing us close to Christ for a permanent union; also, he is the intercom, making communication between Christ and us a reality of our experience; also, he is the spiritual pacemaker, implanted to ensure heart-healthy functioning in love to Christ; and with all this he is the channel through which Christ pours his life and power into us for worship, sanctity, and service. But in all that he does he keeps himself out of sight. When he works in us, Christ, not the Spirit, is the center of attention. "Spiritual" experiences that lead away from Christ, or bypass him, are not from the Holy Spirit at all.

At the heart of Christ's farewell discourse, with explicit teaching about the Spirit flanking it on both sides, stands the Savior's wonderful parable, or analogy, of himself as the vine and Christians as its branches, needing to "abide" (stay steady, stay put) in him if any fruit of divine life is to appear in their lives. There is no more vivid picture of union and communion between disciples and their Lord anywhere in Scripture. It is not said explicitly that this is the heart of life in the Spirit, but the implication is clear.

The Spirit will bring about conviction in the world—that is, among unbelievers—concerning sin, righteousness, and judgment. He will make people realize that their unbelief in Christ is a supreme sin, proving them to be lost souls until they change. He will make them realize that Jesus Christ, whom many thought to be a sinner, a heretic, and a criminal, meriting the crucifixion he suffered, was in every way righteous, as his return to the Father's fellowship in glory shows. And the Spirit will make them realize that the process of divine judgment on sin has now begun, starting with the devil, who through the cross followed by the resurrection was decisively overthrown (16:8–11).

Finally, the Spirit will give disciples the understanding, insight, and power that they need to make true application of the gospel message to the persons to whom they proclaim it, just as Jesus had done before them (20:22–23). Peter's insight into the spiritual state of Simon the sorcerer, and his initial declaration of nonforgiveness for Simon's spiritual lapse (Acts 8:20–23), is an example of the spiritual discernment that is promised here.

Paul's presentation of the Spirit's manifold ministries to Christ's individual disciples covers illumination and the gift of spiritual understanding, new creation through incorporation into the risen Christ, assurance of present salvation, sustained jubilation, moral transformation in holiness and righteousness toward the fullness of the image of Christ, the ninefold fruit of the Spirit building up a change of character, gifting for service in and through the church, and the maintenance of invigorating hope of final glory. (A study of these elements in the Spirit's ministry as Paul lays it out would have to include Romans 5:5; 7:1–6; chap. 8; 14:17 and 15:13; 1 Cor. 2:9–15; 3:16; 6:11; chap. 12 with 2 Cor. 3:14–4:6; Gal. 3:1–13; cf. 4:29, 4:4–6, and 5:15–26; Eph. 1:13–14; cf. 4:30, and 5:18–21, with much beside.) Paul's Christ-centeredness and his view of the Spirit as the means of blessing from and fellowship with Christ, rather than as the focus of attention in himself, fully matches what is in the Gospel of John. All other New Testament references to the Spirit do in fact maintain this perspective as well.

What, now, should we say about the Holy Spirit's ministry with regard to guidance?

Guided by the Holy Spirit?

Here we see ourselves as having to navigate between two extremes, which we label as the *superspiritual* and the *subspiritual* respectively. Let us explain. The *superspiritual* is a mindset that marks out some very devoted believers. Rightly and passionately, they want all their actions to be in line with the will of God, but wrongly, as we think, they look for a distinctive, identifiable nudge from the Holy Spirit to assure them of the rightness of every decision they make and believe that until they have experienced such a nudge they have not received guidance. The most common account of the nudging is of a sense that some thought in one's mind is specially significant; people express this sense by saying, "God spoke to me," and think it is this nudging that Paul refers to when he speaks of Christians as "led by the Spirit" (Rom. 8:14; Gal. 5:18). No matter how clear, therefore, the indicators of the best course of action are—no matter, that is, how unanimous are the pointers from Scripture, the dictates of wisdom, the verdicts of friends and advisors, and the corporate judgment of the church regarding the appropriate move to make—they hang back when they should be moving forward, since they are sure that no firm guidance is ever given without the nudge. On the other hand, however, when they have received what they take to be the divine nudge, they are prepared to break ranks and move out into left field, ignoring contrary urgings from Christian colleagues. Their readiness thus to be eccentric can make them hard to work with, despite the dedication and goodwill that their lives display. Not for one moment would we deny that people sometimes receive clear nudges from God about what they should do or not do, but we see these as exceptional and as ordinarily given only within the frame of seeking guidance for action by the standard means that we have described; and we see this attitude of *always* looking for nudges as opening the door to three mistakes.

First mistake: *undervaluing God's gift of reason*, whereby he has equipped us to work out from Scripture, through wisdom in fellowship, what is the best and most that we can do in his service for his glory. When rational reflection, thorough and tested, has shown us the right path, God always means us to act on it without waiting for anything more.

Second mistake: *overvaluing the grace of patiently waiting.* Granted, God does sometimes keep us waiting for certainty on how to move, and waiting on him patiently at such times is a discipline we must learn to practice. But inappropriate inaction—doing nothing when our situation requires us to do something—will not glorify God, for lagging behind him is as much a lapse as running ahead of him. Inappropriate inaction, however, is likely to result if we make it our habit to wait for nudges from God every time before we act.

Third mistake: *programming the Holy Spirit*, limiting his freedom by specifying in advance what we expect him to do and then waiting for him to do it. Those who follow this procedure certainly believe themselves to be exalting the Holy Spirit, but they are actually doing just the reverse—hobbling him, as we might say, rather than honoring him.

The *subspiritual* extreme, by contrast, is a mindset that has been described in para-trinitarian terms as faith in the Father, the Son, and the Holy Scriptures. It is more common than its superspiritual opposite, partly because of the rationalistic defensiveness that has marked so much popular theology in North America for more than a century; partly because so many of its exponents have constantly before their eyes the danger, as they see it, of losing rational control and lapsing into the superspiritual eccentricity of which we have spoken above; and partly, we think, because Satan dupes us into thinking that faithful Christianity is entirely a matter of believing and doing what Scripture says. What, you ask, is wrong with that? Well, it forgets that basic to the question of what we are called to *do* is the question of what, in terms of godly character and communion with the Father and the Son, we are called to *be*. As Dallas Willard observes: "An obsession merely with *doing* all God commands may be the very thing that rules out *being* the kind of person that he calls us to be"[2] When Bible-believers grow impervious to the insight that *being* is foundational to *doing*, the subspiritual mindset regularly results.

In *Decision Making and the Will of God* (Portland: Multnomah, 1980),[3] Garry Friesen put forward, in place of the idea of guidance by immediate "impressions" or by arresting circumstances, a Bible-based "wisdom" model for determining the will of God with regard to school, marriage, career and all other significant choices, much in line with what we have been affirming in this book so far. But it has been reported that "many . . . came away from his presentation with a great disquiet, a disquiet that arises from a tone that implicitly denies that existential dynamic of the Spirit in the life of the believer and substitutes instead a formula (albeit a thoroughly biblical formula) for determining legitimate options in any situation."[4] And Friesen's book was once roundly critiqued in J. I.'s hearing as a fine statement of the "Deist doctrine of guidance"—a doctrine, that is, that denies, ignores, or otherwise leaves out of account all direct action of God the Holy Spirit in the deep Christian heart and consciousness. It has to be admitted that Friesen's book, however salutary in other ways, does appear overall as an example of this subspiritual mindset in action.

The subspiritual mindset is not prayerless, as the above comments might seem to suggest; but it treats what we have said up to now about obeying Scripture, seeking wisdom, and taking advice as if it were the whole story about guidance, and it is not. Treating it as so, and thus overlooking the full reality of the Holy Spirit's ministry in guidance, opens the door to three mistakes matching those made by the superspiritual mindset, as follows.

First mistake: *overvaluing God's gift of reason.* Reasoning, as we have been trying at length to show, is truly essential to the discerning of God's will, but it is not the only thing that is essential. Human beings are not to be thought of as reasoning and performing machines, like robots and Mr. Spock. That, however, is how the subspiritual outlook in effect regards them, as also did the Pharisees of old, and as do many superficial secular systems of thought of our day. But the Bible shows that human beings are to be understood fundamentally in terms of hearts (i.e., inner selves) that by nature are willfully blind and deaf to God and in terms of deep-rooted, almost instinctive, attitudinal hostility to God, which attitude, directly or indirectly, will express itself in all our thinking about life-agenda and relationships. This is the syndrome that Christians ever since Augustine have labeled "original sin."

And then, we must further understand that when the Holy Spirit changes and renews the heart by instilling in us a recognition of Christ's reality and by uniting us to him in his risen life, our way of thinking is at once altered. Instead of active alienation from and defiance of God, what comes from our hearts is grateful love to God, and a desire to praise and please him. Yet the sinful dynamics of our fallen makeup still operate within us, and incessantly pull against the God-trusting, God-loving, God-serving disposition and motivation that the Spirit has implanted. The result? Paul indicates it when he tells the Galatians: "The desires of the flesh are against the Spirit, and the desires of the Spirit are against the flesh, for these are opposed to each other, to keep you from doing the things you want to do" (Gal. 5:17). Sometimes our knowledge of what we should do is overwhelmed by desire not to do it but to do something else; and again and again we do the right thing in a sluggish, resentful, apathetic, self-pitying, self-absorbed, or self-seeking spirit with hearts that have no deep concern about either the glory of God or the good of others. This happens, not because godly motivation was never there, but because the down-drag of sin in our system has, for the time being, swamped it. We constantly need, therefore, to be asking God to enable us to do the right things in the right way (with love and hope and zeal for God), and only the Holy Spirit who indwells us can bring that about. When, however, all attention is centered on doing the things that Christian reason, informed by the Scriptures, directs us to do, and the question, how we do it (that is, with what attitude and motivation, in what frame of heart) is ignored, as if performance is all that matters, then it can safely be said that reason is being overvalued.

Second mistake: *undervaluing the grace of faithful waiting.* Once reason is entrusted with working out from Scripture what we should believe and do, it craves closure and assumes its own com-petence to achieve it. In the realm of belief, reason does not doubt the propriety of putting God in a box of which reason knows the dimensions. In the realm of behavior, reason does not hesitate to reduce life to the meticulous following out of rigid Bible-based rules, just as the Pharisees did before us. In theology, this is reason losing sight of the mystery of the incomprehensibility of God, the fact that God is greater than we can grasp, and that our knowledge about him and of him is only partial, never complete. In ethics (morality and spirituality) this is reason losing sight of the fact that sometimes God's word of guidance to us is that we should mark time, stay as we are, go on as we are going, and wait for God to change the situation before we attempt anything new. Christian reason, which knows itself called to be enterprising for God, is not of itself able to receive such guidance. Only the Holy Spirit can communicate it. He does this, as we indicated earlier, simply by withholding inner peace in relation to whatever plans of action we had in view.

We saw God doing a version of this in relation to Paul's plans on his second missionary journey, when the Spirit held him back from evangelizing Asia Minor as he had intended (Acts 16:6–7). On the team's first night in Troas, as it seems, Paul received his vision of the man from Macedonia calling on him for help, and that removed all uncertainty as to where they were to go; but doubtless the evening before, at the end of the road they had been following, Paul and his colleagues had stood on the shore at Troas looking out to sea and wondering what God had in store for them, since all they were sure of was that he had not allowed them to leave that road at any particular point on their outward journey. Had they not been sensitive to the Spirit's restraining ministry, however, they would have missed their guidance entirely, and in following their own good plan (evangelizing more of Asia Minor was indeed a good plan), they would have jeopardized God's better plan, namely, evangelism and church-planting in Europe. Readiness to honor God by restraint, when the Holy Spirit nudges us into restraint, rather than barrel ahead with our own rational plans, is an aspect of spiritual life to which subspiritual rationalism is more often than not a stranger, and which it will in fact find it very hard to tune into.

We spoke above of God giving negative guidance ("not that; that is not the way") by a withholding of inner peace, and this calls for fuller comment before we go further. Inner peace is a supremely precious blessing, as appears from what Jesus and Paul said about it. Jesus, in his farewell discourse to his disciples, representatives of all the disciples that were to be, declared: "Peace I leave with you; my peace I give to you. Not as the world gives do I give to you. Let not your hearts be troubled, neither let them be afraid. . . . I have said these things to you, that in me you may have peace. In the world you will have tribulation. But take heart; I have overcome the world" (John 14:27; 16:33). Paul told the Philippians that if they bring all their needs to God in thankful prayer, "the peace of God, which surpasses all understanding, will guard your hearts and your minds in Christ Jesus" (Phil. 4:7). All of Paul's letters without exception, and Peter's two letters, and John's second and third letters along with Revelation—all of these documents begin by wishing the recipients grace and peace from God; the bracketing of peace with grace, which no one doubts is a great and wonderful reality, indicates that peace is a great and wonderful reality too, and this indeed is true.

Peace is a gift from the Father and the Son through the Spirit to all disciples who are seeking to live as such, pursuing a holiness modeled on Christ's, practicing faithfulness to their Lord in all things, observing the tried-and-true joy formula (Jesus first, Others second, Yourself last), and giving credibility to their uncompromising witness by their uncompromised life. The gift is precisely a sense that all is well: my life is on track, my Lord is present with me to protect and help me, my guilt is gone, my hope of heaven is sure, and nothing can separate me from the love of God in Christ. The gift is self-evidencing in one's consciousness, just as is the existence of Christ himself. It is the subjective awareness of an objective reality, in this instance, a reconciled relationship with God. When we have it we know that we have it, and this knowledge brings constant contentment and quiet exhilaration. When anxiety, grief, and distress invade the heart, the peace remains, as the frame within which these traumas are processed.

Withdrawal of God's peace is thus a sign to us that some aspect of our walk with God is not as it should be, and planning to act in a way that would take one out of God's will is a case in point. Withholding peace is one of God's ways of signaling that some rethinking is in order and some adjustment needs to be made.

Third mistake: *restricting the Holy Spirit.* As the superspiritual mindset limited the Holy Spirit by programming him, requiring him always to act in the same way when he guides our decision making, so the subspiritual mindset limits him by effectively reducing his ministry first to the inspiring of Scripture and then to the interpreting of it, in the sense of showing the flow of the story and the instructions in the biblical books—a level of interpretation that non-Christians also can reach. Our point though is that the subspiritual mindset fails to see any need of his direct help to discern how revealed truth bears on our lives, by leading us into heartfelt worship of the God whom we know as real through humbling encounter and by leading us into heartfelt service of fellow beings whom by loving sympathy we see to be needy. Neglecting the need for the Spirit's power to bring about the encounter and the sympathy tends to result in a shallow spirituality of prickly lovelessness.

A fully biblical account of the Holy Spirit's ministry to the children of God will take us on beyond these restrictions (of the superspiritual mindset and the subspiritual mindset) and highlight how very much we owe to the Holy Spirit as we seek at every point to discern and do what will best please our heavenly Father. Such an account, in outline, we offer in our next section.

Led by the Holy Spirit

Twice Paul speaks of being "led" by the Holy Spirit, and the phrase has passed into evangelical jargon: believers say they are being "led by the Spirit" whenever they feel a strong sense of obligation to act in a particular way. But in neither place is Paul talking about being drawn to a specific decision or policy; both times, his theme is overall life-quality, as a sign that one has passed from spiritual death into spiritual life. "If you are led by the Spirit, you are not under the law"—hopelessly and helplessly under condemnation for one's unpaid debt of obedience (Gal. 5:18); "all who are led by the Spirit of God are sons of God"—adopted children who are heirs of glory with Christ (Rom. 8:14).

It is true that the English Standard Version, like most versions, renders Luke 4:1–2: "And Jesus, full of the Holy Spirit, . . . was led by the Spirit in the wilderness for forty days being tempted by the devil." But note (1) that the Greek verb *agō*, used by both Paul and Luke, is a general term for inducing movement as such, rather than a specific term for any one mode of effecting that movement; (2) that here it is used in the imperfect tense (or aspect) meaning that for the forty-day period Jesus was kept on the move; and (3) that the phrase rendered "by the Spirit" is literally "in [*en*] the Spirit," and should be understood as meaning that Jesus was kept at a constant level of high spiritual awareness rather than that the Spirit directly prompted each move from one place to another.

(Had Luke wanted to highlight the Spirit's direct prompting, he would have used a different Greek construction, *hupō* with the genitive, as he does in 2:26.)[5]

The upshot is that in all three cases, being "led by the Spirit" is a phrase that points to living in the Spirit as a personal fact, rather than to particular experiences of guidance, in whatever form.

Here, now, is a quick overview of factors involved in the Spirit-led Christian life.

New birth. The new birth, or regeneration, of a fallen and sinful human being is a work of the same divine power that created the universe, that creates new life in the womb, and that raised Jesus from the dead. In essence, it is the Holy Spirit bestowing a new heart, one that spontaneously expresses itself in faith, hope, and love Godward, in joy that now one knows God savingly, and in overflowing compassion to all around. When Jesus faulted Nicodemus for being "the teacher of Israel"—that is, a supposed Bible expert—yet not understanding what he was saying about being born "of water and the Spirit," (John 3:5, 10), he surely had in mind Ezekiel 36:25–27: "I will sprinkle clean water on you, and you shall be clean from all your uncleanness. . . . I will give you a new heart, and a new spirit I will put within you. And I will remove the heart of stone from your flesh and give you a heart of flesh. And I will put my Spirit within you, and cause you to walk in my statutes. . . ." The New Testament is explicit that from Pentecost on the Spirit effects this cleansing renovation by uniting us to the risen Christ, co-resurrecting us "with" and "in" him (Eph. 2:6; see the whole passage, 1:15–2:10; and Rom. 6:3–11; and Col. 2:11–14). Thereafter the Spirit indwells us (1 Cor. 6:19) as God's seal of ownership (Eph. 1:13–14; 4:30; 2 Cor. 1:21–22), producing in us the fruit of Christlike character (Gal. 5:22–23). So we are not what we were; we are irrevocably changed; we are new creations in Christ (2 Cor. 5:17).

New life. Out of the renewed heart comes "the desires of the Spirit" (Gal. 5:17), matching—indeed, reproducing—the desires that demonstrably drove the Lord Jesus himself: namely, the complex desire to love and serve and please and honor and exalt and glorify his Father, who loves and magnifies his Son. The desire that increasingly drives Christians is to serve and please and exalt the Father and the Son together. The Spirit further instills in us the instinct to commune with the Father and the Son in prayer and prays passionately for us, within us, even when our own power to pray fails (see Rom. 8:15–16, 26; Gal. 4:4–6). Increasingly we become aware that our deepest ambition and longing now is for the closest possible union and communion with Christ, both here and hereafter (Phil. 3:7–14, cf. 1:21). Repeatedly, new insights are given us, making this inbred goal clearer and more vivid to us (Phil. 3:15; cf. 2 Cor. 2:6–16). By these means, "we all . . . beholding the glory of the Lord, are being transformed into the same image from one degree of glory to another. For this comes from the Lord who is the Spirit" (2 Cor. 3:18). Meantime, knowing ourselves to be "created in Christ Jesus for good works" (Eph. 2:10), we labor "to do good, to be rich in good works, to be generous and ready to share" (1 Tim. 6:18), thus fulfilling and expressing our new identity as children of God. So we are not living as once we did; the irrevocable change within us continues; our character is being rebuilt in Christ.

New conflict. Spirit-led life involves conflict in two directions. To start with, there is the outward battle against evil permeating the world, infecting the church, and insinuating spiritual decay into our own lives. This is the spiritual warfare dealt with in Ephesians 6:10–18, where Paul calls on Christians to "be strong in the Lord and in the strength of his might" (v. 10) and to put on the whole armor of God, including the sword of the Spirit, which is the Word of God (v. 17). Clearly it is the Spirit throughout who enables us for this contention.

Also, there is the inward battle against indwelling sin, the anti-God syndrome that once ruled us, that now, though dethroned, is still not destroyed, and that operates within us almost as a devilish second self, distracting us from obedience and dragging us down into flesh-focused self-indulgence, which it deceives us into not seeing what it is and not calling by its proper name, that is, sin. So we find in ourselves the state of things that Paul describes in himself: "I find it to be a law that when I want to do right, evil lies close at hand. For I delight in the law of God, in my inner being, but I see in my members another law waging war against the law of my mind and making me captive to the law of sin that dwells in my members" (Rom. 7:21–23). What we are called to do here is, on the one hand, to mortify sin wherever it raises its head in our lives (Rom. 8:13; Col. 3:5; ESV renders "put to death" both times) and with that, on the other hand, to vivify, cultivate, and strengthen the gracious, Christlike habits that constitute the fruit of the Spirit and are the evidence of our being new creatures in Christ. The discipline of mortification begins with what Jesus said to the dozing disciples in Gethsemane: "Watch [keep alert] and pray that you may not enter into temptation" (Matt. 26:41). The discipline of vivification begins with noting how Scripture portrays godliness and moral excellence both in Christ and in others and thinking out before God what it will mean to follow their examples, as the Spirit within you is urging you to do.

So, though we live joyfully in the peace of God when we are Spirit-led, we do not live peacefully in every sense; instead, we find ourselves having to maintain a two-way conflict that will continue as long as life lasts.

New tasks. The church, says Paul, is the body of Christ, in which, as in a human body, every part has a job to do; and the Holy Spirit gives gifts for service to all Christians so that each may play a full role in the body's life (1 Cor. 12:4–7; cf. 1 Peter 4:10–11). There are gifts of instructive speech, and gifts of straightforward practical helpfulness, and each Christian is tasked with finding, developing, and responsibly using whatever gift or gifts the Spirit has given. Then there is home life in the family, and workplace life, and the life of citizenship and public involvement, all to be lived for God's glory in the power and through the resources that the Holy Spirit supplies. Loving service marks the Spirit-led life at every point. All aspects of the Spirit-led life are universal. No Christian is exempt from anything to which we have referred in the above paragraphs.

Nudged by the Spirit?

What then, in positive terms should we say to those who believe, partly because of what they have been told and partly on the basis of their own past experience, that guidance by divine nudge is frequently God's way of indicating to us what we should do? Simply this, we think:

First, it is not for us to make rules for God or to deny that he made his will known this way when someone testifies that he did. We recognize that God sovereignly may renew today any of the modes of communication that he used in Bible times—visions, dreams, voices, inner promptings, whatever.

Second, this kind of guidance is most likely to be authentic and healthy when it comes at a time when one is not looking for it but is seeking to discern God's will by the methods described in the foregoing chapters. Then the peace of God in the heart finally confirms the rightness of the thinking.

Third, if we are looking for a kind of spiritual experience that God himself, teaching us in Scripture, has not told us to look for, Satan, who is very good at imitating genuine spiritual experience, may fool us again and again by giving us his version of what we are looking for and will thereby lead us astray.

Fourth, while it is always important to check our conclusions as to what God wants us to do by consulting wise folk in the church, it is supremely important to do this when we believe we have received guidance by unusual means. Sin and Satan operate by deceit and the corrupting of good judgment, which makes lone rangers in this matter of direct guidance more than ordinarily vulnerable. If the wise folk agree in giving us reasons to doubt whether our experience really was God revealing his will to us, we should doubt it too.

Fifth, direct guidance will never breach biblical boundaries or cut across biblical directives. Inner urgings to do either of these things most certainly do not come from God.

A Gracious, Willing Guest

We began our survey of the truth about guidance by highlighting Psalm 23 as the biblical classic on the subject. We set ourselves to understand its picture of faithful shepherding and reminded ourselves that to get its full message to us we should view it within the full New Testament frame of spiritual reality that the Old Testament order foreshadowed. As we started to do this, the psalm opened up to us as a source of tremendous reassurance and confidence for all the people of God at all times.

The psalm teaches us to see ourselves as sheep who belong to, and are shepherded by, Yahweh, the LORD, the God of grace, who has covenanted with us his people and who always keeps his promises, and his covenant commitment means that his caring for us, his giving to us, and his rejoicing over us, will never end. And one aspect of the loving care that marks his ministry to us is giving us guidance. "He leads me in paths of righteousness for his name's sake" (v. 3)—that is, to display the praiseworthiness of his love and power here and now in a way that will evoke endless praise for the glory of his grace in thus conveying us to our eternal home. "Paths of righteousness" is a phrase carrying the thought of a journey of which every step in retrospect is seen to have been *right*—right for us, for others, and for God; right in terms of God's standards and intentions; right in its response to every situation and circumstance through which the shepherd brought us; right in handling each obstacle that the shepherd helped us to surmount; right in terms of every short-term frustration and disappointment becoming a source of long-term maturity, humility, strength, and triumph; and right in terms of our experience bringing benefit to others, and enabling us to show the depth of our loyalty to the God who loves us. "He leads me" are words pointing to the certainty that God will always reveal his will for my forward steps, so that I shall always know how to be faithful to him, even when I am totally puzzled and discouraged about everything else. The verse is a wonderful promise, wonderfully phrased.

As New Testament Christians, we know that Israel's covenant God is in truth tripersonal. He is the Father, the Son, and the Holy Spirit, three distinct persons living together in love within the unity of a single divine reality consisting of a single divine life and energy. We know too that the second person, the Son, who two millennia ago became man in the land of Israel for our salvation, announced himself as the Good Shepherd, the shepherd of God's people *par excellence*, and echoed Psalm 23 directly in describing his own shepherding ministry (John 10:1–16). We have offered some thoughts on the shepherding work of both the Father and the Son. We have yet, however, to relate the multiple services that the Spirit renders us in David's picture of shepherding by God. But that we propose to do now, as we draw this chapter and this book to a close.

Some verses of a somewhat sugary nineteenth-century hymn on the Spirit's ministry that was much sung in J. I.'s youth will set us on our way.

> Our blest Redeemer, ere He breathed
>   His tender last farewell,
> A Guide, a Comforter, bequeathed
>   With us to dwell.
>
> He came sweet influence to impart,
>   A gracious, willing Guest,
> Where He can find one humble heart
>   Wherein to rest.
>
> And His that gentle voice we hear,
>   Soft as the breath of even,
> That checks each fault, that calms each fear,
>   And speaks of heaven.
>
> And every virtue we possess,
>   And every conquest won,
> And every thought of holiness
>   Are His alone.

What part, now, does the Holy Spirit play in the shepherding ministry of the holy Three?

The first thing to say is that though the ministry of the Spirit toward us is distinctive to him, his work is always done in union and communion with the Father and the Son, and we must keep this fact constantly in view as we analyze it. The Father and the Son were together in sending the Spirit on his Pentecost mission to the world (see John 14:16, 26; 15:26; 16:7; Acts 2:33; cf. Gal. 4:6), and the implication is that they were together also in sending the Spirit into the lives of each person who has ever received him—including ourselves who write this and you who read it.

It follows that when the Spirit works in human hearts to bring them to faith and repentance, when he renews those hearts so that faith and repentance are exercised, and when he indwells them thereafter for character transformation, he acts as the agent of the Father and the Son. Indeed, both the Father and the Son indwell Christian hearts through the Spirit's agency there (John 14:23; Col. 1:27). Those in whom the Spirit thus works become members of Christ's flock, conscious of his calling them by name and knowing them personally as he leads them to their place of pasture (John 10:3–4, 9).

By means that (let us admit it) we never fully grasp, since they involve the hidden depths of our hearts, the Spirit makes Christ in the power of his cross and resurrection indisputably real to us, and induces in us a full-hearted commitment of faith and hope in him and love toward him; and the Spirit sustains this commitment at times when our commitment is becoming temporarily blurred and unsteady through muddle in our minds or temptations in our hearts. Thus he fulfills his role as Helper and Comforter.

All the processes of mind and heart, all the thinking and all the praying through which divine guidance is discerned through Scripture, wisdom, and help from fellow believers, as we have sought to spell out, are prompted and sustained by the Spirit. So are the peace-laden resonatings in the heart that correct false steps, motivate renewed resolves, and fix our attention once more on the Lord Jesus when our gaze is beginning to wander. We have already seen that the Father and the Son are committed to bring back to the flock any sheep that are inclined to stray or have actually done so; what we are speaking of now is the Spirit's share in that ministry.

Finally, the Spirit both prompts and energizes all the good works, all the acts of obedience, all the fruit of Christlike behavior, all the witnessing and all the ministry, that become part of each Christian's life. All these things, as the hymn said, "are His alone."

Thus the God who is Three-in-One, the *they* who are *he*, "leads me"—and you, and all believers with us—"in paths of righteousness for his name's sake." Thus the Holy Spirit joins with the Father to further the glory of the Good Shepherd. Thus the Holy Spirit, while keeping out of sight, exerts the full power of creation to achieve the fullness of new creation in every believer's life and to bring to each one a full perception of the guidance of God.

Praise to the Father; praise to the Son; praise to the Holy Spirit. Amen.

Epilogue

An End to Fear

I will instruct you and teach you in the way you should go;
I will counsel you with my eye upon you.

Psalm 32:8

Ninety-five percent of knowing the will of God consists in being
prepared to do it before you know what it is.

Donald Grey Barnhouse

This book was born out of anxiety for the many whose anxiety
about guidance gives them nightmares as to what might happen
to them if they make a mistake at this point. We saw their fear as
having a twofold source: failing to appreciate the greatness of the
grace of God and falling into superstition about the way guidance
is given. We wrote accordingly.

In these chapters we have tried to make three things clear. First,
God's guidance is a covenanted aspect of his larger ministry of
graciously guarding us against sin's folly and Satan's malice in order
to bring us safe and sound to glory. Second, our quest for guidance
should be thought of as essentially a quest for the wisdom we need

to cope with all the demands for decision that come to us in our waking lives, rather than with just a few big ones. Third, the gift of God-centered peace of heart as we contemplate and embrace the best, wisest, and most God-honoring option open to us is God's ordinary way of confirming to us that we have attained the wisdom that we sought by observing circumstances, praying for a clear head and discerning heart, searching the Scriptures, consulting experienced friends, and thinking hard before the Lord. This peace, be it said, is not any sort of informative nudge; it is, rather, a sense that the quest is ended, the solution has been found, and no more puzzling over the matter is necessary.

Christians fall into superstition when they posit causative forces and causal connections of which the Bible knows nothing, or which it explicitly rules out by denying them to be real. Thus, expecting benefits from worshipping unreal gods (idolatry), or real demons (Satanism), or supposing that the structure of creation somehow limits the Creator (process theology, deistic liberalism, open theism), or imagining that we can manipulate God and harness his supernatural powers to our own wishes (magic), or thinking that some sort of meritorious performance earns from God favor that was not ours before (legalism), are all superstitions; and so is the idea that one condemns oneself to being a permanently second-class Christian by getting one's guidance wrong on a major matter. Unbiblical superstition must be rejected in all its forms.

Faithful God

When we look at landscapes and landmasses from miles up in the air, as satellite images now enable us to do, we sometimes see parallels that escape us when our vantage point is at ground level. And when we take a bird's-eye view of the two Testaments in our Bible, we similarly see a likeness that we may miss while doing detailed textual study. Both Testaments have, basically, two parts: first, a great redemption story, and then a mixed bag of narrative, admonition, and response, addressed to the redeemed as they seek, often shakily, to live up to the privilege and hope that redemption has brought them. The New Testament proclaims what was God's goal from the start—total redemption from sin and death through the living, dying, rising, reigning, and future return of Jesus Christ, the incarnate Son of God. The Old Testament proclaims a foreshadowing of this—total redemption from slavery in Egypt for what should have been an idyllic life in Canaan, the Promised Land. The New Testament redemption story is told in four parallel accounts of Jesus's three-year ministry in Israel. The Old Testament redemption story extends over forty years and fills four books that come from Moses, Exodus to Deuteronomy inclusive. In both stories the divine Redeemer is the sovereign (absolute ruler) and at the same time the shepherd (the covenant-keeping shepherd of Psalm 23; the Good Shepherd of John 10). The sovereign shepherd faithfully guards and guides his people as he leads them to their true home, and though what surrounds them, obstructs and threatens them, they are safe under his care.

We began this book with some reflections on God's shepherding. We return to that theme as now we draw to a close. In the narrative of how Israel got from Egypt to the Promised Land (Moses's story) three things stand out. The first is the huge reality of miraculous divine deliverance, achieved through the long-term providential preparation of Moses, the ten plagues, the Passover, the opening of the Red Sea for Israel to cross and its closing to destroy the Egyptian forces, the provision of food and drink in the desert, and the guidance given throughout by the pillar in the sky (cloud by day, fire by night).

The second thing that stands out is the huge reality of Israel's multiple mistrustings of God—their grumbling, complaining, disobedience, and defiance, culminating in their irrational and irreverent refusal to invade Canaan, which prompted God to prolong their wanderings by thirty-eight extra years. As Moses reminds them in his farewell address: "You are a stubborn people. Remember and do not forget how you provoked the LORD your God to wrath in the wilderness. From the day you came out of the land of Egypt until you came to this place, you have been rebellious against the

Lord. . . . You have been rebellious against the Lord from the day that I knew you" (Deut. 9:6–7, 24).

The third thing that stands out is the huge demonstration of God's unfailing faithfulness to the wanderers, in spite of their constant lapses from faithfulness toward him. A stunning expression of this is God's own utterance given to Moses as his prophet to relay to the people and repeated by Moses in his farewell speech: "The Lord your God has blessed you in all the work of your hands. He knows your going through this great wilderness. These forty years the Lord your God has been with you. You have lacked nothing" (Deut. 2:7). Such generous grace, in face of childish and extreme provocations that nearly drove Moses out of his mind, fairly takes one's breath away. God at Sinai had identified himself to Moses as "the Lord, a God merciful and gracious, slow to anger, and abounding in steadfast love and faithfulness, keeping steadfast love for thousands, forgiving iniquity and transgression and sin. . . ." (Exod. 34:6–7); and his forty years of mercy to perverse and pigheaded Israel proved the truth of his words.

We said at the beginning of our book that for some Christians the guidance of God is a theme that awakens anxiety, even panic. When we wrote that, we were thinking particularly of depressives, for whom the fear of getting God's guidance wrong is a bogey constantly haunting their minds. "Whoever fears has not been perfected in love," wrote John (1 John 4:18)—nor in wisdom, either! We cannot shout it too often or too loudly: once God takes us into covenant with himself, as he does the moment we put faith in Christ and are born again by the Holy Spirit, our relation to God is of child to Father and sheep to shepherd, and that means that the Father, the Son, and the Spirit will hold us fast and not let go of us, even if in moments of madness or sadness, or just plain badness, we stray into the wilderness of sin and death. The Shepherd searches for the lost sheep until he finds it; the Spirit troubles our conscience as we wander; the Father waits to welcome and restore his child when sanity and repentance set in. And if God so restores Christians who have lapsed with their eyes open, none should fear that he will abandon any who, while seeking to see and do God's will, inadvertently get their guidance wrong.

And suppose we become convinced that in good faith we really have made a major wrong decision—married the wrong person, taken the wrong job, embarked on the wrong career, moved to the wrong place, joined the wrong church, or whatever—and for the time being due to circumstances we are unable to do anything about it? That puts us on a par with Israel, obliged to spend thirty-eight further years in the wilderness because of their wrong decision when God told them to invade Canaan. Remember, now, that it was of those years that God could and did move Moses to tell the people: "These forty years the LORD your God has been with you. You have lacked nothing." If you wait on God, acknowledging your mistake and affirming to him that his will is what you still want to do, you will find that God makes these words equally true of you. You have nothing to fear. God is good, and he is yours forever.

Faith-filled Prayer

There has been little about prayer in these pages (though we have published a whole book on it elsewhere[1]), but something must be said on the subject as we close, for in finding God's guidance, prayer plays an important part. When we speak of prayer, we have in mind a following, at least in spirit, of biblical models. These prayers are conversational and petitionary: they address God with the expectation that he will respond, both in dealing with the need prayed about and also, perhaps, by giving us a special sense of his presence in our prayer session itself. The staple ingredient of these prayers is the need that God is being asked to meet.

In the Old Testament, the Psalms are the supreme instances of such praying; in the New Testament, the Lord's Prayer itself is perhaps the front-running example. So when we pray for anything, whether alone or in company, silently or aloud, we should first invoke God, however briefly, as who and what he is; we should thank him for past benefits; and then we should ask him for what we and others need, giving him reasons why we think that for him to give what we ask will truly make for his glory, as well as furthering our own and others' welfare. All our prayers, in intention anyway, should be reducible to "Hallowed be thy name (i.e., may you be glorified), thy kingdom come, thy will be done." The basis for biblical Christian prayer is the covenant relationship whereby the God, who through Christ is our father, and the Lord Jesus, who because of our adoption is now our elder brother in God's family, stand pledged to hear and answer the prayers of believing people (see John 14:13–14; 16:23–24; 1 John 5:14–15).

When praying for guidance, we should always start by asking to be delivered from stupidity, pride, and pigheadedness, and all forms of motivational perversity that would skew our thinking, and we should ask for sensitivity, pure-heartedness, and clarity to discern what course of action will bring about the most good and honor God most fully. This line of prayer needs to be constantly churning in our hearts as we do the reading, thinking, talking, and listening that our quest for discernment requires of us.

At the outset of this book we looked at Psalm 23, as the Bible's classic witness to God's way in guidance. As God had the first word, so he shall have the last: some verses from Psalm 25 form a classic prayer for guidance, and our final word to our readers is: go, and pray likewise. Your fears and problems regarding guidance will melt away as you do.

> Make me to know your ways, O LORD:
>   teach me your paths.
> Lead me in your truth and teach me,
>   for you are the God of my salvation;
>   for you I wait all the day long. . . .
>
> Good and upright is the LORD;
>   therefore he instructs sinners in the way.
> He leads the humble in what is right,
>   and teaches the humble his way.

All the paths of the LORD are steadfast love and
    faithfulness,
    for those who keep his covenant and his testimonies. . . .

Who is the man who fears the LORD?
    Him will he instruct in the way that he should
    choose. . . .
My eyes are ever toward the LORD,
    for he will pluck my feet out of the net.

Psalm 25:4–5, 8–10, 12, 15

Appendix

John Newton on Divine Guidance

Answer to the question, "In what manner are we to expect the Lord's promised guidance to influence our judgments, and direct our steps in the path of duty?"

Dear Sir,

It is well for those who are duly sensible of their own weakness and fallibility, and of the difficulties with which they are surrounded in life, that the Lord has promised to guide his people with his eye, and to cause them to hear a word behind them, saying, "This is the way, walk ye in it," when they are in danger of turning aside either to the right hand or to the left. For this purpose, he has given us the written Word to be a lamp to our feet, and encouraged us to pray for the teaching of his Holy Spirit, that we may rightly understand and apply it. It is, however, too often seen that many widely deviate from the path of duty, and commit gross and perplexing mistakes, while they profess a sincere desire to know the will of God, and think they have his warrant and authority. This must certainly be owing to misapplication of the rule by which they judge, since the rule itself is infallible, and the promise sure.

The Scripture cannot deceive us, if rightly understood; but it may, if perverted, prove the occasion of confirming us in a mistake. The Holy Spirit cannot mislead those who are under his influence; but we may suppose that we are so when we are not. It may not be unseasonable to offer a few thoughts upon a subject of great importance to the peace of our minds, and to the honor of our holy profession.

Many have been deceived as to what they ought to do, or in forming a judgment beforehand of events in which they are nearly concerned, by expecting direction in ways which the Lord has not warranted. I shall mention some of the principal of these, for it is not easy to enumerate them all. . . .

[Some people], when in doubt, have opened the Bible at a venture, and expected to find something to direct them in the first verse they should cast their eye upon. It is no small discredit to this practice that the heathens, who knew not the Bible, used some of their favorite books in the same way; . . . for if people will be governed by the occurrence of a single text of Scripture, without regarding the context, of duly comparing it with the general tenor of the Word of God, and with their own circumstances, they may commit the greatest extravagances, expect the greatest impossibilities, and contradict the plainest dictates of common sense, while they think they have put the Word of God on their side. Can the opening upon [i.e., opening the Bible at] 2 Samuel 7:3, when Nathan said unto David, "Do all that is in thine heart, for the Lord is with thee," be sufficient to determine the lawfulness of our Lord's words to the woman of Canaan (Matt. 15:28), "Be it unto thee even as thou wilt," amount to a proof that the present earnest desire of the mind (whatever it may be) shall be surely accomplished? Yet it is certain that matters big and with important consequences have been engaged in, and the most sanguine expectation formed, upon no better warrant than dipping (as it is called) upon a text of Scripture.

A sudden strong impression of a text, that seems to have some resemblance to the concern, upon the mind has been accepted by many as an infallible token that they were right and that things would go just as they would have them: or, on the other hand, if the passage bore a threatening aspect, it has filled them with fears and disquietudes [i.e., anxieties] which they have afterwards found were groundless and unnecessary. These impressions . . . have frequently proved no less delusive [than the practice of dipping]. It is allowed that such impressions of a precept or a promise as humble, animate or comfort the soul be giving it a lively [i.e., vivid] sense of truth contained in the words are profitable and pleasant; and many of the Lord's people have been instructed and supported (especially in a time of trouble) by some seasonable word of grace applied and sealed by his Spirit with power to their hearts. But if impressions or impulses are received as a voice from heaven, directing to such particular actions as could not be proved to be duties without them, a person may be unwarily misled into great evils and gross delusions; and many have been so. There is no doubt but the enemy of our souls, if permitted, can furnish us with Scriptures in abundance in this way, and for these purposes.

Some persons judge of the nature and event of their designs [i.e., the outcome of their plans] by the freedom which they find in prayer. They say they commit their ways to God, seek his direction, and are favored with much enlargement of spirit; and therefore they cannot doubt but what they have in view is acceptable in the Lord's sight. I would not absolutely reject every plea of this kind, yet without other corroborating evidence, I could not admit it in proof of what it is brought for. It is not *always* easy to determine when we have spiritual freedom in prayer. Self is deceitful; and when our hearts are much fixed and bent upon a thing, this may put words and earnestness into our mouths. Too often we first secretly determine for ourselves, and then come to ask counsel of God; in such a disposition we are ready to catch at everything that may seem to favor our darling scheme; and the Lord, for the detection and chastisement of our hypocrisy (for hypocrisy it is, though perhaps hardly perceptible to ourselves), may answer us according to our idols (see Ezek. 14:3–4). . . .

Once more a remarkable dream has sometimes been thought as decisive as any of the foregoing methods of knowing the will of God. That many wholesome and seasonable admonitions have been received in dreams, I willingly allow; but, though they may be occasionally noticed, to pay a great attention to dreams, especially to be guided by them, to form our sentiments, conduct, or expectations upon them, is superstitious and dangerous. The promises are not made to those who dream, but to those who watch.

Upon the whole, though the Lord may give to some persons, upon some occasions, a hint or encouragement out of the common way, yet expressly to look for and seek his direction in such things as I have mentioned is unscriptural and ensnaring. . . . I have seen some presuming they were doing God service, while acting in contradiction to his express commands. I have known others infatuated to believe a lie, declaring themselves assured, beyond the shadow of a doubt, of things which, after all, never came to pass; and when at length disappointed, Satan has improved [i.e., taken advantage of] the occasion to make them doubt of the plainest and most important truths, and to account their whole former experience a delusion. By these things weak believers have been stumbled, cavils [i.e., objections] and offences against the gospel multiplied, and the ways of truth evil spoken of.

But how then may the Lord's guidance be expected? After what has been premised negatively, the question may be answered in a few words. In general, he guides and directs his people by affording them, in answer to prayer, the light of his Holy Spirit, which enables them to understand and to love the Scriptures. The Word of God is not to be used as a lottery; nor is it designed to instruct us by shreds and scraps, which, detached from their proper places, have no determinate import; but it is to furnish us with just principles, right apprehensions to regulate our judgments and affections, and thereby to influence and direct our conduct. They who study the Scriptures in an humble dependence upon divine teaching are convinced of their own weakness, and are taught to make a true estimate of everything around them, are gradually formed into a spirit of submission to the will of God, discover the nature and duties of their several situations and relations in life, and the snares and temptations to which they are exposed. The Word of

God dwells richly in them, is a preservative from error, a light to their feet, and a spring of strength and consolation. By treasuring up the doctrines, precepts, promises, examples, and exhortations of Scripture in their minds, and daily comparing themselves with the rule by which they walk, they grow into an habitual frame of spiritual wisdom, and acquire a gracious taste, which enables them to judge of right and wrong with a degree of readiness and certainty, as a musical ear judges of sounds. And they are seldom mistaken, because they are influenced by the love of Christ, which rules in their hearts, and a regard to the glory of God, which is the great object they have in view.

In particular cases, the Lord opens and shuts for them, breaks down walls of difficulty which obstruct their path, or hedges up their way with thorns, when they are in danger of going wrong, by the dispensations of his providence [i.e., by his providential ordering of their circumstances]. They know that their concernments [i.e., concerns] are in his hands; they are willing to follow whither and when he leads; but are afraid of going before him. Therefore they are not impatient: because they believe, they will not make haste, but wait daily upon him in prayer; especially when they find their hearts most engaged in any purpose or pursuit, they are most jealous of being deceived by appearances, and dare not move farther or faster than they can perceive his light shining upon their paths. I express at least their desire, if not their attainment: thus they would be. And though there are seasons when faith languishes, and self too much prevails, this is their general disposition; and the Lord, whom they serve, does not disappoint their expectations. He leads them by a right way, preserves them from a thousand snares, and satisfies them that he is and will be their guide even unto death.[1]

John Newton (1725–1807),
Forty-One Letters on Religious Subjects, Letter 28

For Discussion and Reflection

Chapter 1: The Shepherd and His Sheep

1. "The Taste of Fear" titles this book's prologue. When have you tasted fear as you considered God's guidance?

2. Some Christians see God's guidance as primarily a personal but partially hidden road map, where if you make a wrong turn, nothing in your life will be quite as good as it might have been (see prologue pp. 9–12). What do you know of God's character that might soften that fear?

3. Read the warning that Agabus gave to Paul in Acts 21:10–11. If you had been one of Paul's advisors, what factors would you want Paul to consider as he decided how to respond to the words that Agabus said came from the Holy Spirit?

4. Look again through the section of text subtitled "Covenant Context." If God's guidance is part of his covenant care for you, what all would you expect that guidance to include?

5. Slowly read aloud Psalm 23 pausing after each phrase to savor the image. Thank God for what you see of him and of yourself there.

6. Under the subhead "Theological Framework," the authors speak of four theological principles at work in this psalm: God as Trinity, God's covenant care of his people, God's salvation of his people, and practical aspects of real-life shepherding. Read Psalm 23 again and pick out several examples of each category. Which of the categories speaks most strongly to you at this phase of your life? Why?

7. Phillip Keller describes occasions when one of his sheep would fall over onto its back, then lie there, feet helplessly kicking in the air—until he came and set it upright again (pp. 25–26). It is this image that Keller uses to describe what God does when "he restores my soul." When and how do you experience a similar restoration from God?

8. Psalm 23 says, "He leads me in paths of righteousness for his name's sake." What does this statement convey to you about how and why God will guide you? Give several examples of what that guidance would look like or not look like.

9. Read again the final paragraph of the chapter. Do you find these statements worrisome or encouraging, or both. Why?

10. Pray, expressing to God your response to his shepherdlike guidance.

Chapter 2: Some Tangled Tales

1. Thoughtfully read the quotations from John Henry Newman and from Psalm 23 that open this chapter. What do you find here that draws you to desire God's guidance?

2. "God's holiness is his righteousness in intention, and his righteousness is his holiness in action" (p. 32). Consider the meaning of this statement by reviewing the first two paragraphs under "The Nature of Righteousness." Then create several endings to a sentence that begins, "Because God is righteous. . . ."

3. "Righteousness is love with wisdom; love is righteousness with good will." . . . "The decisions we make should always have in view the twin goals of maximum service to others and maximum pleasing of God" (pp. 32–33). Bring to mind one decision (large or small) that you need to make in the near future. What direction do you think these principles of righteousness would turn that decision?

4. Read through the two dozen quotations of Scripture on pages 34–35 and find one that is particularly encouraging or challenging to you. What would it mean for you to seriously take this passage to heart? (Consider spiritual, emotional, practical impact.)

5. Review the three paragraphs under "The shape of guidance" (pp. 36–37). What steps could you take to weigh with discernment any guidance you think that you are receiving from God?

6. In the section titled "Signs and Certainty" (pp. 39–44), the authors give six reasons to support the section's final two sentences. To what extent do you agree or disagree. Why?

7. The section titled "Guided Endurance" (pp. 44–52) asserts that God-guided people often suffer that their lives are not necessarily easy, and that hardship is not a reliable indicator that they are on the wrong path. Who have you known or read of whose apparently God-guided life included significant suffering?

8. Read 1 Kings 22:1–28 and Jeremiah 19:15–20:8. Do the biblical accounts of Micaiah and Jeremiah encourage or frighten you? Why?

9. As you reflect on various turning points in your own life, as J. I. Packer does on pages 50–51, recall at least one point where hindsight reveals that God's guidance was at work. Did subsequent events after that turning point bring you ease or pain, or both? What were the long-term spiritual results?

10. Pray now for someone whose life is now difficult partly *because* he or she is following God's guidance.

Chapter 3: Your Good Health

1. What are some ways that you evaluate spiritual health in yourself?

2. Do you agree that a periodic spiritual checkup is important? Why, or why not?

3. Principle One: *Health* for the soul is the fruit of holiness in the heart (pp. 63–67). When we ask God to "unite my heart to fear your name" (Ps. 86:11), what are we asking God to do?

4. Principle Two: Holiness of life is the fruit of *habits* in the heart (pp. 67–73). Focus again on the ninefold fruit of the Spirit as described on pages 68–73. How and why have you appreciated one of these "habits of the heart" in another person?

5. Which of these nine habits of the heart do you hope that God will develop more fully in your own heart? How can you begin to move toward better spiritual health in that area?

6. Principle Three: Habits of living are the fruit of desires of the *heart* (pp. 73–80). According to this section of the chapter, habits grow out of desires of the heart (pp. 74–75). Bring to mind two of your own habits: one good habit and another not so good. What desires led you to each habit?

7. As you read pages 73–80 what do you find here that you would like to cultivate as a heart desire? What steps can you take to nurture that desire and its resulting habits?

8. Principle Four: *Holiness* of life leads to discernment in the heart (pp. 80–84). If we are to discern God's will, we must cultivate: (1) holiness of heart and life, (2) a mind seeking deeper and fuller renewal from God, and (3) the willingness to think hard in exploring and comparing possible courses of action. "Subtract any or all of the first three, and the fourth [discerning God's will] will suffer" (p. 84). To what extent do you agree or disagree with this statement? How does it contribute to your understanding of God's guidance?

9. If you were to work with a spiritual director for a time of "spiritual midwifery" (p. 63), what subject would you most likely concentrate on? Why?

10. Slowly read aloud Romans 12:1–2 below.

> I appeal to you therefore, brothers, by the mercies of God,
> to present your bodies as a living sacrifice,
> holy and acceptable to God,
> which is your spiritual worship.
> Do not be conformed to this world,
> but be transformed by the renewal of your mind,
> that by testing you may discern what is the will of God,
> what is good and acceptable and perfect.

Pray now, in writing, your response to God.

Chapter 4: Guided by the Word of God

1. Give a brief summary (in writing, in speaking, or in thinking) of your present practice of using Scripture. Consider frequency of reading, motive, amount and method of study, ways Scripture does or does not touch your life after you have closed the book, your sense of being guided by Scripture, relevance or irrelevance of what you find there, your own consistency of approach to Scripture, and how you feel about the Bible and its contents.

2. "The human being has in the past been defined as a tool-making animal. We here are defining ourselves, biblically we believe, as discerning, direction setting, and decision making creatures of God, and seeking to understand ourselves and our lives, first to last, in these terms" (p. 86). What differences do you see in the two definitions of what it means to be human? What does the second definition suggest about our potential relationship with God?

3. Under the section, "Guided by God's Commands" we read, "As our Creator and as our Redeemer [God] is entitled to

say to us, 'Now this is what you must and must not do'"
(p. 88). This statement might trigger a number of responses:
thanks, anger, frustration, security, stubbornness, humility,
confidence, confusion, or some other response. Select one
or two that best fit your current response. Explain.

4. John wrote, "For this is the love of God, that we keep his
   commandments. And his commandments are not burdensome" (1 John 5:3). Meditate in silence on this statement
   of God's love and yours. Do not neglect to consider those
   areas of command that have at times felt troublesome to
   you.

   After several moments of mediation, pray your response to
   God. As you consider how best to pray your response, select
   one or more areas of ACTS praying: Adoration, Confession,
   Thanksgiving, Supplication.

5. "God is gracious and good—he meets people where they
   are, and often showers beginner Christians with insights for
   their personal guidance as they take their first hesitant steps
   in forming the habit of daily Bible reading" (p. 92). How
   is your "habit of daily Bible reading" progressing? Create a
   written "note to self" about any adjustments that you need
   to make.

6. Reread the paragraph beginning, "Freedom exists when not
   only have we been freed *from* whatever oppressed us, but
   are also now enjoying the state of dignity, happiness, fulfillment, and contentment that we were freed *for*. Freedom
   is thus two-sided" (p. 99). Do you think you would have
   more freedom with or without God's law? Explain? (Notice
   particularly the illustration of a boat's anchor.)

7. When and how is God's law an anchor for you?

8. The second commandment given in Exodus 20 says, "You
   shall not make for yourself a carved image." The authors of
   this book suggest that "all who begin, 'My idea of God is . . .'
   or 'I prefer to think of God as . . .' are ordinarily breaking
   the second commandment already, before they finish their
   sentence" (p. 108). Suppose in conversation with a close

friend, you hear this kind of statement. If you are guided by God's mind, how might you respond?

9. Near the end of the chapter (p. 108) the authors warn that following God's guidance sometimes has a *"double effect, or unintended and undesired consequences."* In other words, in some situations, even our best effort to follow all that we know of God's commands, his Book, his law, and his mind, will cause pain and hardship—because there is no good solution to the problem. Here we must decide for something that brings about less evil than the alternatives. Bring to mind a present or past dilemma of this sort from your own experience. How does being guided by the Word of God encourage you in this setting?

10. Read slowly aloud this patterned outline of what the Bible says about itself. Pause after each line to think and pray.

All Scripture is
B R E A T H E D   O U T
by God
and profitable
for teaching,
for reproof,
for correction,
and for training in righteousness,
that the man of God may be competent,
equipped for every good work.

Chapter 5: The Way of Wisdom

1. When and how have you benefited from someone else's wisdom?

2. What events of your life has God used to make you more wise?

3. When considering the centrality of wisdom, the authors observe that the core responsibility of Christian life is to

love and serve God and others with imagination and devotion, with a sense of privilege and a spirit of self-giving, with a self-forgetful humility and a joyful awareness of self-fulfillment. To grow in wisdom . . . is simply to realize . . . that this is how Jesus Christ, our Savior, our Lord, and our life, wants to express himself in the new renewed personhood that he is developing within us (p. 118).

Select one phrase of this definition of a Christian life that is guided by wisdom. How can you visualize that phrase lived out in your own life?

After a time of discussion or reflection, reread aloud the last sentence of the quote.

4. Reread the paragraph on page 122 which lists seven topics of biblical wisdom. Select one of these that you would like to experience more deeply and reread the section on pages 122–31 that speaks to that particular area. How can you use the resources found in those paragraphs to better develop the *nature* of wisdom in your life?

5. "One mark of a wise person . . . is that one is willing to accept instruction and correction and to learn to know things better than one does at the moment" (p. 125). How have you seen this lived out in a person that you care about? What is one situation where you would like to better live it out yourself?

6. The apostle Paul says in Philippians 2 that "it is God who works in you, both to will and to work for his good pleasure." How might an increased appreciation for this truth lead you to better work, better wisdom, and better worship?

7. "We ask for wisdom in times of trial, wisdom that will enable us to face up to our present situation (even if that situation is cancer, job loss, divorce, or children on the road to ruin) and see what is best for us to do and enable us also to keep rejoicing in God's gift of present salvation and promise of future glory as we battle through" (p. 133). If this statement were pointing to your own current circumstances, what particularly would you be expected to do?

8. Review Jesus's assessment of the way of wisdom when he chose to stop teaching and to bless the children instead (pp. 134–35). How might looking at "kingdom issues" help you to make a wise assessment in one of your current decisions?

9. Review the story of three servants in Matthew 25:14–30. If you were to insert the term "wisdom" into that parable as your "talents," what steps would this parable encourage you to take or not take?

10. Where do you most need wisdom right now? Ask God for it right now.

Chapter 6: With a Little Help from Our Friends

1. What are some practical rules that you follow when it comes to giving and receiving advice?

2. "Individuality and individualism are in fact two very different things" (p. 141). Reread the section subtitled "Individuality and Individualism." Then give three examples of what *individuality* says, does, and thinks, and then what *individualism* says, does, and thinks.

3. Why is individuality so difficult and individualism so tempting?

4. The Greek word *koinōnia* signifies "the act and consequence of sharing what God has given to each of us: I give to you what I have to share, you give to me what you have to share, and we both end up enriched and encouraged beyond where we were when we started" (p. 142). When and how have you experienced *koinonia*? Or, when and how do you wish you had a better experience of *koinonia*?

5. The church is "our corporate, spiritual friend" (p. 144). In what ways does your church guide and guard you?

6. How can you contribute to the spiritual well-being of others in your church?

7. Proverbs 11:14 says, "In an abundance of counselors there is safety." Does this mean that if you want God's guidance as

you make a major decision, you should poll your Christian friends and then make the decision advised by the largest number of friends? Why or why not?

8. Slowly and thoughtfully read the six proverbs quoted on pages 149–50 pausing to reflect after each one. Select one as a needed corrective for yourself. When, why, and how do you hope to implement it?

9. Read the story of Agabus giving advice to the apostle Paul—and Paul rejecting that advice (Acts 20:22–21:14). What do Paul's actions here suggest to you about the way you ought to weigh advice even when given with good intent from godly friends?

10. In prayer, bring to God one area where you need his guidance. As you pray, ask yourself and God these questions from page 146:

- What is the best I can do for the glory of God?
- What is the best I can do for the good of others?
- What is the best I can do for the advancing of God's kingdom?
- What is the best witness to God's truth and power, and to the grace of my Lord Jesus Christ?

Chapter 7: Modeling

1. J. I. Packer points to two role models who helped shape the person that he is: Richard Baxter and George Whitefield (pp. 164–65). Who has been in some way a role model to you? (Consider those whose lives are contemporary to your own as well as people of the past whose lives or writings have drawn you to model them in some way.)

2. Whom would you *like* to model? Why?

3. In expounding the phrase "He leads me in paths of righteousness for his name's sake" from Psalm 23, the authors say, "If the sheep supposed that the shepherd's eye was off it while it trotted along in the flock, the sheep would be

wrong. Similarly, we must understand that God in his sovereign providence is leading and guiding us through each day of our lives, whether that day calls for new, far-reaching decisions or not" (pp. 165–66). Survey your most recent past, full day, measuring it from top to bottom. Upon reflection about that day, where do you sense "God in his sovereign providence . . . leading and guiding"?

4. How does this sheep's-eye view of the shepherd inform your understanding of God's guidance, even if you did not notice it that day?

5. Review the threefold answer to the question, What can models do for us? (pp. 167–70)

- Models will enlarge our vision
- Models make us realize what could and should be in our lives
- Encountering a model can help us vocationally

Select the one most relevant to your current setting and reread that section. What is the best way you can respond to this particular purpose of a model?

6. Read aloud Hebrews 11:1–12:2 as if you were proclaiming it as a sermon about models for the people of God. As you survey the "cloud of witnesses" in chapter 11, what person or qualities would you like to model? How?

7. Read once more Hebrews 12:1–2. "This is the climax, to which the tour of the heroes' gallery was, it now appears, simply the preliminary. Jesus, centrally and definitively . . . must be the model for his followers" (p. 172). When you are "looking to Jesus" as your model, what do you see?

8. "In God's church everybody is a leader to somebody . . ." (p. 175). Read Peter's instructions to us in 1 Peter 5:2–3. Who in the church are likely to see you as a model or a shepherd? Which of Peter's instructions here can you take as corrective guidance so that you can better serve as a shepherd in your own church setting?

9. What warning do you find in the statement from Jeremiah 22:22: "The wind shall shepherd all your shepherds" (p. 177)?

10. In Matthew 11:28–30, Jesus says, "Come to me, all who labor and are heavy laden, and I will give you rest. Take my yoke upon you and learn from me. . . ." Picture yourself attached by a yoke to Jesus as described on page 173. What would you want to say to this divine model with whom you share the yoke of your life? Write and then pray your response.

Chapter 8: Guided Life Commitments

1. As you reflect on your life thus far, what do you see as one of the most important decisions that you have made? How did you go about making that decision?

2. Under "Vocational Guidance: Its Nature," the authors note that they see some Christians as being guided by God mainly through rational understanding of Scripture, opportunity, and skills or interest. Others seek for God's guidance through "feelingitis." Which approach is closest to your usual sense of God's guidance in your decisions? Reread the paragraph beginning "Yet the way to pray . . ." (p. 184). What shift might the suggestions in this paragraph have on your own praying for guidance during times of decision?

3. Part of God's vocational guidance includes commitment to our families. "If anyone does not provide for his relatives, and especially for members of his household, he has denied the faith and is worse than an unbeliever" (1 Tim. 5:8). What examples can you think of by which this principle is lived out—or ignored? What personal challenge does this text present to you (p. 187)?

4. "Family members of people with 'special needs' make life-long career adjustments in order to provide. . . ." (p. 187). How have you seen this principle at work in ways that

you admire? Pause now to pray for a family that includes someone with special needs.

5. Reflect on the life commitments of Moses, Nehemiah, and Paul (pp. 187–94). Which of these appeals to you as paralleling your own experience in some way? How?

6. "Commonly, if not invariably, God orchestrates circumstances that bring to a head the issue of life commitment to a vocational task" (p. 190). As you think about your own current vocational commitment (student, homemaker, worker, or other), what was one primary trigger to your commitment to this role? How, if at all, do you see God's guidance as part of that trigger?

7. Notice the closing statements as Moses, Nehemiah, and Paul each came to the end of his life (pp. 191–92). Write one sentence that you hope would similarly comment on your life.

8. God guided Moses and Paul, as he does many of us, through vocational course corrections—which might have looked initially like failure. As you look back on your life thus far, how has God used what looked like failure as a guided correction in the course of your life?

9. If you are enduring a current disappointment or failure, what hint of God's guidance toward a course correction can you explore? How?

10. The section heading titled "Conclusions" (p. 194) raises five questions. Select one of these that is most relevant to your current setting. How might you act on the help offered in that brief paragraph?

Chapter 9: Situation Ethics

1. Peruse the three quotations that open this chapter (p. 197). What does each quotation reveal about the speaker's view of circumstances?

2. What examples have you seen (or experienced) of self-indulgent situation ethics (p. 198)?

3. We can make decisions by calculating consequences. We can decide what to do based on which course of action will lead to the most good and the least harm (p. 198). What do you find helpful about this criterion for decision making? What limitations do you see in it?

4. "Bible-believers . . . see that law and love belong together, that law is love's eyes, that love for God and humankind is the law's heart, and that the conjunction remains a non-negotiable of Christianity" (pp. 198–99). If this is a true statement, what does it reveal about God's nature? What does it suggest about an appropriate ethic for God's people?

5. The authors observe that life-situations are "a field of God's sovereignty" but are also "a field of Satan's endeavor," and finally life-situations are "a field of personal responsibility" (pp. 199–202). Bring to mind one of your own life-situations of the past week. How can you draw on all three of these observations as you respond to that situation?

6. Review the story of Aaron's golden calf as summarized on pages 203–4 and Exodus 32. What things went wrong in Aaron's response to his situation?

7. Read Luke 4:1–13, which records the temptation of Christ (pp. 205–7). As you look at the various responses Jesus made to the three situations Satan introduced, what do you see that you might want to imitate in your own response to difficult situations?

8. Review David's story as summarized on pages 207–208. In what ways is David both an example and a caution to you?

9. In the section titled "Situational Guidance" (pp. 208–210), the authors list a series of seven steps that can lead to good situational decisions. Write out one choice that you must now make. Begin to work your way through these steps as you seek God's guidance. What do you expect to find most helpful about this process?

10. As you continue to reflect on your own troubling situation, write or speak a prayer of trust in God for his guarding, guiding presence in this matter.

Chapter 10: Guarded and Guided by the Holy Spirit

1. Quietly meditate on the words of Simon Browne that open this chapter (p. 211). If this were to be your own prayer, what things would you be saying about yourself? about God? Begin by praying this prayer aloud for yourself, or your discussion group, or your church.

2. Review the section titled "Introducing the Holy Spirit" (pp. 213–18). Suppose you were in conversation with a person who believed that there is only one God but had no concept of Trinity. What would you want that person to understand about the Holy Spirit?

3. Augustine understood that "in all the acts of God all three persons of the Trinity are involved, expressing their unity" (p. 214). How can this truth influence the way you pray for the Spirit's guidance?

4. This section is littered with Scripture passages. Select one; read and study it. What does it contribute to your understanding of God's guidance?

5. Review the section "Guided by the Holy Spirit?" (pp. 218–25). Which category best describes your approach to guidance by the Holy Spirit: superspiritual or subspiritual? How and why?

6. Consider the "three mistakes" explained under your most preferred approach to guidance. What do you find helpful (or not helpful) here? Explain.

7. In the section titled "Led by the Holy Spirit" (pp. 225–28), the authors describe a Spirit-led person as having new birth, new life, new conflict, and new tasks. Focus on one of these as you reflect on the work of God's Spirit in your life. Describe some of the ways in which you see God currently at

work in your life in that particular area. What challenges do you face as a result?

8. Read Romans 8:1–17, one of the great New Testament passages on the Holy Spirit. Select one sentence from this passage that challenges or encourages you. Write or speak or pray your response.

9. What is one step that you could take as you further explore God's guidance of you through the Holy Spirit?

Epilogue and Appendix of Reflections from John Newton

1. The epilogue is titled "An End to Fear" (pp. 234–40). On a scale of 1 to 5, how would you rate your "fear factor" regarding God's guidance? Explain.

2. Paragraph three of the epilogue (p. 235) warns against five forms of superstition that Christians sometimes fall into when they try to find God's guidance. Which of these "superstitions" do you find in your own natural inclination? How can you become appropriately cautious in this area?

3. What do you find in a bird's-eye view of the whole sweep of Scripture's narrative that strengthens your faith in God as a faithful God? (pp. 235–37)

4. What do you find in the last two paragraphs of the section titled "Faithful God" (pp. 237–38) that softens your own fears about God's guidance?

5. "All our prayers, in intention anyway, should be reducible to 'Hallowed be thy name'" (p. 239). If you were to take this statement as a consistent goal of your own praying for guidance, how might you pray differently? What might you expect from God as a response to this kind of praying?

6. Bring to mind one of your own current needs for God's guidance. What specifically could you say to God if your primary goal in that situation is "Hallowed be thy name"?

7. What do you find helpful in John Newton's letter answering the question, "In what manner are we to expect the Lord's

promised guidance to influence our judgments, and direct our steps in the path of duty?" (p. 244).

8. If you were able to write a responding letter to John Newton, what more would you want to ask him?

9. Return to the excerpts from Psalm 25 on pages 239–40. Softly read the selected verses of this psalm aloud, stopping after each verse to meditate and pray. Thank God for all that he is, and that this God is your guard and your guide.

Notes

Chapter 1 The Shepherd and His Sheep

1. Phillip Keller, *A Shepherd Looks at Psalm 23* (Grand Rapids: Zondervan, 1970).

2. Ibid., chapter, 10, 114ff.

3. Ibid., 35ff.

4. Ibid., 45ff., 49ff.

5. Ibid., chapter 7, 92ff.

6. Ibid., chapter 8, 92ff.

7. Ibid., 37.

8. Ibid., 100–103.

Chapter 2 Some Tangled Tales

1. Elisabeth Elliott, *A Slow and Certain Light* (Waco: Word, 1973), 46.

2. Ibid., 105.

3. J. A. Motyer, *The Message of Philippians: Jesus Our Joy* (Leicester, UK; Downers Grove, IL: InterVarsity, 1984), 208.

4. Phillip D. Jensen and Tony Payne, *The Last Word on Guidance* (Homebush West, NSW: Anzea/Sydney, St. Matthias, 1991), 68.

5. Bruce Waltke, *Finding the Will of God: A Pagan Notion?* (Gresham, OR: Vision House, 1995), 67–68.

6. Dallas Willard, *Hearing God* (Downers Grove, IL: InterVarsity, 1999), 111–12.

7. Waltke, *Finding the Will of God*, 68–69.

8. Elisabeth Elliot, *Through Gates of Splendor* (Wheaton, IL: Tyndale, 1981); idem., *Shadow of the Almighty* (New York: Harper & Row, 1979), idem., *These Strange Ashes* (London: Hodder & Stoughton, 1976); idem., *The Savage My Kinsman* (Ann

Arbor: Servant, 1981); see also idem., *A Slow and Certain Light*; and her novel based on some of her experiences, idem., *No Graven Image* (New York: Harper & Row and London: Hodder & Stoughton, 1966).

9. Alister McGrath, *To Know and Serve God* (London: Hodder & Stoughton, 1997); idem., *J. I. Packer* (Grand Rapids: Baker, 1997). An earlier, slighter account was contained in Christopher Catherwood, *Five Evangelical Leaders* (London: Hodder & Stoughton; Wheaton, IL, Harold Shaw, 1985).

10. Interestingly, Dr. Tidmarsh was to play a significant role in the story of the Waorani (Auca) and five missionary martyrs. See Olive Fleming Liefield, *Unfolding Destinies* (Grand Rapids: Discovery House Publishers, 1998); *The Journals of Jim Elliot*, ed. Elisabeth Elliot (Old Tappan, NJ: Revell, 1978), 174–75, 219, 225, 261, 264, 368–72, 413, 426–27, 451.

11. Willard, *Hearing God*, 180–81.

12. In the 1950s this people group was called "Auca" by their first visitors, but later communication with the tribe showed that they called themselves "Waorani," meaning "The People." Further the term "Auca" has pejorative meaning to them since it was commonly used to mean "savage." Documents written after that time usually refer to some variation of the term "Waorani" as their tribal name. See Kathryn Long and Carolyn Nystrom in *Christian History* 89 (Summer 2005).

13. *The Journals of Jim Elliot*, 15–16.

14. Elliot, *The Savage My Kinsman*, from Capa's foreword.

Chapter 3 Your Good Health

1. John Piper, *Desiring God: Meditations of a Christian Hedonist*, 3rd ed. (1986; Sisters, OR: Multnomah, 2003).

2. Jonathan Edwards, *The Miscellanies, a-500*, ed. Thomas Shafer *Works of Jonathan Edwards*, XIII (New Haven: Yale University Press, 1994), 495, quoted in John Piper, *The Dangerous Duty of Delight* (Sisters, OR: Multnomah, 2001), 19. The statement is also found in Edwards's treatise *The End for Which God Created the World* (1729), reprinted in John Piper, *God's Passion for His Glory: Living the Vision of Jonathan Edwards* (Wheaton, IL: Crossway, 1998), 242.

3. Richard Baxter, "A Treatise of Self-Denial," in *Practical Works* (Ligonier, PA: Soli Deo Gloria, 1990), 3.372.

Chapter 4 Guided by the Word of God

1. See further J. I. Packer, *"Fundamentalism" and the Word of God* (Grand Rapids: Eerdmans, 1958); idem., *God Has Spoken*, 3rd ed. (Grand Rapids: Baker, 1988); idem., *Truth and Power* (Downers Grover, IL: InterVarsity, 1996), idem., "Theology and Bible Reading" in ed. Elmer Dyck, *The Act of Bible Reading* (Downers Grove, IL: InterVarsity, 1996).

2. Roman Catholics see Jesus's words as showing that marriage is indissoluble; whereas, most Protestants, noting that Jesus seems to specify adultery and Paul desertion as warranting divorce (see Matt. 19:7–9; cf. 5:32; 1 Cor. 7:12–16), understand Jesus as indicating simply that divorce is always a sad lapse from God's ideal, whatever the circumstances. We cannot further explore this difference here.

Chapter 5 The Way of Wisdom

1. See Oswald Chambers, *The Complete Works of Oswald Chambers* (Grand Rapids: Discovery House Publishers, 2000), 1194 (emphasis added).
2. Calvin, *Institutes of the Christian Religion*, 3.10; trans. F. L. Battles (Philadelphia: Westminster, 1960), 719–20.
3. Charles Simeon quoted in Hugh Evan Hopkins, *Charles Simeon of Cambridge* (London: Hodder & Stoughton, 1977), 205.
4. See J. I. Packer, "Hot Tub Religion: Toward a Theology of Enjoyment," and "Joy: A Neglected Discipline," in *God's Plans for You* (Wheaton: Crossway, 2001), 47–72, 107–126.
5. Derek Kidner, *Proverbs* (London: Tyndale, 1964), 158.

Chapter 6 With a Little Help from Our Friends

1. An anecdote given in Olive Fleming Liefeld, *Unfolding Destinies: the Ongoing Story of the Auca Mission* (Grand Rapids: Discovery House Publishers, 1998), 17.
2. *Our Children: The Church Cares for Children Affected by AIDS* (Nairobi: World Relief; 2003) 45.
3. For a fuller account of Ryle's call to Liverpool and outstanding leadership there, see J. I. Packer, *Faithfulness and Holiness* (Wheaton: Crossway, 2002), 51–59; Ian D. Farley, *JC Ryle, First Bishop of Liverpool* (Carlisle, UK: Paternoster, 2000); Eric Russell, *That Man of Granite with the Heart of a Child* (Fearn, UK: Christian Focus, 2001), 133–209.
4. C. S. Lewis, *Mere Christianity* (New York: Simon & Schuster, 1996), 74–75. First Touchstone edition under Simon & Schuster in 1996; earlier copyrights by Macmillan in 1943, 1945, 1952, renewed 1980.

Chapter 9 Situation Ethics

1. Willard, *Hearing God*, 215.

Chapter 10 Guarded and Guided by the Holy Spirit

1. J. I. Packer, *Knowing God's Purpose for Your Life* (Ventura: Regal, 2000), 395ff.
2. Willard, *Hearing God*, 11.
3. Garry Friesen with J. Robin Maxim, *Decision Making and the Will of God: A Biblical Alternative to the Traditional View*, rev. and updated ed. (1980; Portland: Multnomah, 2004).
4. M. James Sawyer in *Who's Afraid of the Holy Spirit?* ed. Daniel B. Wallace and M. James Sawyer (Dallas: Biblical Studies Press, 2005), 264.
5. Matthew and Mark both come closer to the idea of the Spirit's specific prompting than Luke does. Matthew uses a compound of *agō* in the aorist aspect, with *hupō* and the genitive expressing personal agency, to tell us that "Jesus was *led up by the Spirit* into the wilderness" (4:1). Mark, a very forthright writer, uses

a different, stronger word, saying that "the Spirit immediately *drove him out* into the wilderness" (1:12).

Epilogue

1. J. I. Packer and Carolyn Nystrom, *Praying: Finding Our Way through Duty to Delight* (Downers Grove, IL: InterVarsity, 2006).

Appendix

1. John Newton, "Of the Lord's promised Guidance," letter 28, *Forty-One Letters on Religious Subjects*, in *The Works of the Rev. John Newton Late Rector of the United Parishes of St. Mary Woolnoth & St. Mary Woolchurch Hall*, vol. 6 (1774; New York: Williams & Whiting, 1810), 294–301. The letter as reprinted here has been very modestly edited (e.g., capitalization and numerical Scripture references) along with the addition of some bracketed clarifications.

J. I. Packer is Board of Governors' Professor of Theology at Regent College in Vancouver, British Columbia, and an executive editor for *Christianity Today*. He is the author or editor of more than thirty books, including the bestselling classic *Knowing God*.

Carolyn Nystrom is a freelance writer and the coauthor with Mark Noll of *Is the Reformation Over?*